CABINETS & BUILT-INS

26 Custom Storage Projects

CREATIVE HOMEOWNER®, Upper Saddle River, New Jersey

Writers: Herb Hughes, Ken Oberrect, and
         Bob Flexner (author of *Understanding
         Wood Finishing*)
Editorial Director: David Schiff
Editors: Joseph Wajszczuk, William Sampson,
          Rich Ziegner, Laura Tringali
Assistant Editor: Patrick Quinn
Copy Editor: Diane DiBlasi

Art Director: Annie Jeon
Graphic Designer: Michael James Allegra
Technical Illustration: Frank Rohrbach
Opening Illustrations: Paul M. Schumm
Photography: Jim Roberson

Cover Design: Annie Jeon
Cover Photograph: Freeze Frame Studio
Back Cover Illustrations: Paul M. Schumm

Current Printing (last digit)
10 9 8

Cabinets & Built-Ins
Library of Congress Catalog Card Number: 94-69650
ISBN: 1-880029-41-3

CREATIVE HOMEOWNER®
A Division of Federal Marketing Corp.
24 Park Way
Upper Saddle River, NJ 07458
Web site: **www.creativehomeowner.com**

Safety First

Though all the designs and methods in this book have been tested for safety, it is not possible to overstate the importance of using the safest construction methods possible. What follows are reminders; some do's and don'ts of basic carpentry. They are not substitutes for your own common sense.

- *Always* use caution, care, and good judgment when following the procedures described in this book.

- *Always* be sure that the electrical setup is safe; be sure that no circuit is overloaded and that all power tools and electrical outlets are properly grounded. Do not use power tools in wet locations.

- *Always* read container labels on paints, solvents, and other products; provide ventilation, and observe all other warnings.

- *Always* read the manufacturer's instructions for using a tool, especially the warnings.

- *Always* use hold-downs and push sticks whenever possible when working on a table saw. Avoid working short pieces if you can.

- *Always* remove the key from any drill chuck (portable or press) before starting the drill.

- *Always* pay deliberate attention to how a tool works so that you can avoid being injured.

- *Always* know the limitations of your tools. Do not try to force them to do what they were not designed to do.

- *Always* make sure that any adjustment is locked before proceeding. For example, always check the rip fence on a table saw or the bevel adjustment on a portable saw before starting to work.

- *Always* clamp small pieces firmly to a bench or other work surface when using a power tool on them.

- *Always* wear the appropriate rubber or work gloves when handling chemicals, moving or stacking lumber, or doing heavy construction.

- *Always* wear a disposable face mask when you create dust by sawing or sanding. Use a special filtering respirator when working with toxic substances and solvents.

- *Always* wear eye protection, especially when using power tools or striking metal on metal or concrete; a chip can fly off, for example, when chiseling concrete.

- *Always* be aware that there is seldom enough time for your body's reflexes to save you from injury from a power tool in a dangerous situation; everything happens too fast. Be *alert!*

- *Always* keep your hands away from the business ends of blades, cutters, and bits.

- *Always* hold a circular saw firmly, usually with both hands so that you know where they are.

- *Always* use a drill with an auxiliary handle to control the torque when large-size bits are used.

- *Always* check your local building codes when planning new construction. The codes are intended to protect public safety and should be observed to the letter.

- *Never* work with power tools when you are tired or under the influence of alcohol or drugs.

- *Never* cut tiny pieces of wood or pipe using a power saw. Cut small pieces off larger pieces.

- *Never* change a circular- or table-saw blade or a drill or router bit unless the power cord is unplugged. Do not depend on the switch being off; you might accidentally hit it.

- *Never* work in insufficient lighting.

- *Never* work while wearing loose clothing, hanging hair, open cuffs, or jewelry.

- *Never* work with dull tools. Have them sharpened, or learn how to sharpen them yourself.

- *Never* use a power tool on a workpiece—large or small—that is not firmly supported.

- *Never* saw a workpiece that spans a large distance between horses without close support on each side of the cut; the piece can bend, closing on and jamming the blade, causing saw kickback.

- *Never* support a workpiece from underneath with your leg or other part of your body when sawing.

- *Never* carry sharp or pointed tools, such as utility knives, awls, or chisels, in your pocket. If you want to carry such tools, use a special-purpose tool belt with leather pockets and holders.

Table of Contents

TECHNIQUES

The real mark of an experienced woodworker is not the number of tools that he or she owns, or the square footage of his shop, but rather the techniques he has developed over the years. An accomplished craftsperson will have a few well rehearsed ways of accomplishing a given task and will stick with these methods because he has learned that they best suit his specific needs and equipment. In comparison, a less experienced person may waste time and materials trying to figure out how to perform the same operation. For the most part, technique is something refined over time, but starting off with good basic techniques will prevent you from wasting time, effort, and materials.

The techniques explained here include those that are widely applicable for the projects in this book. Some techniques, such as those for building drawers and doors, appear in this chapter so that they needn't be repeated with each project. Wherever necessary, these techniques have been conveniently cross-referenced throughout the book.

WORKING WITH PLYWOOD

Plywood is the material of choice for most of the projects in this book for several reasons. Plywood cabinets are easier to build because you are already starting with large panels that, unlike solid wood, will not shrink or swell significantly with changes in humidity. This means that joinery can be less complicated. Building cabinets of plywood is also less expensive than using solid wood. However, one of the main

Making the Straight-Cutting Jig

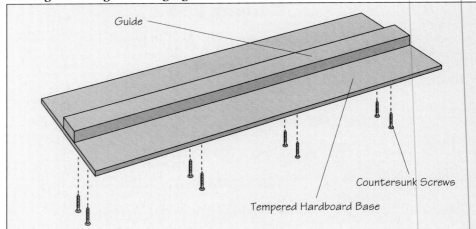

Guide

Countersunk Screws

Tempered Hardboard Base

drawbacks to using plywood is that the large 4x8-foot panels are awkward to handle and can be difficult to cut accurately.

Cutting and Trimming Plywood

Because a full plywood panel is large and heavy, it is usually easier and safer to cut the panel with a portable saw or router instead of trying to maneuver the panel over a table saw or router table.

One way to break panels down to a manageable size is to make freehand cuts with a portable circular saw, running the saw along a layout line. However, freehand cuts are not accurate enough for most cabinet work. So, begin by using a portable circular saw to rip panels about 1/4 inch oversize. Then rip them to final width on the table saw, guiding the factory edges against the rip fence.

Even after panels are ripped to width, many are too long and wide to crosscut to length on the table saw.

Instead, make your crosscuts with the portable circular saw, guiding the saw against a straightedge, or better yet, make a straight-cutting jig.

Making the Straight-Cutting Jig. Guiding a circular saw along a simple straightedge is a bit tricky because the straightedge must be offset from the cut line by a distance that is exactly equal to the distance between the edge of the saw base and the blade. The straight-cutting jig is custom-cut to your saw and blade so you can set the edge of the jig right on the cut line without worrying about an offset.

The jig is simply a straight-edged board that is glued to a hardboard base. For your straightedge, use any length of plywood or solid lumber that has two straight edges and is at least 2 inches wide. Glue the straightedge to a length of 1/8-inch-thick tempered hardboard, allowing about 8 inches of hardboard on both sides. Fasten the straightedge onto the hardboard with glue and screws. Screw through the hardboard into the

Splinter-Free Plywood Cuts

When marking plywood, score the layout lines with a utility knife instead of drawing a pencil line. Scoring has two advantages over drawing lines. First, your knife is a more accurate marking tool than a pencil. The second advantage is that by cutting through the veneer, the knife line will help prevent chipping and tear-out when you make the cut.

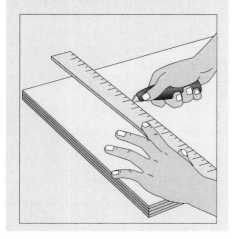

straightedge and countersink the screws slightly.

Once the glue has dried, trim off one side of the base. To do this, square the blade to the base of the saw, adjust the depth of cut to 1/4 inch and place the jig on a scrap of ply-

wood. When you make the cut, run the edge of the circular saw's base against the straightedge. This will create a straight base edge that shows the saw's exact cutting line.

To use the jig, clamp it onto the workpiece and align the edge of the base along the cutting line. Place the clamps along the extra hardboard on the untrimmed side of the jig so that the saw's motor won't run into clamps during the cut. When you get a new saw blade, retrim one side of the jig so you know the cut line will coincide precisely with the edge of the jig.

Finishing Edges

One of the problems with plywood is the appearance of its edges. Unless you are working with a premium plywood material, such as Baltic birch ply, most plywoods have voids within their laminations, leaving unsightly gaps visible along the edges. Many of the joinery techniques used in cabinetmaking conceal most of the plywood edges, but there will be those occasions when you will have to take measures to conceal an ugly edge. If the plywood will be painted, you can fill the rough edge and sand it smooth. Otherwise, you can conceal the edge with wood tape or solid-wood edge banding.

Filling an Edge. Thin down latex wood putty with water until it is easily spreadable and apply it along the edge with a putty knife. After the putty has dried completely, lightly sand the edge with 150-grit sandpaper.

Wood Tape. Most home centers now stock wood tape to match commonly sold plywood panels. Some kinds of wood tape come with pressure-sensitive or heat-activated adhesive so the tape can simply be pressed or ironed onto the edge of the plywood. After the tape is firmly attached to the plywood, lightly sand the edges with 150-grit sandpaper. Installing wood tape to cover a plywood edge is fast, easy, and economical, but it isn't the most durable edge treatment.

Molding and Solid Wood. You can get a more durable edge that's almost as easy to apply as wood tape simply by gluing solid wood directly onto the edge of the plywood. Screen and half-round molding are both good choices; wider trim will give the appearance of a more substantial panel. You can use masking tape to hold the molding in place while the glue dries. After the glue dries, you can sand or plane the edge flush with the plywood, but it's easier to use a piloted flush-trimming bit in your router.

Wood Tape

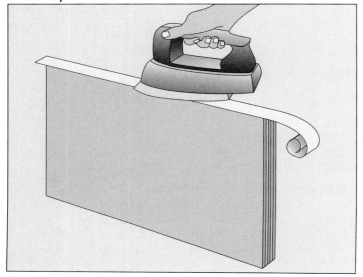

Molding and Solid Wood

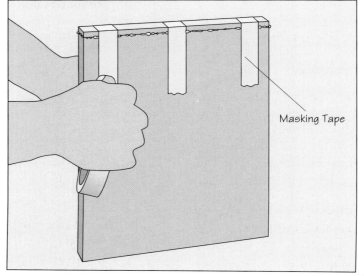

Masking Tape

EDGE-GLUING STOCK

Sometimes you need a panel for a project, and plywood just won't do. You want the look of solid wood, but today's lumberyards rarely have solid wood in wide panels. The solution is to edge-glue smaller boards to make a wider panel. If you are careful to match grain, it will be hard to tell that the panel is not one wide board.

1. **Cut stock and joint edges.** The key to successful edge-gluing is perfectly straight glue surfaces on the edges. The easiest way to achieve such edges is with a jointer, but if you don't have one you can carefully plane the edges square and flat with a hand plane. Use the largest plane you have for the flattest edge.

2. **Arrange the boards.** Check the ends of the boards for the direction of the annual growth rings in the wood. Orient all the boards in the same direction. This way, if the panel has any tendency to warp, the boards will all move in the same direction, and fasteners will more readily control the warping. If you alternate the growth rings up and down as some books recommend, the panel will turn into a washboard.

3. **Glue and clamp the panel.** Apply glue to all the edges to be glued. Using as many bar or pipe clamps as necessary, clamp the panel together. Make sure you alternate the clamps above and below the panel for even clamping pressure. Check that all the boards are aligned with no edges sticking up.

4. **Finish the panel.** Don't wait until the glue dries hard to clean up the squeeze out. It's easier to scrape off the excess glue if you do so when it has reached a rubbery consistency; then it just peels off cleanly. In any case, make sure you get all the glue off before you plane. Glue will quickly dull the plane's blade. Once the glue is cured, plane or sand the panel smooth.

Cutting Stock and Jointing Edges

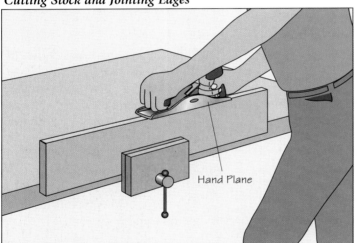

Hand Plane

Arranging the Boards

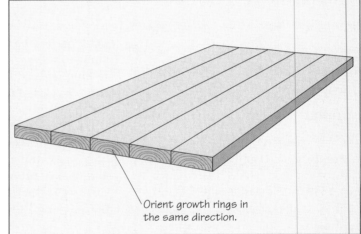

Orient growth rings in the same direction.

Gluing and Clamping the Panel

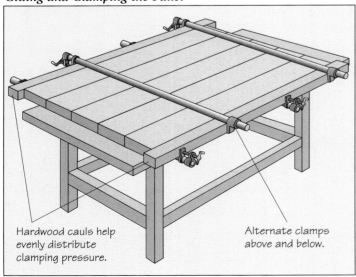

Hardwood cauls help evenly distribute clamping pressure.

Alternate clamps above and below.

Finishing the Panel

Stop

JOINERY

You can join wood in a variety of ways, ranging from the simple butt joint, to the stronger, more sophisticated dovetail joint, to a whole range of other types of joints that vary in strength and complexity. However, only a few simple joints are called for in the projects in this book. The cabinet carcases are assembled with butt, rabbet, dado, and miter joints. For the frame and panel doors, you will also need to learn how to make simple mortise-and-tenon joints.

Butt Joint

A butt joint is simply two pieces of wood butted together. It is typically secured with glue and some other type of fastener. Although it's a weak

Butt Joint

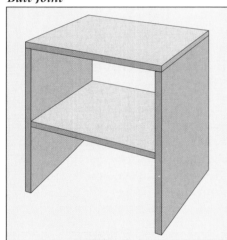

Miter Joint

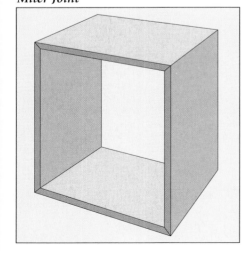

joint, it can be easily reinforced. Butt joints are commonly used in face frames where strength is not important because the face-frame members are usually glued to the cabinet. However, face-frame butt joints are often reinforced with dowels or biscuits, which not only add strength but help align the pieces during glue-up.

Miter Joint

A miter joint is essentially an angled butt joint. Like the butt joint, the miter joint requires additional reinforcement with fasteners. Use a miter joint where two pieces of trim or molding meet at a corner. You can also use a miter joint on a plywood carcase so that none of the unsightly plywood edge shows along the joint line.

Reinforcing Joints with Dowels

Wood dowels can increase the strength and improve the accuracy of butt joints. In face-frame construction, the joint usually includes two dowels glued into each end of a rail (the horizontal member) and then into corresponding holes in the stiles (the vertical members).

1. **Locate the dowel holes.** To locate dowel holes accurately, temporarily position the two mating pieces in place. Strike a line on both members indicating the dowel locations. Transfer that mark onto the edge of each piece with a square.

2. **Drill the holes.** Use a doweling jig to ensure that the dowel holes are drilled exactly equidistant from the two faces of the piece. Use a stop collar or a piece of tape on the bit to indicate when you have drilled to the correct depth.

3. **Assemble the parts.** Apply glue to the dowels and insert them in the holes in one of the parts to be joined. Attach the mating part and clamp the assembly until the glue has set.

Locating the Dowel Holes

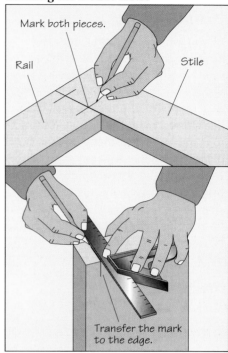

Drilling the Holes

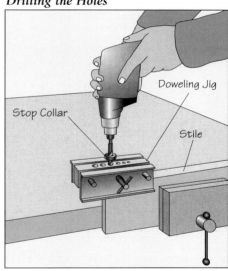

Assembling the Parts

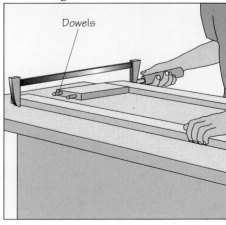

Reinforcing Joints with Biscuits

Biscuit joinery is quickly replacing dowel joinery because these strong joints can be made more quickly. Biscuit joinery uses wooden biscuits that are pieces of pressed wood shaped like flat footballs. The biscuit joining machine or plate joiner cuts slots in the pieces to be joined. The slots are perfectly aligned from top to bottom. The biscuits are slightly shorter than the slots to allow a bit of lateral adjustment during glue-up. This is very handy because face surfaces are automatically flush but you can move pieces back and forth a bit during glue-up to make sure ends are absolutely flush and square.

Making Biscuit Joints

1. **Locate biscuit slots.** Mark the locations of biscuit slots on the faces of parts to be joined just as you would dowel holes, but you don't have to extend the lines to the edges. Make sure that the workpieces are thick enough or wide enough to accept the elliptically-shaped biscuits without having them stick through the sides. Also make sure you use the right size biscuit for the job and that the plate joiner is set to the correct depth of cut for the biscuit size you are using. The three most common biscuit sizes are 0 (smallest), 10 (medium), and 20 (largest and most commonly used in 3/4-inch sheet stock).

2. **Make the cuts.** Clamp the workpiece to a stable work surface. Align the biscuit joiner with the marks you made and move the cutter into the wood. Make sure you hold the machine firmly and properly aligned during the cut.

3. **Apply glue and assemble the parts.** Spread glue in the slots and along the edges of the parts to be joined. Don't put glue on the biscuits. One of the major reasons why biscuits are so strong is that they expand when they come in contact with the glue. If you put glue on them first, the biscuits won't fit in their slots. Once you've spread the glue, tap the biscuits into their slots. Clamp the parts until the glue is dry.

Dadoes, Grooves, and Rabbets

Dadoes and grooves are identical except for their relationship in respect to the wood's grain: Dadoes are actually a type of groove that runs across the grain; grooves that run with the grain are not dadoes. For the sake of clarity, we'll use the term groove to

Locating Biscuit Slots

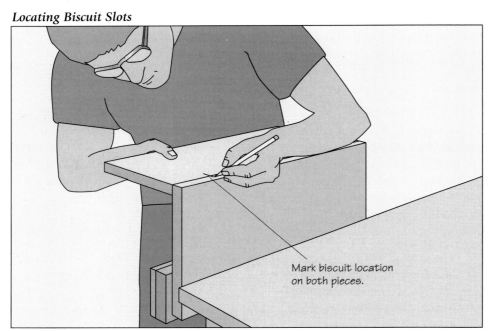

Mark biscuit location on both pieces.

Marking the Cuts

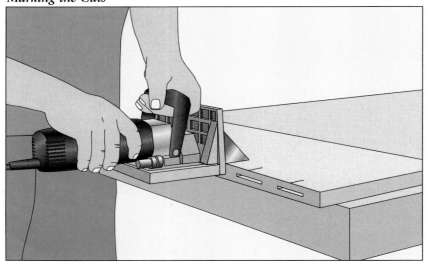

Applying Glue and Assemblying the Parts

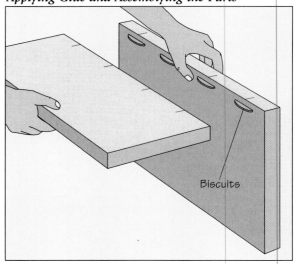

Biscuits

Dadoes, Rabbets, and Grooves

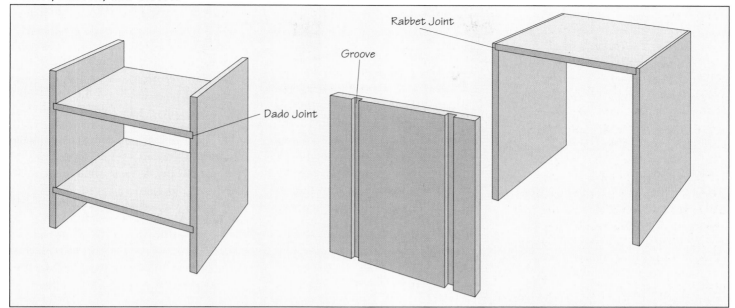

describe only grooves that run with the grain. A rabbet is like a ledge cut along one edge of a piece. Dadoes are commonly used for fitting shelves and partitions into cabinet panels. Grooves are commonly used for fitting partitions and insetting shelf standards, while rabbets most often are used for joining cabinet panels and insetting cabinet backs.

Making Dadoes and Grooves with a Table Saw

Making dadoes and grooves on a table saw employs the rip fence. As a result,

this method is most suited to making long grooves. For example, this is a very handy setup for making grooves for insetting shelf standards. Once you have the fence and blade set up, you can just run panels through knowing all your grooves will be equidistant from the panel edges.

You can use the table saw to make dadoes as well, but the longer the panel is, the more awkward this operation will be. You will find that the router is usually the better tool for making dadoes in large cabinet sides.

1. **Make a test cut.** Unplug the saw and replace your regular saw blade with a dado cutter. Use either the wobble-style or stacked cutter setup for the desired cut. Adjust the cutter for the proper depth of cut and set the fence to the desired distance from the cutter. Before you make the cut on your project, make a test cut in scrap wood to make sure your settings are correct.

2. **Make the final cut.** To cut the groove or dado in your panel, simply run the panel over the blade and make the cut. Always use push blocks and hold-downs where appropriate

Making a Test Cut

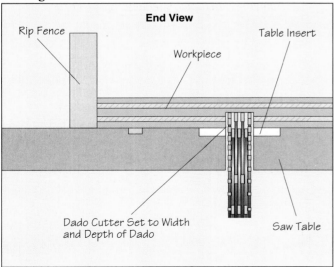

Making the Final Cut

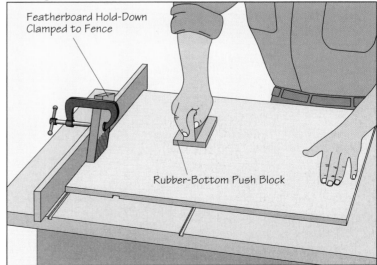

to keep the workpiece from lifting off the saw table or kicking back. You can make a featherboard hold-down simply by kerfing the end of a small board that has had its ends cut on the diagonal. Such a device is shown in *Making the Final Cut*. If you need to make a matching dado or groove an opposing panel, be sure you do it before you change the fence adjustment.

Note: When working with a stacked or wobble-type dado blade, you may need a different throat plate with a wider opening than the one used with an ordinary blade. Once you install the dado head, turn the blade by hand to make sure that it has adequate clearance. If it does make contact with the throat plate, you will have to make a replacement wooden throat plate. Refer to your saw's owner's manual for specific instructions.

Making Rabbets with a Table Saw

Cutting rabbets on the table saw is similar to cutting grooves and dadoes, but you will need to equip your saw with an auxiliary wood fence so that the blade can run right up against the edge. Again, because the rip fence is used, this operation is more suitable for cutting rabbets along the edges

Making Dadoes and Rabbets without a Dado Blade

It is possible to make dadoes and rabbets without a special dado blade. Set up your regular saw blade just as you would a dado head and run the panel over the blade. After the first pass, shut the saw off and move the fence about 1/8 inch from the blade for the second pass. Continue making passes in 1/8-inch increments until the dado or groove is cut to the desired width.

of long panels than it is for cutting rabbets along the top or bottom of long panels.

1. **Make and mount the auxiliary fence.** Make the auxiliary fence from 3/4-inch plywood. Make the auxiliary fence the same length as the rip fence and a couple of inches higher than the rip fence. Screw the auxiliary fence onto your rip fence (refer to your owner's manual for specific directions). Install the cutter in your saw and drop the blade below the saw-table surface.

2. **Cut a blade cove.** To make the dado cutter easy to adjust, cut a blade cove into the auxiliary fence. With the dado cutter lowered beneath the

saw's table, move the fence so that it extends over the blade by approximately 5/8 inch, and lock it in place. Make a pencil mark on the left face of the auxiliary fence 1 inch above the saw table. Turn the saw on and slowly raise the dado cutter until it hits the pencil mark.

3. **Install and adjust the cutter.** After mounting a dado cutter to the saw arbor, set the cutter to the proper blade height and adjust the auxiliary fence to the desired rabbet width.

4. **Make the Cut.** Make a sample cut on a piece of scrap to check your measurements and saw settings. When the setting is perfect, put the workpiece

Making and Mounting the Auxiliary Fence

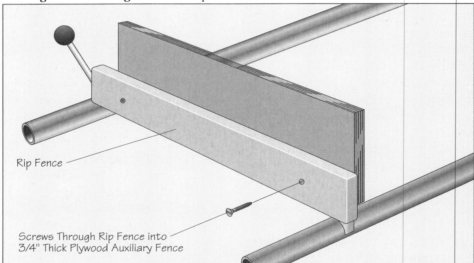

Rip Fence

Screws Through Rip Fence into
3/4" Thick Plywood Auxiliary Fence

Cutting a Blade Cove

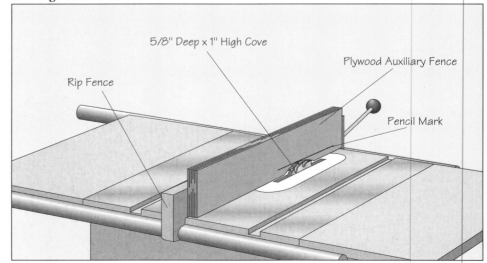

5/8" Deep x 1" High Cove

Plywood Auxiliary Fence

Rip Fence

Pencil Mark

Installing and Adjusting the Cutter

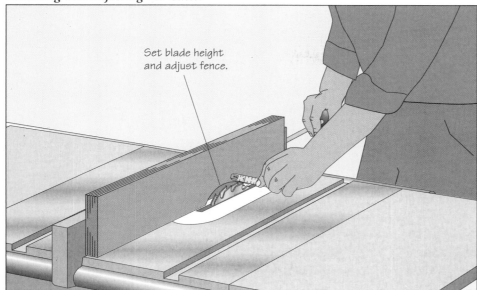

Set blade height and adjust fence.

Making the Cut

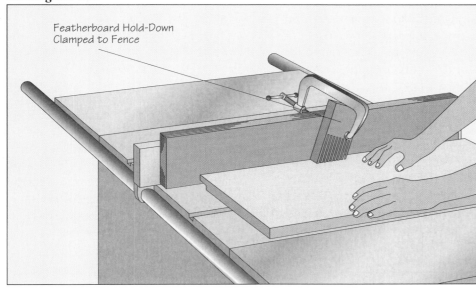

Featherboard Hold-Down Clamped to Fence

on the table and run the piece over the blade.

Making Dadoes with the Router

In cabinetmaking, if you are making a dado in a panel, chances are you'll be making a matching dado in an opposing panel. The easiest way to make sure opposing dadoes are perfectly aligned is to cut them both in the same pass. You can do this by using a simple straightedge as a guide, but you will find it is really worth your while to make a T-square router guide.

When cutting dadoes with a router, it is very tricky to get the cutting edge of the bit exactly the right distance away from the straightedge guide. With the T-square guide, you cut a dado into the crosspiece, then simply align the dado to your layout line on the workpiece. The other advantage is, of course, that the T-square makes sure your dadoes are perfectly square to the edges of the workpiece. By routing one dado on each side of the crosspiece, you can use the guide for dadoes of two different widths.

1. **Make the T-square router guide.** Make this guide from two pieces of 3/4-inch-thick plywood. Make the crossbar about 3 x 14 inches long. Make the guide 3 inches wide and about 3 inches longer than the width of your workbench. Assemble the guide with three screws posi-tioned as shown in *Making the T-Square Router Guide.* When the glue has dried, fit your router with a straight bit whose diameter matches the dado width you want to cut. Set the bit to the desired dado depth. Guiding the router against the guide, cut a dado in one side of the crossbar. Later, when you need a dado of a different width, you can make a cut in the other side of the crossbar.

2. **Cut the dadoes.** To use the cutting guide, align the dado in the crossbar to the dado layout on the workpiece. Clamp the workpiece to a stable work surface. Clamp both ends of the jig to the work surface. Or if the workpiece is narrower than the work surface, you can clamp one end of the guide to the work surface, sand-wiching in a clamping block that is the same thickness as the workpiece as shown.

Making the T-Square Router Guide

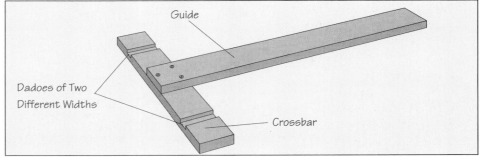

Guide

Dadoes of Two Different Widths

Crossbar

Cutting the Dadoes

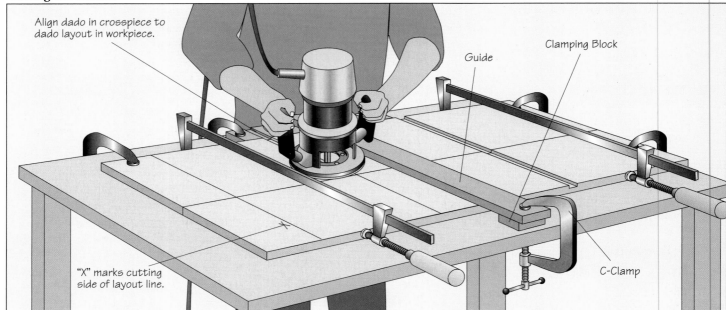

Align dado in crosspiece to dado layout in workpiece.

Guide

Clamping Block

"X" marks cutting side of layout line.

C-Clamp

When running a router against a straightedge guide, always work from left to right when the router is between you and the guide.

Making Rabbets with a Router

You can make rabbets with your router, a straight bit, and an straightedge guide. Another option is to purchase special bits specifically designed for cutting rabbets. The best rabbeting bits have ball bearing tips that roll easily

along the workpiece and prevent burning the edges of the wood. You can buy the bits in different sizes or in a kit that includes a carbide-tipped bit with interchangeable bearings for making rabbets of different dimensions.

Regardless of which technique you use, remember always to run the router through the stock against the rotation of the router bit. This will keep the bit from skating dangerously along the stock.

SQUARING A CARCASE

One of the benefits of working with plywood in carcase construction is that you can build a large carcase with just a few panels. However, carcase assembly can still be a real headache. Often, you are working with large, heavy panels, trying to position them exactly in place and long enough to drive a screw, or until the glue has had enough time to adequately set

Rabbeting with a Router and a Straightedge

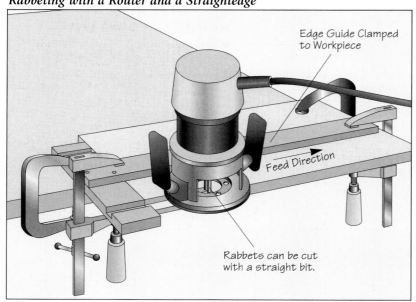

Edge Guide Clamped to Workpiece

Feed Direction

Rabbets can be cut with a straight bit.

Rabbeting with a Ball Bearing Guide

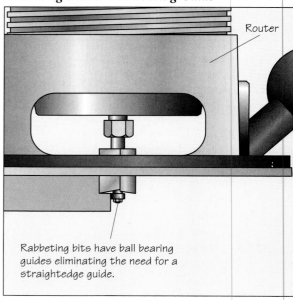

Router

Rabbeting bits have ball bearing guides eliminating the need for a straightedge guide.

the joint. Once they are in place, it is essential that the corners are perfectly square and that they stay this way.

Always check a carcase for square as soon as it is assembled and before the glue is set. To check for square, measure diagonally from corner to corner. If the measurements match, the carcase is square.

If measurements don't match, you can reposition clamps or apply clamping pressure diagonally to bring the carcase into square before the glue sets.

Using the Back to Square a Carcase

It's possible to square up your cabinet accurately without ever reaching for a measuring tape or framing square. As long as at least one corner of the back panel was cut with a square corner

(the corner is made of two factory-cut edges), it will true up the rest of the carcase as it is installed. The key to this procedure is to install the back immediately after assembling the carcase, while the glue is still wet and will allow you to shift things around a bit.

1. Install the back. Apply glue to the back edges and drop the back into position. Align the square corner with one top corner of your carcase and secure it with an appropriate screw or finishing nail.

2. Align the carcase. Next, shift the carcase so that it is flush along the bottom edge of the carcase and drive one fastener through the bottom corner opposing the fastened top corner. Shift the carcase as necessary until the sides are aligned. Secure the remain-

ing corners, then drive fasteners as necessary along the perimeter to clamp the back panel until the glue sets.

MAKING CABINET DOORS

Most cabinet doors fit into one of two categories: slab doors or frame-and-panel doors.

Slab Doors

This type of door can be as simple as a flat piece of wood or a panel of plywood, or it can be adorned with trim or faced with veneer for a more elegant effect.

Frame-and-Panel Doors

These consist of a pair of rails and stiles that frame a center panel. This panel can be as simple as a piece of glass or plywood, or it can have beveled edges that create a raised panel. A frame-and-panel door is essential if you make the door out of solid wood. This kind of construction allows the door panel to expand and contract with changes in humidity. With a plywood panel, the frame-and-panel design is more decorative than functional because plywood is much more stable than solid wood.

Building a Slab Door

1. Cut the panels. Because slab doors are made of plywood, the exposed edges need to be covered with 1/4-inch wide strips of solid wood. So begin by cutting plywood panels that are 1/2 inch narrower and shorter than the final width and length you need.

2. Cut the edge strips. Usually, you will want to make the edge strip stock out of the same wood species as the face veneer of the plywood you are using. This way, the edging will blend in with the panel, especially on the

Squaring a Carcase

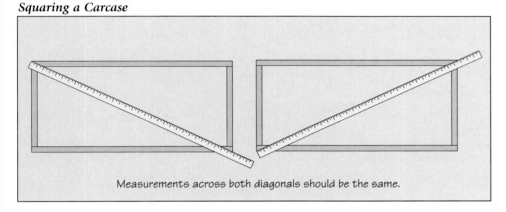

Measurements across both diagonals should be the same.

Using the Back to Square a Carcase

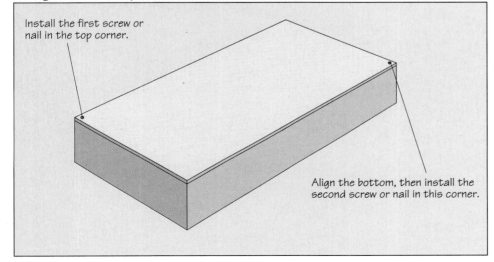

Install the first screw or nail in the top corner.

Align the bottom, then install the second screw or nail in this corner.

edges that run parallel to the panel's grain. Cut the edging about 1/8 inch wider than the panel thickness. For example, if your doors are 3/4 inch thick, make the edging 1/4 inch thick and 7/8 inch wide.

3. **Glue the edging in place.** Cut lengths of edging that are about 1 inch longer than the edges they'll cover. Edge the top and bottom of each door first. Apply glue to the edge and then put the edging in place so that it overhangs the panel on all sides. Secure the edging to the panel with masking tape. See "Molding and Solid Wood," page 7. After the glue has set, saw each end of the edging flush with the sides of the door. Scrap off the excess glue, then use a block plane to pare the edging flush with the faces of the door. (Be careful not to nick the panel's face veneer.) Now install the edging on the sides of the door the same way, letting the side edging overhang the top and bottom edging. When the glue sets, trim the side edging. Sand the edging smooth.

Building a Frame-and-Panel Door

1. **Cut the rails and stiles.** Cut the stiles to door height. Cut the rails to door width plus the length of the two tenons less the width of the two stiles. For example, if the door is 20 inches wide with 2-inch-wide stiles, and you want 3/8-inch tenons, you would cut the rails 16¾ inches long (20 + 3/4 - 4 = 16¾). Do this work with the miter gauge on the table saw.

2. **Groove the stiles and the rails.** Adjust the dado cutter in your saw to a width that matches the thickness of your door panels. Measure the panel to be sure: Even if the plywood is nominally 1/4 inch thick, it's likely to be thinner. Position your rip fence to guide the frame member sides when milling the panel grooves. It's impor-tant that the grooves are centered on

Building a Slab Door

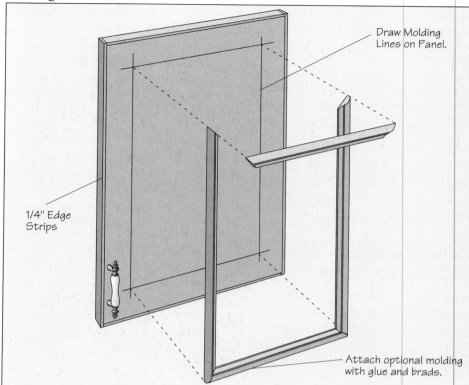

Draw Molding Lines on Panel.

1/4" Edge Strips

Attach optional molding with glue and brads.

Building a Frame-and-Panel Door

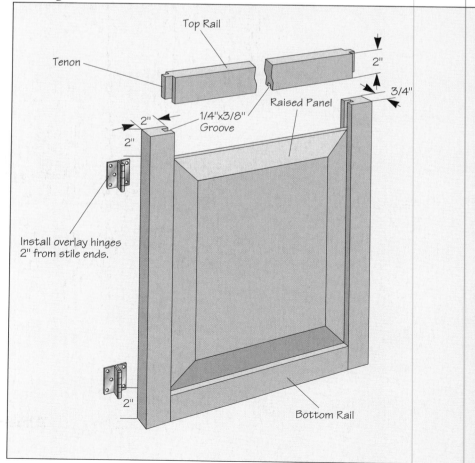

Top Rail

Tenon

2"

3/4"

2"

1/4"x3/8" Groove

Raised Panel

2"

Install overlay hinges 2" from stile ends.

2"

Bottom Rail

the frame edges. To test your fence position, turn on the saw and guide a scrap cutoff against the fence and through the cut. Now turn the piece around, and with the groove facing down, guide its opposite side against the fence to make a second pass. If your fence is set correctly, the width of the groove shouldn't increase with the second pass.

3. **Cut the tenons.** Each rail tenon is as thick as the door panel and is 3/8 inch long. Lay out a sample tenon on a piece of rail stock. Adjust the dado cutter's height to 1/4 inch. Screw a piece of stock to your table saw's miter gauge so it will support stock close to the blade. Clamp a stop block to the rip fence ahead of the

blade. Adjust the fence and stop block so that it positions the shoulder layout to the blade. Hold or clamp the rail securely to the miter gauge and slide it past the stop block and over the dado cutter. This way there is no danger of pinching the work between the cutter and the rip fence. Flip the rail over and cut the other side of the tenon. Before cutting the actual rails, cut some scrap wood stock to check the tenon's fit in the groove. Then adjust the stop block or cutter height until you get a perfect fit. Cut the tenons on both ends of each of the rails.

4. **Cut and raise the panel.** The panel in a frame-and-panel door should be 1/8 inch shorter and narrower than the groove measurements of the frame.

The easiest way to determine this is simply to test-fit the stiles and rails and to measure the opening where the panel is to fit. (This will also give you a chance to see how the frame fits together.) Square up the frame, then measure the height and width of each opening. Add 5/8 inch to each measurement to get the finished dimensions of each panel for a door that has 3/8-inch grooves. Cut the panel to size then raise it. See "Making a Raised Panel," below.

5. **Assemble the Door.** Glue the tenons and assemble the door around the panel. Be careful that you do not accidently glue the panel into the groove. The idea is to give the panel freedom to expand and contract with changes in humidity without pushing the frame apart. Draw the stiles against the rails with bar or pipe clamps and let the door stand overnight.

Making a Raised Panel

A raised panel is a board with beveled or tapered ends and edges so the stock is thicker in the center than at its perimeter. The center, unbeveled part of the panel is called the field. The panel is usually mounted in a frame that allows it to expand and contract

Grooving the Stiles and Rails

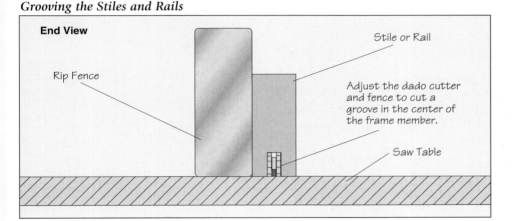

Cutting the Tenons

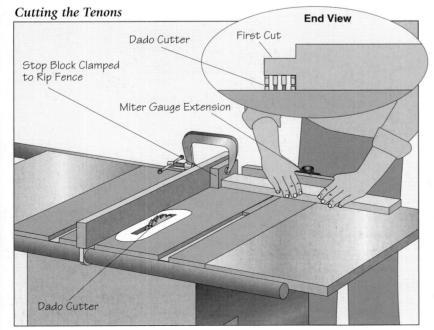

Assembling the Door

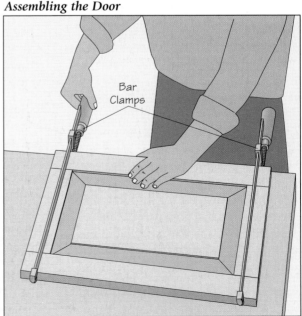

without otherwise stressing the rest of the project. The easiest way to bevel the ends and edges is with your table saw.

The raised panel bevels can run directly to the field as shown in *Raised Panel Styles*, or for a more formal look, you can add a shallow step between the bevel and the field. In either case, the bevel must be angled to fit within its groove without splitting the sides of the groove or being too loose in its frame. For the projects in this book, a 15-degree angle will fit nicely as long as you use 3/8 x 3/8-inch grooves in the door stiles and rails.

With the directions presented here you can make raised panels in 5/8-inch-thick stock or 3/4-inch stock, with or without steps for either thickness.

1. **Install an auxiliary fence.** You'll need an auxiliary fence tall enough to support the wide panel. Make the fence from a piece of 3/4-inch plywood or a straight 1x6 or wider board, and bolt it onto your saw's fence according to your saw's instructions.

2. **Raise the panel.** For 3/4-inch panels that will have a step, or for 5/8-inch thick panels without a step, raise the blade to 1½ inches. For 3/4-inch panels without a step, raise the blade to about 2 inches. For 5/8-inch panels that will have a step, raise the blade to 1 inch. Tilt the blade away from the fence 15 degrees from vertical. Set the fence 1/4 inch from the blade's near teeth. Back the panel against the auxiliary fence. Select a scrap of 1x3 or 1x4 that is a little longer than the panel. Place this scrap guide board on top of the auxiliary fence and clamp it to the panel as shown in *Raising a Panel on the Table Saw*. Press firmly on the guide board as you run the panel through the saw. Cut the two bevels that go across the grain first. That way, any tear-out will be eliminated when you cut the bevels that run with the grain.

Note: On most table saws the blade tilts to the right of the operator's side.

Raised Panel Styles

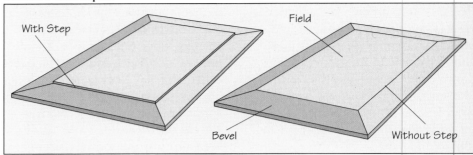

Raising a Panel on the Table Saw

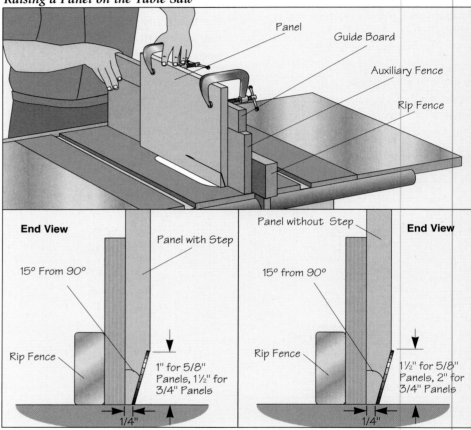

In this case, you will have to place the fence to the left of the blade.

3. **Square the step.** This procedure applies, of course, only if you will have a step. The step won't be square to the field because the blade was tilted to cut the bevel. To square the step, place the panel on the saw table. Raise the blade to the step depth as shown in *Squaring the Step*. Then set the rip fence to the edge of the panel. Cut the step square on all four sides. Use a sanding block to remove all saw marks from the panel.

Squaring the Step

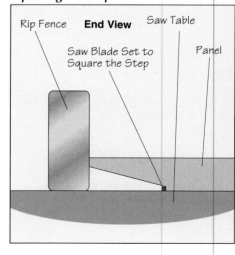

INSTALLING DOORS AND HINGES

Three types of hinged doors are used in cabinets: flush-fit, overlay (also called surface mounted), and inset (sometimes called lipped). Overlay doors are the easiest to fit because the door overlaps the face frame of the cabinet rather than fitting into an opening. Inset doors have a rabbet around the inside face so that the doors fit into the opening but have a lip that closes over the face frame. Inset doors must be fit more exactly than overlay doors, but the lip does provide a little margin of error. Inset doors fit into the opening so that they are flush with the face frame. They require the most exacting fit because the gap between door and cabinet must be even all around. Each door type has different hinging requirements. A wide variety of hinges are available to meet the requirements of each door type. *Types of Hinged Doors* shows the most common method for hinging each door type.

Installing Flush-Fit Doors

It is always a good idea to make flush-fitting doors after you make the cabinets, so you fit them to the actual size of the cabinet. If the cabinet will be built-in, install it before you install the door. After installing the cabinet, make sure that the frame is plumb and level before hanging the doors. Doors hung before cabinet installation could bind if the cabinet flexes.

1. **Fit the door.** Measure the height and width of each door and allow yourself a 3/32-inch gap on all edges. To make installation a little easier, some cabinetmakers bevel the edges of flush-fit doors 3 to 5 degrees toward the back.

2. **Select the hinges.** With solid-wood doors or doors with solid-wood frames, you can use butt hinges. Or, for a more Colonial look, you can use fully exposed hinges as shown in *Flush-Fit Hinge Options*. Butt hinges are unsuitable for plywood or particleboard doors because these materials aren't strong enough to support fasteners in their edges. You can use fully exposed hinges for plywood or particleboard, but flat panel doors such as these usually look better with

Types of Hinged Doors

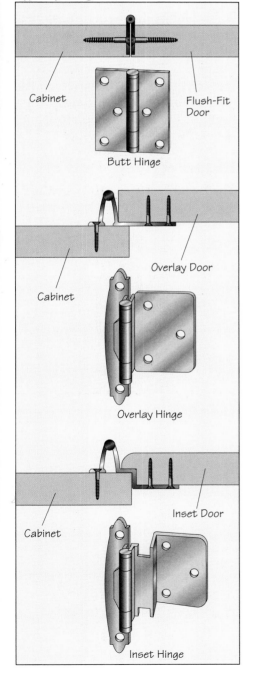

Cabinet

Flush-Fit Door

Butt Hinge

Overlay Door

Cabinet

Overlay Hinge

Inset Door

Cabinet

Inset Hinge

Fitting a Flush-Fit Door

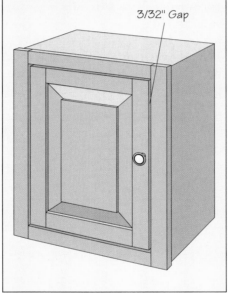

3/32" Gap

Flush-Fit Hinge Options

Fully Exposed Hinges

Concealed Wraparound Hinges

a concealed wraparound hinge as shown. Attach whichever hinges you choose to the door. The position of the hinges along the length of the door is mostly an aesthetic decision, but you usually want to stay between 2 and 5 inches from the top and bottom of the door.

Scoring the Hinge Mortise

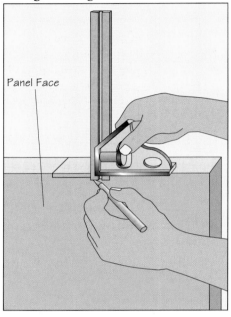

Panel Face

3. **Score the hinge mortises.** If the hinges you choose must be mortised into the door, start by clamping the door in a bench vise with the edge to be mortised facing up. Position the hinge on the door and score the perimeter with a knife. Remove the hinge and carefully deepen the score cuts to the depth of the hinge. Then use the thickness of one hinge leaf to set the ruler on a combination square. Use the square and a knife as shown in *Scoring the Hinge Mortise* to score the hinge depth on the face of the door.

4. **Cut the mortises and install the hinges.** Cut the mortises with a chisel. First, use a hammer and chisel to chop the waste areas into sections as shown in *Cutting the Mortises.* Then use the chisel to pare out the waste. Mark the locations of screw holes and drill pilot holes. Install the hinges on the door.

5. **Install the hinges on the cabinet.** Hold the door in position using shims. Then mark the hinge locations with a pencil. If you need to mortise the hinges into the cabinet, cut the outlines of the mortise with a knife. Cut the mortise with a chisel. Mark the screw holes and drill pilot holes. Install the hinges and door.

Installing Overlay Doors

1. **Install the hinges on the doors.** You'll find overlay hinges available in a variety of styles and finishes. Mark the hinge locations and drill pilot holes for hinge screws. Install the hinges in the door.

2. **Install the hinges on the cabinet.** After the cabinet has been installed, set the doors in place with the hinges already attached. With the doors correctly positioned, mark the face frame for the hinge-screw pilot holes. Drill the holes in the face frame, attach the door pulls, and hang the door.

Installing Inset Doors

1. **Measure for Door Size.** After the cabinet has been installed, measure the door opening and add 1/2 inch to the height and 1/2 inch to the width.

Cutting the Mortises

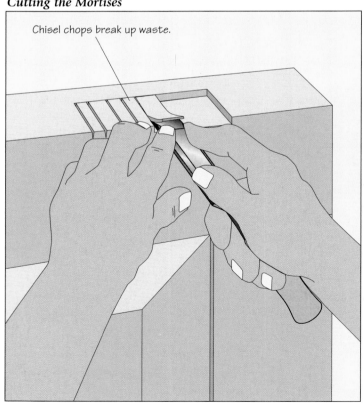

Chisel chops break up waste.

Installing the Hinges in the Cabinet

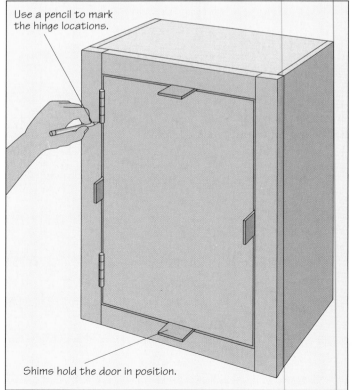

Use a pencil to mark the hinge locations.

Shims hold the door in position.

Measuring for Door Size

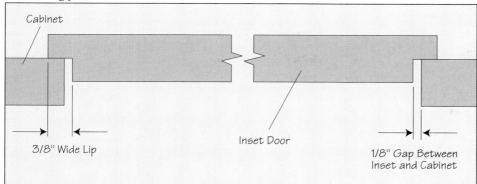

Cabinet

3/8" Wide Lip

Inset Door

1/8" Gap Between Inset and Cabinet

Cutting the Rabbets and Roundovers

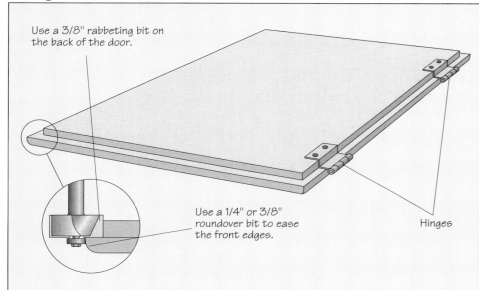

Use a 3/8" rabbeting bit on the back of the door.

Use a 1/4" or 3/8" roundover bit to ease the front edges.

Hinges

ADJUSTABLE CABINET SHELVES

If you want to make cabinet shelves that are adjustable for height, there are two common ways to do it. One way is to use pins in holes drilled inside the cabinet, the other is to use metal shelf standards.

Both are easy to use and install. Whichever you choose, check the hardware before you build your shelves. Different shelf-support hardware may require different clearances that may affect the size of the shelf.

Installing Metal Standards

Cut shelf standards to length with a hacksaw, cutting them all off at the top end so they will align to each other when registered to the bottom of the cabinet. Shelf standards can simply be screwed to the inside of the cabinet, but it is much more elegant to inset them into grooves. Cut the grooves on the table saw as described in "Making Dadoes and Grooves with a Table Saw," page 11.

This will give you a 3/8-inch-wide lip, while giving the inset portion of the door 1/8 inch of clearance all around.

2. **Cut the rabbets and roundovers.** Use a router and a 3/8-inch rabbeting bit to mill a 3/8-deep rabbet along all four sides of the back of the door. Then, if you like, use a 3/8-inch roundover bit to round over the front edges of the door.

3. **Install the hinges on the door.** Mark the locations of screw holes and drill pilot holes. Install the hinges in the door.

4. **Hang the door.** Hold the door in position in the cabinet and mark the locations of the hinges and screw holes. Drill pilot holes and hang the door.

Shelf Standards

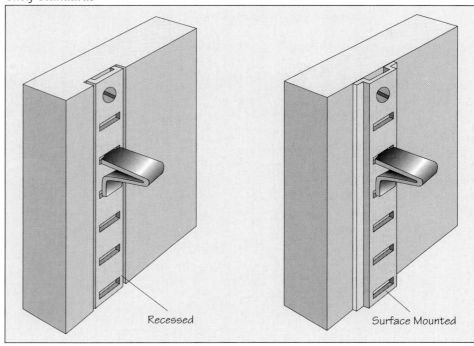

Recessed

Surface Mounted

Installing Shelf Pins

Shelf pins come in a variety of styles. Some include brass insets that you tap into the holes, dressing them up a bit and making them more durable. Most shelf pins require a 1/4-inch-diameter hole, but this varies.

1. Make a shelf pin hole template. The trick to drilling holes for shelf pins is making sure every set of four holes is in perfect horizontal alignment. If they aren't aligned horizontally, the shelves will rock. If the holes are slightly misaligned to the front and back of the cabinet, it won't affect their function.

To ensure perfect horizontal alignment, make a simple drilling template from a scrap of 1/4-inch-thick plywood. Rip the scrap to about 5 or 6 inches wide and make it about 5 inches shorter than the inside height of the cabinet. Mark one long edge of the

template as the "register edge." On this template, lay out the hole spacing you want. A good spacing is to make the holes two inches from the register edge. Lay out the first hole about 8 inches from the bottom of the template and then lay out a hole about every 1½ inches from the bottom of the template. Stop about 3 inches from the top of the template.

2. Drill the holes. Use a stop collar or a piece of tape on the drill bit to mark the depth you want to drill. Align the register edge of the template to the front edge of the cabinet. Make sure the bottom of the template rests on the bottom of the cabinet. Clamp the template in place and drill the holes. Now flip the template over so you will be drilling through the other side. Push the register edge against the back of the cabinet. Drill the holes. Repeat this process for the holes in the opposing panel.

Aligning the Shelf Pin Hole Template

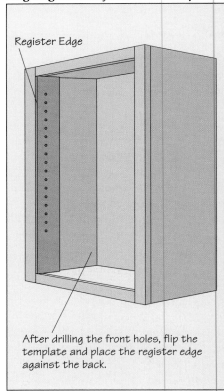

After drilling the front holes, flip the template and place the register edge against the back.

Shortening the Bottom for a Square Drawer

You might find it a little difficult to square up a drawer after the bottom is installed. Some cabinetmakers recommend making the drawer bottom 1/32 inch shorter in length and width to allow some room for adjustment.

Test-fit the bottom before permanently installing it. Clamp the panel in place and check for square. If you find that you cannot coax the drawer square, plane or sand the edges off the bottom panel to provide a little more leeway.

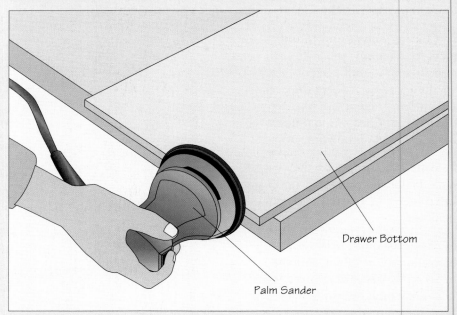

Drawer Bottom

Palm Sander

Making a Shelf Pin Hole Template

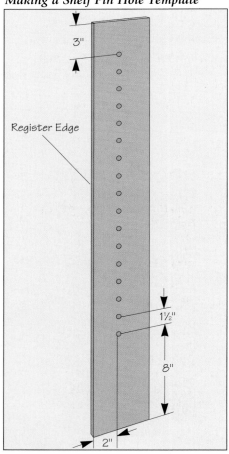

3"

Register Edge

1½"

8"

2"

BUILDING DRAWERS

The most important rule in drawer construction is squareness: If the drawer is not square, it will not function, period.

Bigger drawers require thicker stock. For the projects in this book, drawer sides and end panels can be 3/4-inch-thick solid wood or 3/8- to 3/4-inch plywood. Use plywood for drawer bottoms. For light-duty drawers, you can get away with 1/4-inch drawer bottoms, but 3/8-inch bottoms are recommended for larger drawers or cabinets that you expect to receive heavy-duty use.

There are many different joints for attaching drawer fronts to sides, but for the purposes of this book, you will do quite well with a few simple options. Butt joints are the least glamorous, but they are the simplest to master, and when reinforced with nails or dowels and glue, they are more than adequate for the applications in this book. Rabbet and dado joints are also used in this book for added strength and better appearance.

Size the drawer to fit the opening and the hardware you are going to use. What follows is a common method for making drawers, using primarily plywood.

Drawer Construction

The instructions and drawings here assume your drawers will overlay the face frame. Cut the parts for each project according to the dimensions in the Materials List accompanying the project.

1. Groove the side and front panels. Set the table saw blade 1/4 inch above the table and 1/4 inch away from the fence. Run the front panel and each side panel over the blade to create a 1/8-inch-wide by 1/4-inch-deep

Drawer Construction

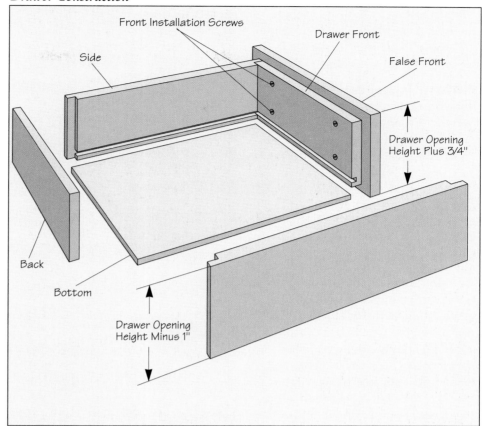

Grooving the Side and Front Panels

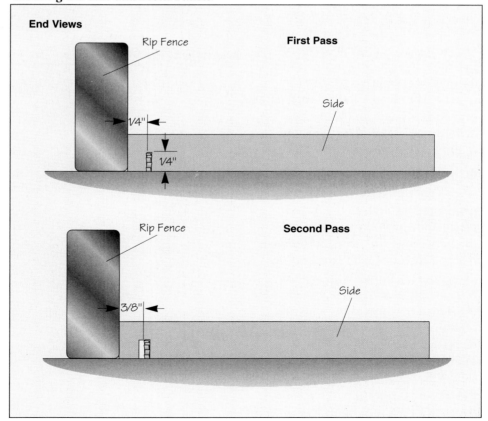

groove in each panel. Move the fence 1/8 inch further from the blade, and run each piece through again to widen the groove to 1/4 inch. Leave the fence set as it is for the next step.

Note: If you are using 3/8-inch-thick wood for a heavy-duty drawer bottom, then you will have to make a third run over the table saw blade to make a 3/8-inch groove. Also, if you are using bottom-mounted drawer slides, you may need to raise the bottom panel to 3/8 inch or 1/2 inch from the bottom edge of the sides. Always purchase the hardware you will use before making drawers.

2. Trim the rear panel. Don't move the rip fence, but raise the blade about 1/2 inch. Rip 1/2 inch off the rear panel. (Be sure to use a push stick, not your hand, to move this narrow piece between the fence and blade.) Now the rear panel will be precisely the right height to fit above the drawer bottom.

3. Rabbet the sides. Set the dado cutter for a width that matches the thickness of your back pieces. Raise the cutter to 1/4 inch above the table saw. Remove the fence from the saw. Use the miter gauge to mill a 1/4-inch-deep rabbet that has a width that matches your wood. Rabbet each end of each side panel. In the absence of a dado cutter, make each rabbet with multiple passes over the saw blade.

4. Assemble the drawer box. Apply glue to the front rabbets in the side panels and the ends of the front panel, and attach the side panels to the front panel with three 3d finishing nails on each side. Slide the bottom panel into position, all the way forward. Apply glue to the rear rabbets in the side panels and to the ends and bottom edge of the rear panel. Put the rear panel in place, flush with the top of the side panels and nail on the sides. Check the drawer for square; then secure the bottom to the rear panels with 3/4-inch brads.

Trimming the Rear Panel

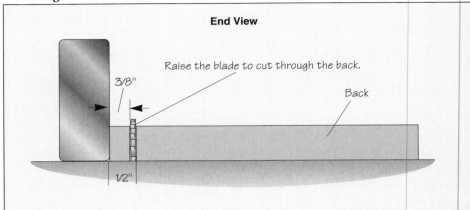

End View

3/8"

Raise the blade to cut through the back.

Back

1/2"

Rabbeting the Sides

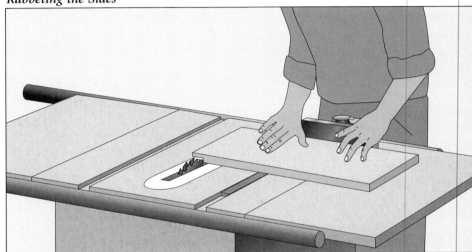

Assembling the Drawer Box

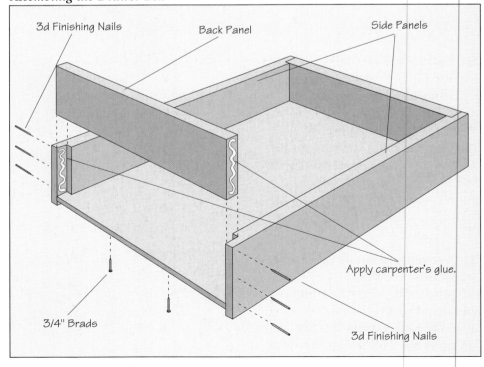

3d Finishing Nails

Back Panel

Side Panels

Apply carpenter's glue.

3/4" Brads

3d Finishing Nails

5. Attach the drawer front. If your project has inset doors and you want your drawers to match, rout a 3/8x3/8-inch rabbet all the way around the inside face of the false front. (Keep in mind, this will make the drawer travel 3/8 inch further into the opening, so you may have to shorten the drawer sides accordingly.) After the false front has been raised, routed, or otherwise readied for finishing, attach it to the front end panel with four #6x1¼-inch wood screws driven through countersunk pilot holes near each front inside corner of the drawer.

If your project doesn't have inset doors, there is no need to rout. Attach the false front with four #6x1¼-inch wood screws as described above.

DRAWER SLIDES

There are several options for drawer slides depending on how you build the cabinet. The simplest drawer slide system is the drawer that just fits inside its drawer opening and is supported on wooden runners. However, this system doesn't work well for drawers that will carry heavy loads, such as kitchen drawers. It's also not recommended for drawers with plywood sides because the plywood edges won't hold up.

Another option is wooden slides which can be built in several ways. But the problem with all wooden slides is that they change dimensions with changes in humidity, causing drawers to bind or be sloppy in their openings. Wood drawer slides also wear out faster when subjected to heavy use.

For heavy use and guaranteed smooth operation, metal slide hardware is the way to go. There are commercial slides for every need, and some models can even handle loads from 75 to 100 pounds. For the projects in this book, side-mounted and bottom-mounted slides are used. In general, follow the manufacturer's instructions for instal-

Attaching the Drawer Front

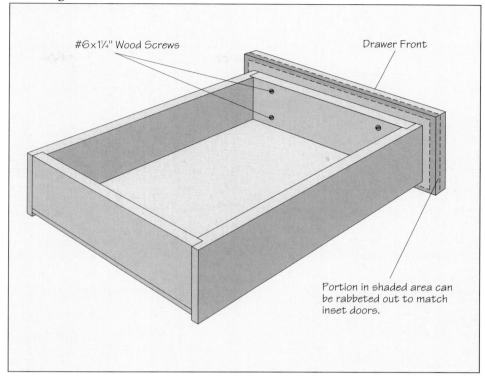

#6 x 1¼" Wood Screws

Drawer Front

Portion in shaded area can be rabbeted out to match inset doors.

lation. Here are some basic instructions for installing the most common side-mounted drawer slides.

Installing Drawer Slide Hardware

1. Install the drawer slides. Use the screws supplied to attach the drawer slides to the bottoms of the sides,

locating the rollers at the rear of the drawer. The non-roller end should touch the back of the drawer front.

2. Install the drawer guides in the cabinet. Align the drawer guide perpendicular to the cabinet front and resting on the bottom of the cabinet opening with the wheel at the front of the opening. Most slides have both oblong

Installing Drawer Slides

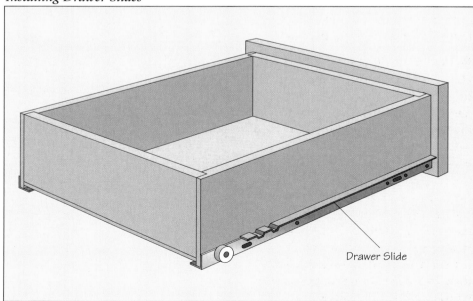

Drawer Slide

Installing Drawer Guides

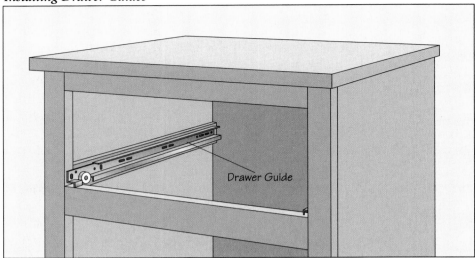

Drawer Guide

Countertop Options

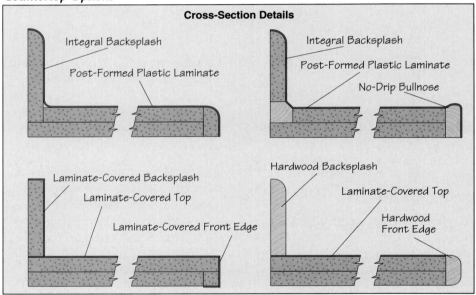

Cross-Section Details

Integral Backsplash

Post-Formed Plastic Laminate

Integral Backsplash

Post-Formed Plastic Laminate

No-Drip Bullnose

Laminate-Covered Backsplash

Laminate-Covered Top

Laminate-Covered Front Edge

Hardwood Backsplash

Laminate-Covered Top

Hardwood Front Edge

Plastic Laminate Cutting Jig

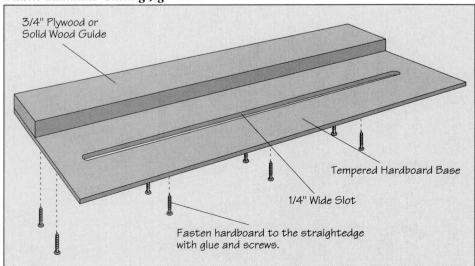

3/4" Plywood or Solid Wood Guide

Tempered Hardboard Base

1/4" Wide Slot

Fasten hardboard to the straightedge with glue and screws.

and round holes for mounting screws. If you first mount the guides to the sides of the cabinet using the oblong holes, you can make fine adjustments before permanently positioning the guides using the round holes.

COUNTERTOPS

You'll need to consider countertop options for the cabinets that you will install in the kitchen, bathroom, or utility room. The right countertop will provide you with a convenient and durable work surface.

Plastic laminate is a durable, stain-resistant material that has many applications. Laminate comes in various lengths, widths, textures, and colors to match just about any job and to fit into any project budget. You will find that the 0.05-inch general-purpose grade is the most common laminate for countertops, cabinets, and furniture.

Be extra careful when working with sheets of laminate. The sheets can crack or chip quite easily before you attach them to a substrate. If you can, have large sheets cut to size at a home center or a cabinet shop.

You can build plastic laminate countertops in your own shop or you can purchase factory-made countertops which are available in several standard sizes in most home centers. When building your own, use two layers of 3/4-inch-thick plywood or particleboard. Some stores can even cut panels to order. These countertops come pre-laminated with a special post-forming grade of plastic laminate that can be bent into gentle curves. These "post-formed" counters feature integral backsplashes and curved front edges or no-drip, bullnose profiles.

Cutting Plastic Laminate

While it is possible to cut plastic laminate with a saber saw and a special laminate-cutting blade, it's slow work.

Cutting Plastic Laminate

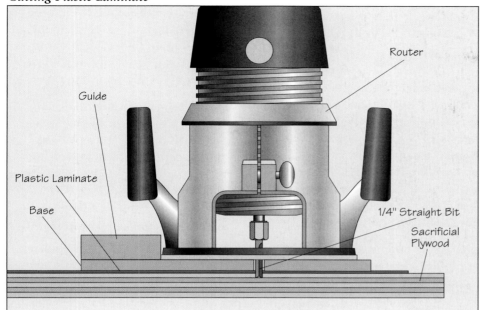

There is also a chance that you will damage the material during the cut, or at least not get a smooth finish.

The best tool for cutting plastic laminates is your router and a 1/4-inch straight-cutting bit. Use a carbide-tipped bit; plastic laminate will dull a steel-tipped bit in seconds. To guide the router when cutting laminate, make a jig similar to the straight-cutting jig on page 6. In fact, if you have made the straight-cutting jig you can use it as a laminate-cutting jig simply by routing a 1/4-inch slot in the side of the jig you are not using to guide the circular saw.

When you use the laminate-cutting jig, set the laminate on top of a sacrificial piece of plywood. Align the cutting slot to your cutting layout line. Clamp the laminate and the jig to the plywood. Set the router cutting depth to go through the laminate and slightly into the plywood.

Cut edge strips for any project about 1/4 inch wider than you need. (You will trim the excess off with a router and a flush-trimming bit after installation.) Cut countertops, coverings for doors and drawer faces, and other flat surfaces about 1/2 inch larger on all dimensions.

Gluing Laminate to Substrate

Use contact cement to attach plastic laminate to plywood or particleboard substrate. Make sure you have plenty of ventilation and stay away from any source of flame.

Applying Adhesive to Edges

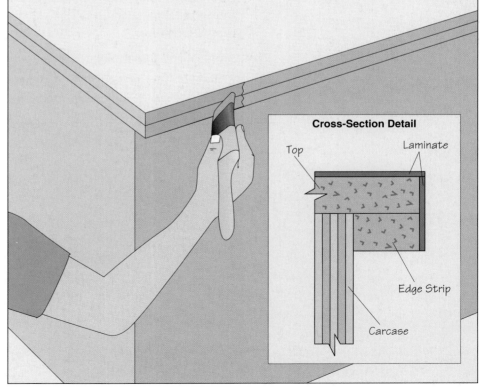

1. **Apply adhesive to the edges and edge strips.** With a brush or small roller, coat the edges of the substrate and the back of the laminate with contact cement. In most cases this includes the edges of the countertop and the edges of doors and drawers. For these smaller areas, use a brush or smaller roller. Allow the adhesive to dry at least as long as recommended on the can (it should be dry to the touch).

2. **Install and trim the edge strips.** Install the edge strips, making sure they overhang both sides of the surface. Use a laminate roller (a rolling pin also works well in a pinch) to firmly seat the piece. Trim both sides of the laminate with a flush-trimming bit in the router.

3. **Laminate the countertop.** Next, apply contact cement to the horizontal surfaces and the bottom of the laminate. The easiest way to do this is to pour some cement right on the surface and spread it out with a short-napped paint roller, a large brush, or even a scrap of laminate. When the cement is dry to the touch, cover the substrate with plain brown wrapping paper or small strips of lath. Leave about 1/2 inch of exposed surface along one edge of the substrate. Carefully lay the laminate on the paper or lath. Do not allow it to touch the substrate yet or it will tack immediately.

Align the laminate and press it in place where you left the exposed cement. Gradually remove the paper or lath and press the laminate in place to work out any bubbles. Use a laminate roller or a rolling pin to ensure that the laminate is properly seated. Use a router and flush-trimming bit to trim the overhanging edges of laminate flush with the surface.

Trimming the Edge Strips

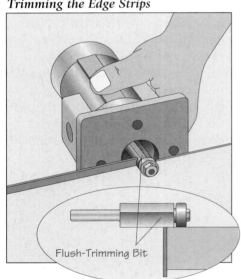

Flush-Trimming Bit

INSTALLING CABINETS AND BUILT-INS

Installing cabinets and other built-in projects is not difficult, but it can be an exercise in patience. Your cabinets must be installed plumb and vertical, which can be a challenge if your wall or floor is out of whack. If you find installation to be a sometimes slow but always methodical job, you're probably doing it right.

You might have to remove some molding before installation. See "Removing Trim," page 30, for more details.

Finding Studs

Wall materials such as plaster and drywall don't have the strength to support heavy cabinets or built-ins. Cabinets should be supported by framing inside the wall, which usually means screwing through the wall surface into studs. Studs are typically installed on 16-inch centers, so once you've located one, you can measure along the wall to find other fastening points.

A magnetic stud finder is one of the simplest and least expensive ways to find studs. These nifty gadgets detect the nails or screws used to attach the wallboard to the wood. A bit more expensive but even better than the magnetic stud finders are the electronic stud finders now available in home centers and hardware stores.

In the absence of a stud finder, you can probe the wall with a small nail or a small-diameter bit as long as you are sure that the holes you are making will be covered by the cabinet after installation.

Removing Wallboard

Some of the projects in this book require you to remove wallboard so the cabinet can be installed inside the wall. Before planning such a project, make sure there will be no plumbing or electrical wiring where you want to install the cabinet, otherwise you will have to plan to relocate pipes or wiring.

Even if you think that there are no wires in the wall you wish to remove, go to the circuit box and switch off power to that portion of the house to be safe.

Use a reciprocating saw or drywall saw to cut through the wallboard and remove the material. Be warned that this will be a dusty operation, so cover adjacent areas and be sure to wear a dust mask and safety glasses.

Laminating the Countertop

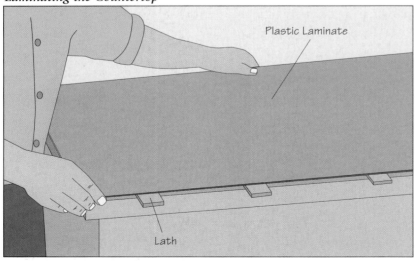

Plastic Laminate

Lath

Removing Wallboard

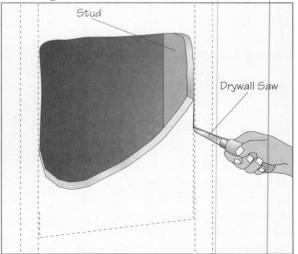

Stud

Drywall Saw

Removing Carpet

If you are planning to install your project over preexisting hard floor coverings, such as wood, tile, or vinyl, just install the project right over it, there's no need to remove anything. However, if the room is carpeted, you will need to remove the carpet before installation.

Before you cut the carpet, measure the base of your project without baseboard or trim molding. Transfer those measurements to the floor, exactly where the project will be installed. Use a straightedge and a carpet knife or utility knife to remove both the carpet and the pad.

Measuring the Cabinet

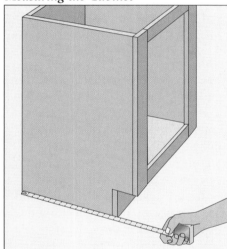

Cutting the Carpet

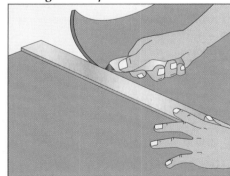

Installing Base Cabinets

There is no such thing as a perfectly level floor or plumb wall. Even the best walls have a slight ripple; the best laid floor may slope away from the wall imperceptibly. These minor imperfections can ruin a perfectly

good finish. Fortunately, it's easy to adjust for these imperfections during installation.

1. **Find the floor's high point.** Use a level to find the high spot in the floor where you are installing the cabinet. To do this, set a level on the floor and check if the floor is level. If it isn't, slide the level along to the high side until the bubble shifts to the other side of the vial. Mark that spot as the high point of your floor.

2. **Scribe a level line.** Measure up the wall from the floor's high point, and make a mark at cabinet height. Use the level to scribe a level line along the wall for the full length of the cabinet.

3. **Install the cabinet.** Slide the cabinet against the wall, and check it against the level line. Use wood shims at the back of the cabinet to level it from front to back. Use shims under the cabinet to level it from side to side. Once the cabinet is level and plumb, attach it to the studs with 3½-inch screws. Trim the shims with a utility knife or chisel.

4. **Finish the kickplates.** There are at least three ways to cover the gaps caused by shimming. An easy and ideal solution for kitchens and baths where floors will get wet is to use vinyl base molding. You can attach vinyl molding with construction adhe-

Scribing a Level Line

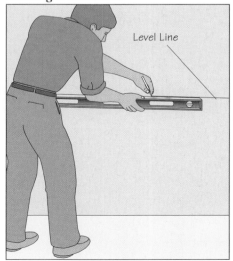

sive or contact cement. It is flexible enough to allow you to press it into place and then trim it at the top with a utility knife.

Leveling a Base Cabinet

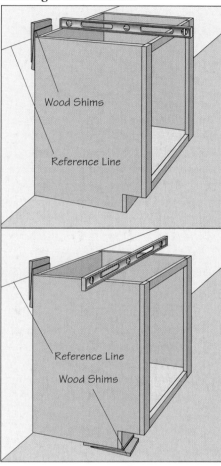

Wood Shims

Reference Line

Reference Line

Wood Shims

Covering the Shim Gaps

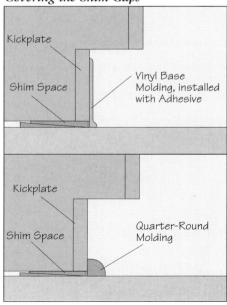

Kickplate

Shim Space

Vinyl Base Molding, installed with Adhesive

Kickplate

Shim Space

Quarter-Round Molding

For dry areas, such as the living room where vinyl molding might not look appropriate, you can face the kickplate with strips of 1/4-inch-thick plywood. Or you can add a run of quarter-round molding. The quarter-round looks particularly appropriate if it has been used as a shoe molding on the baseboard in the room.

Installing Wall Cabinets

Wall cabinets are a little more difficult to install than base cabinets because they must be hung. Even positioning small units in place can be exhausting, unless you have a means of supporting them. One of the most basic ways of doing this is to screw a temporary rail, or ledge, along the bottom line of the cabinets. Not only will the rail ensure that the cabinet is hung level, but you never have to worry about its arms getting tired.

1. **Install the ledger.** Using a level, draw a line along the wall indicating the bottom of the wall cabinets. Using 2-inch screws, secure a temporary ledger along that line. Make sure that you've screwed into studs, and that the board is perfectly level before continuing to the next step.

Installing a Temporary Ledger

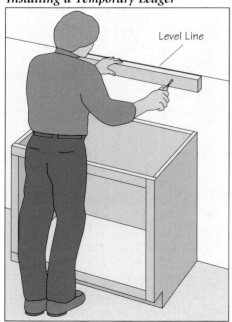

Level Line

2. **Hang the cabinets.** Lift the cabinet onto the ledge and position it as close to the wall as possible. Drive two 3-inch screws through the upper hanging cleat just tight enough to hold the cabinet in place. Check for level from front to back. You may have to do a little shimming. Secure the bottom of the cabinet to the wall by driving two 3-inch screws through the lower hanging cleat and into the studs.

3. **Apply molding.** Depending on how flat and plumb the walls are, there will probably be gaps between the walls and the cabinet. These can be easily concealed by installing quarter-round or other molding along the cabinet.

TRIM AND MOLDING

Besides adding another level of decor to your project, molding can be used to conceal screw holes, nailholes, and other blemishes that are inevitable in construction. Typically, molding is used as a transition piece to cover up the gap between a cabinet and a wall, a cabinet and the floor, or a cabinet and a cabinet.

Hanging the Cabinets

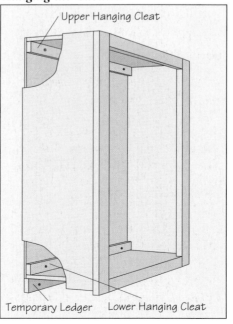

Upper Hanging Cleat

Temporary Ledger   Lower Hanging Cleat

Removing Trim

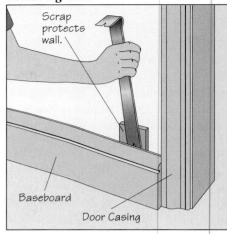

Scrap protects wall.

Baseboard

Door Casing

Removing Trim

You will have to remove any baseboard or crown molding before you can install the built-in units. If you carefully remove these moldings, you will be able to reinstall them later.

The best place to start removing trim and molding is where it begins—at a door or corner. If the joint at the corner is coped, remove the coped piece first, then the butted piece. Starting at the end, coax the molding away from the wall with a pry bar. Pry as near the nails as possible, and use a thin scrap of wood behind the pry bar to protect the wall. After you've pried part of the the trim or molding away from the wall, move to the next nail. Continue this process until you gradually pry away the entire length of material.

If a strip of molding won't come loose, drive the nails through the piece with a nail set. It's much easier to patch these holes later than to fix broken trim.

Replacing Trim

Replace any molding and trim you removed earlier, and add new matching trim and molding as required. Wherever possible, use the existing nailholes. Nail removal will have enlarged the holes, so use larger nails during replacement. Fill the nailholes and do any necessary touch up.

Nail Safety

One of the most potentially painful sights around a construction site is a board with a nail (or nails) in it. Remove nails from trim as soon as you remove the trim from the wall. The best way to pull finishing nails from trim without damaging the face of the trim wood is to pull the nails completely through the back of the piece. Use slip-joint pliers or nail nippers to grab the point of the finishing nail and lever the nail out by rocking the tool. If the molding is damaged, or if you are not planning to reuse a piece, make it a habit to bend the nails over with a hammer.

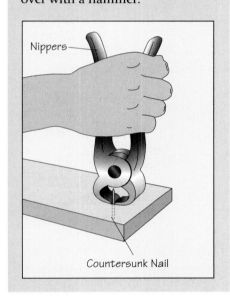

When replacing molding, you'll have to fit pieces together around corners. Miter joints are the way to go for outside corners. But for inside corners, it is better to use cope joints. Done properly, a coped joint looks seamless, allowing the profile to continue smoothly around the corner. Coped joints are less likely to open up than inside miter joints.

Making a Coped Joint

1. **Miter the molding to be coped.** To make a coped joint, first miter the piece of molding as if you were fitting an inside miter. Pencil a 90-degree angle at the top edge of the molding. Then run the pencil along the profile revealed by the miter cut.

2. **Cope the joint.** Using a coping saw, back-cut the molding by following the line where the miter meets the front of the molding. If the molding has curves across its entire face, cope all the way across. If it is a molding such as a baseboard with a large flat field, you may want to complete the cut with a miter saw. Test-fit your coped piece and fine tune it with a chisel or small file.

3. **Finish the installation.** Once the coped joint is in position, butt the cope against the existing baseboard molding and allow the opposite end to run long. Mark the back of the long end and square-cut it to the correct length.

Cutting and Installing Crown Molding

Whether you're adding new molding to a project or re-cutting and replacing molding you removed for cabinet installation, you should have no trouble making the simple cuts with a miter box and backsaw or power miter saw. One type of molding that might give you some trouble, however, is crown molding. Because of its design, it gets installed differently and must be cut differently.

Crown molding leans at a 45-degree angle from the vertical surface where it's attached—whether the surface is a wall where it meets the ceiling, or at the top of a cabinet or bookcase. The trick to cutting crown molding is to lean it in the miter box at that same angle. The easiest way to do this is to turn the molding upside down when it's in the miter box or miter saw. To keep the molding in place when you lean it, attach a stop block to the fence or table. Use a strip of 3/4-inch-square stock and screw or clamp it in place.

Mitering the Molding

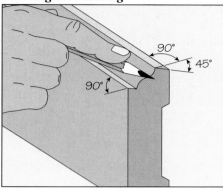

Coping the Joint

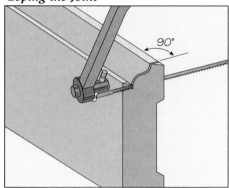

Cutting Crown Molding

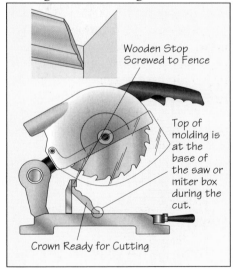

Installing Crown Molding

Attaching crown molding to a wall is simple—just tilt it into position against the wall and ceiling, and nail it in place. If you're using it on a cabinet, you can install it the same way. You may need to bevel-cut some blocking material and attach that at the top of the cabinet to provide additional support for wider moldings.

TOOLS

GETTING STARTED

Many people new to woodworking and do-it-yourself projects are surprised to learn how much they can accomplish with simple hand tools and a few portable power tools. It doesn't take a shop full of expensive machinery to build practical and attractive furnishings. What's more, as your skills develop, you'll be able to build pieces by hand that are in many ways superior to those that roll off an assembly line.

If you've tackled other do-it-yourself projects, or have done home repairs and maintenance, you may already own most of the hand and power tools necessary to build the projects in this book. There are many other sophisticated tools that can simplify tasks, but there is no need to run out and buy them all at once. It makes sense to start slowly, adding tools as the need arises. This way, you'll be sure to purchase only what you really need.

ESSENTIAL HAND TOOLS

Here's a list of the hand tools you'll need to complete the projects in this book. Below this list you'll find a list of tools that aren't essential, but will help you work more efficiently.

Steel Tape Measure

Tape measures commonly come in lengths from 6 to 50 feet. A 16-footer will serve fine for any project in this book. If you want to use the tape measure for carpentry work as well, choose a 25-footer.

Squares

The four most common squares in the home workshop are the carpenter's or framing square, angle square, try square, and combination square. They're used for measuring, marking, and checking the inside and outside squareness of right angles.

Framing Square. This square is available in a few sizes. The larger version has a 24-inch-long blade and 16 inch-long tongue, and is the tool of choice for house framing work. You may find one of the smaller models, measuring 8x6 or 12x8 inches, more convenient for smaller projects.

Angle Square. Often called by the brand name Speed Square, this durable triangular square has many uses both in the shop and on the construction site. Use it as a depth gauge, protractor, and for scribing lines at 45 and 90 degrees. It also doubles as a circular saw guide for crosscutting and miter cutting.

Try Square. This square has a broad blade attached to a stock at a right angle. The blade, which may be graduated for measurement, is available in lengths from 2 to 12 inches. Use a try square to test, or try, the squareness of right angles, to scribe lines, and to calibrate tools. One type, called a try-and-miter square or just a miter square, has a 45-degree angle built into the top of the handle so that it can also try and scribe miters.

Combination Square. This tool consists of a 6-, 12-, or 16-inch graduated steel blade with a sliding handle that can be tightened at any position. Most come equipped with a spirit level and scratch awl built into the handle.

Hand Tools

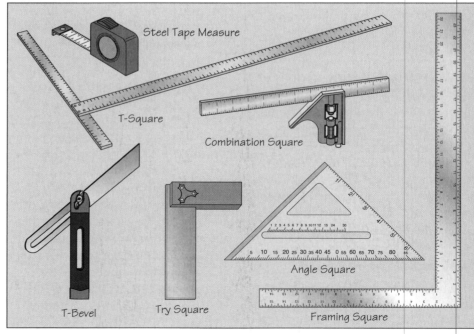

Steel Tape Measure

T-Square

Combination Square

T-Bevel

Try Square

Angle Square

Framing Square

The combination square is one of the most useful tools in any woodworker's shop. You can use it horizontally to check for level, vertically to check for plumb, or diagonally as a miter square. It serves as an inside try square, outside try square, depth gauge, marking gauge, and straight edge. It's also the ideal tool for locating and centering screw holes and scribing layout lines.

T-bevel. Also known as the sliding T-bevel or bevel square, this simple tool consists of a handle or stock attached to a 6- or 8-inch slotted blade. The T-bevel can function as a try-and-miter square, but it is more commonly used for transferring and duplicating angles other than 90 degrees.

T-square. Another useful square—and one that's ideal for working with gypsum wallboard, paneling, plywood, hardboard, and other sheet stock—the 48-inch T-square is sometimes called a drywall square. Although smaller T-squares are available, you'll need one this long for scribing lines across standard-sized sheet stock. This square also works well as a cutting guide for utility and acrylic knives and glass cutters.

Hammers and Related Tools

Every woodworker should be armed with at least three basic hammers: a claw hammer, a tack hammer, and a mallet. Each is indispensable for its own specific task. A claw hammer is the first choice for driving and removing nails and brads. But when it's necessary to drive tacks or brads that are just too tiny to grip, you'll appreciate the magnetic head on your tack hammer. A wooden mallet or soft-faced hammer should be used whenever a metal hammer might damage a surface, as when tapping in wood plugs, or a tight-fitting tenon, or when working with wooden-handled chisels and gouges.

Nail Sets and Center Punches. A nail set is used to drive finishing nails below the work surface without denting the surface, so the holes can be easily filled. A set rests on top of a nail or brad, enabling you to safely sink the nail without damaging the surrounding wood. The standard three-piece set—consisting of 1/32-, 1/16-, and 3/32-inch nail sets—will handle most of the jobs for the home workshop.

A center punch looks like a nail set, except that its sharp, conical point tends to stick into wood. You'll need one for locating and punching starter holes for twist-drill bits to keep them from "walking" off their mark during the initial drilling. Starter holes are also handy when hand-driving screws.

Miter Box and Backsaw

One of the most important hand tool combinations in any woodworker's shop is the miter box and backsaw. Miter boxes come in a variety of styles and prices, ranging from inexpensive three-sided wooden boxes with blade slots for cutting at 90 and 45 degrees, to relatively expensive metal models that are adjustable for making cuts at any angle between 90 and 45 degrees. Backsaws come with blades ranging from 12 to 30 inches.

When cutting long boards and strips of molding, be sure to support the stock that extends beyond the miter box table. You can stack wood scraps and other objects on your workbench or saw horses, invest in adjustable supports designed for such purposes, or build your own supports.

Hammers and Related Tools

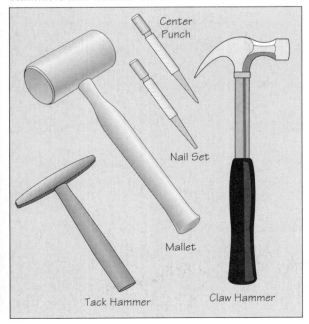

Center Punch

Nail Set

Mallet

Tack Hammer

Claw Hammer

Miter Box and Backsaw

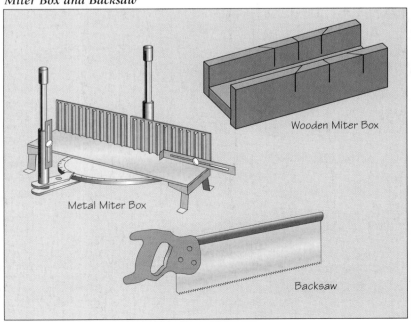

Wooden Miter Box

Metal Miter Box

Backsaw

Levels

Levels are made of wood, metal, or plastic. They are used to determine whether a surface is horizontal (level) or vertical (plumb). New electronic digital levels are also capable of checking other angles. Levels come in lengths from 9 inches to more than 72 inches. Pick up a 2-footer to start with; it is small enough for working in tight quarters, yet long enough to provide an accurate reading.

Planes

Although you could build every project in this book without ever having to reach for one, few tools can remove paper-thin shavings of wood or smooth a rough board as quickly or precisely as an old-fashioned hand plane.

Today, good new planes are relatively expensive, but used planes are often in good supply at bargain prices at secondhand stores and antique shops. If you have to do without a hand plane, don't despair. Since the development of efficient power tools that can make short work of most trimming and smoothing chores, as well as the widespread availability of surfaced lumber, hand planes aren't as much of a necessity in the typical home workshop as

they once were. But once you get the hang of using such basic planes as the block plane, smooth plane, and jack plane, you'll find them a valuable addition to your toolbox.

The block plane is the most versatile plane in the home workshop. Designed for trimming end grain, called blocking or blocking in, this little plane can also be useful for other small trimming jobs, such as easing the backs of mitered joints or planing down edging flush with a plywood panel.

Jack planes and smooth planes are easy to handle and good for general use. They look very similar to each other, with both having blades about 1¾ to 2 inches wide, but they differ in length. Jack planes are between 11 and 14 inches long. Smooth planes range from 6 to 10 inches long. They both are excellent for taking care of rough areas in wood and for removing saw and mill marks.

Wood Chisels

Designed for removing wood in chips, chunks, and shavings, wood chisels can be driven with a mallet or manipulated by hand for precise paring. They are particularly handy for making quick work of hinge mortises. A

four-chisel set including 1/4-, 1/2-, 3/4-, and 1-inch chisels will see to most needs in the home workshop.

An old shop rule warns against striking a chisel with anything but a wooden or leather mallet. This rule still holds with wooden chisels; the blade tangs can split the handle if the tool is used improperly. Modern plastic-handled chisels, however, are much more durable and can be used with ordinary steel hammers.

Other Helpful Hand Tools

In addition to the hand tools listed above, you'll need some other tools to help with the projects.

Saws. You'll need a hand saw for cutting wood and wood products and a hacksaw for cutting metal. For some of the decorative curves you may find a need for a coping saw. For flush-cutting chores such as cutting off wood plugs you might want to buy a special flush-cutting saw.

Utility Knife. Not only is a utility knife useful for the projects listed in this book, but it's a great tool to have for other tasks. Always make sure the blade is sharp because dull blades aren't as precise and may slip off the

Level, Planes, and Wood Chisels

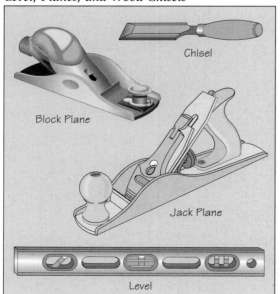

Chisel

Block Plane

Jack Plane

Level

Other Helpful Hand Tools

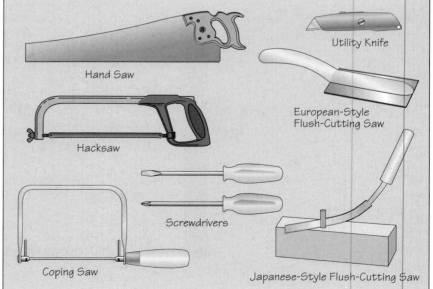

Hand Saw

Utility Knife

Hacksaw

European-Style Flush-Cutting Saw

Screwdrivers

Coping Saw

Japanese-Style Flush-Cutting Saw

mark. Be sure that the blade is retracted when not in use.

Screwdrivers. Although they may rank as one of the simplest tools found in any toolbox, a good set of screwdrivers is essential for the do-it-yourselfer. The two most common types of screwdrivers are the slotted and the Phillips head. The best way to avoid stripping screw heads is to have a good selection of different size screwdrivers to properly fit the different size screws you will encounter.

Clamps

No shop ever has enough clamps, yet these essential tools are most often overlooked by beginning do-it-yourselfers. Clamps are designed for such jobs as edge-gluing boards and attaching trim to plywood edges. It won't take long for you to discover how valuable they can be throughout your shop. Use clamps to secure workpieces for sawing, routing, drilling, or sanding. A good basic starter set consists of a pair or two of 4-inch C-clamps and at least one pair of pipe clamps.

Bar Clamps and Pipe Clamps. Bar clamps provide greater reach than most other clamps and are ideal for drawing frame members and cabinet panels together. They range in size from about 1 to 8 feet. Bar clamps of 24 to 36 inches will see to many chores in the home workshop and aren't prohibitively expensive. Big bar clamps, however, might prove too costly for the do-it-yourselfer on a tight budget.

Pipe clamps offer a less expensive alternative, especially for big clamping tasks. These clamps, consisting of cast-iron fixtures that you thread onto lengths of separately purchased black-iron pipe, are available from home centers, hardware stores, and mail-order sources. You should be able to buy threaded pipe at a home center, otherwise you may have to go to a store that specializes in plumbing supplies. A pair of 48-inch pipe clamps will take care of most jobs. When you need something bigger, you can simply join two pieces of pipe with a pipe coupler.

Corner Clamps. These clamps are designed to hold two pieces of material together at a right angle for gluing, nailing, or screwing. Start with a basic set of four to assemble miter-cut frames, as well as any other frame or box joined at right angles.

POWER TOOLS

To build the projects in this book, you'll need an electric drill, saber saw, circular saw, router, and an electric sander. You can get by without any stationary power tools, but a table saw can save a lot of time when you need to cut sheet stock, mill grooves or rabbets, and tackle a great variety of other sawing chores.

Drill, Bits, and Accessories

Look for a 3/8-inch, variable-speed, reversible drill for everyday use. Cordless drills may be more expensive, but they are the most convenient because they can be used anywhere without an extension cord. Today there are 12-volt cordless drill/drivers powerful enough to handle most tasks. Many come with keyless chucks, adjustable clutches, and driver-bit storage. If you decide to purchase one, consider buying an extra battery so you will always have a backup power supply.

Basic Bits. Invest in a set of twist-drill or brad-point bits with sizes from 1/16 to 1/4 inch; you can always buy the larger sizes as they are needed. Brad-point bits cost a little more, but are better for drilling wood. Their pointed tips are less apt to skid across your work, and they generally bore cleaner holes. For most larger wood-boring chores, you can get by with inexpensive spade bits for holes up to $1\frac{1}{2}$ inches in diameter and hole saws for boring holes up to $2\frac{1}{2}$ inches in diameter.

You'll also want screwdriver bits, which you can buy individually or in sets for standard slotted, Phillips, and other types of screws.

Countersink and Counterbore Bits. You'll want to invest in a set of inexpensive countersink bits for drilling and countersinking holes for screws

Clamps

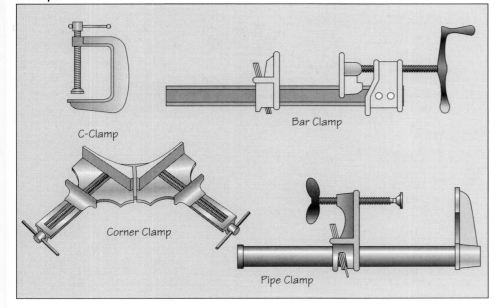

C-Clamp

Bar Clamp

Corner Clamp

Pipe Clamp

in sizes from #4 to #12. Although you can drill, countersink and counterbore screw holes with ordinary drill bits, counterboring bits can perform all three functions in one step.

Doweling Jig. For assembling furniture and cabinets with dowels, you'll need a doweling jig. It will enable you to drill perfectly aligned holes in parts to be joined.

Portable Power Saws

Saber Saw. Use a saber saw with a saw guide to cut straight lines or freehand to make pocket cuts, circular cuts, and other cuts of unusual shape. A saber saw is excellent for cutting and trimming panel stock, back-cutting large moldings, and making cutouts in countertops. With the right blade you can use a saber saw to cut metal, plastic pipe, laminates or Plexiglass. Look for a saw that has orbital action (which advances the blade on the cutting stroke), for faster cutting speeds and longer-lasting blades.

Circular Saw. This workhorse is as indispensable in the home workshop as it is on a commercial construction site. The standard saw uses a 7¼-inch

blade that can crosscut or rip stock up to 2½ inches thick, which means this saw will easily handle nominal 1-inch and 2-inch lumber and all sheet stock.

There are various blades available for the circular saw designed for crosscutting, ripping, and other specific chores and materials, as well as general-purpose combination blades that will do several jobs fairly well. Generally, the more teeth a blade has the finer it will cut; a 7¼-inch circular blade, with 36 to 40 carbide-tipped teeth will provide a reasonably splinter-free cut.

Circular Saw and Router Guides. Without any kind of guide, a circular saw can make cuts that are straight enough for carpentry work. However, to make cuts straight and square enough for cabinet work, you'll need a guide. Router bits designed to shape edges have their own pilots, but a guide is essential to mill dadoes and grooves with the router.

You can buy a guide that attaches to a circular saw and runs along the edge of the board as you make a cut. This kind of guide works only for cuts that are within a few inches of the edge. As a result, it is useful mainly for making

rip cuts along the length of a board or panel. This can be handy if you don't have a table saw for ripping. You can buy a similar sort of guide to attach to your router, but you won't need one for the projects in this book.

A more versatile approach to guiding both the circular saw and the router is to use a straightedge guide that you clamp to the work. You can buy metal guides that have clamps built in. Plans for a shop-built guide that works for both the router and circular saw can be found on page 6. On the same page you'll find plans for a T-square guide that ensures that your router cuts are square.

Router, Bits, and Accessories

The router ranks just behind drills and saws in popularity among woodworkers. This versatile tool deserves its place in the workshop because of

Portable Power Saws

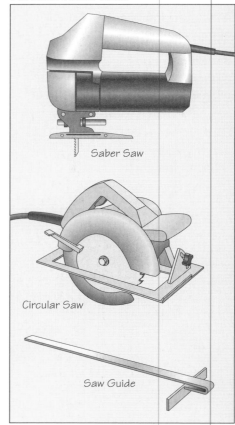

Saber Saw

Circular Saw

Saw Guide

Drill, Bits, and Accessories

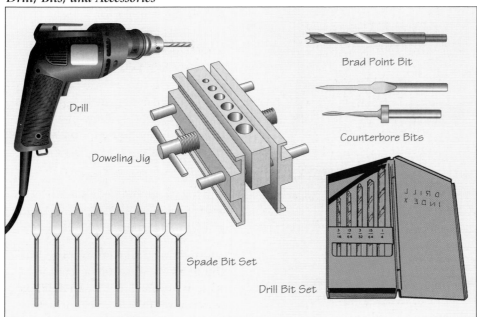

Drill

Doweling Jig

Spade Bit Set

Drill Bit Set

Brad Point Bit

Counterbore Bits

its capacity to perform a tremendous variety of tasks such as making rabbets, dadoes, and grooves; routing decorative edges in wood; making moldings, and cutting plastic laminates.

All routers are basically a motor mounted on a base. The wide range in prices largely reflects differences in power: 1/3- to 1/2- horsepower (hp) models are considered light-duty, while heavy-duty models are powered with 2- to 3- hp motors. Also, some routers can plunge the bit into the work, a feature you won't need for the projects in this book. If you are purchasing one router for general purposes, get one with about 1½ horsepower.

Router, Bits, and Accessories

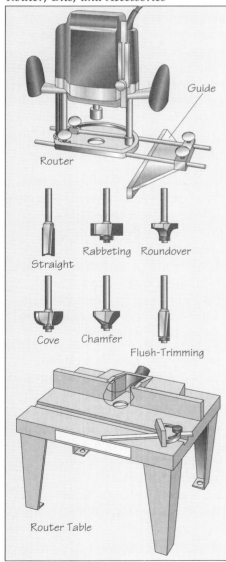

Basic Bits. Outfit your router with a set of basic bits including straight, round-over, rabbeting, cove, and chamfering bits. If you plan to laminate your countertops, you'll also need a flush-trimming bit. All of these bits, except the straight bit, are piloted edge-shaping bits. The ones illustrated are piloted by a ball bearing that runs along the edge of the wood. Bits are also available with fixed pilots that spin with the bit. These are cheaper, but the friction of the spinning pilot often burns the edge of the wood.

Router Table. You can buy or build a router table. This accessory lets your router function like a small shaper. A table is ideal for many applications where it's easier or safer to bring the material to the tool, instead of vice versa. This is the preferred way to make your own moldings and to mill decorative edges on panels such as drawer fronts.

Sanders

No chore is as tedious as hand sanding. A general-duty electric sander will save untold amounts of time and will help produce a more uniform finish.

Sanders

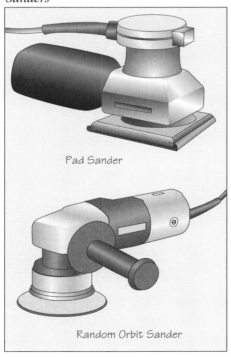

Pad Sander

Random Orbit Sander

Pad Sander. Also known as finishing sanders, pad sanders are available in three popular sizes to accommodate 1/4, 1/3, or 1/2 sheets of sandpaper. The 1/3-sheet and 1/2-sheet sanders are designed for two-handed operation, while the 1/4-sheet models, often called palm sanders, are for one-handed use. Pad sanders sand in an orbital motion for fast material removal or straight-line motion for fine finishing; some can be switched between the two modes.

Random-Orbit Disc Sander. This sander is popular with woodworkers because it removes wood faster than a pad sander while its random orbit eliminates the swirls you get with a pad sander.

Plate Joiner

One of the most versatile new tools finding its way into home shops is the plate joiner, sometimes called a biscuit joiner. Once reserved for professionals, this tool has become attractive to do-it-yourselfers because it quickly and precisely makes strong joints to join panels or cabinet parts. The tool cuts a precise semi-circular kerf in which a plate or biscuit is inserted. The biscuit is a pressed wafer of wood that expands with the moisture of glue to make for very tight joints.

Table Saw, Blades, and Accessories

By far, the most valuable and versatile tool for any serious home workshop is the table saw. It's available in a wide variety of sizes and prices, ranging from inexpensive 8-inch bench-top models for just over $100 to the 12-inch industrial powerhouses that cost more than $2,000. The saw most popular among woodworkers uses a 10-inch blade. Most bench-top and some free-standing models are "motorized." This means the saw arbor is attached directly to the motor. Better saws are belt-driven, which makes them work smoother, stronger, and quieter than motorized saws.

Blades. Steel blades are priced between $10 and $20; carbide-tipped blades go from $10 to more than $200. The usual rule applies: Buy the best you can afford. Carbide blades are initially more expensive than steel blades, and high quality carbide blades cost more than lower quality ones, but the better blades will cut cleaner and stay sharp longer. For general purposes, buy one of the 40- or 50-tooth combination blades. For making clean, splinter-free cuts in plywood and other materials, buy an 80-tooth, carbide-tipped blade designed for such purposes. Here's a hint: Motorized saws are generally less powerful than belt-driven saws. If you intend to rip a lot of hardwood with a less powerful saw, invest in a new, thin-kerf blade before the job. The sharpness of a new blade, combined with the reduced resistance of the narrower thin-kerf blade, goes a long way toward compensating for the lack of a powerful saw.

Dado Cutters. A table saw equipped with a dado cutter can make short work of cutting dadoes, grooves, and rabbets. Depending on the style and manufacturer of the cutter, most are capable of cutting widths ranging from 1/4 to 13/16 inch.

Safety Equipment

Common sense should tell you not to attempt any project without adequate eye and ear protection. Wear safety goggles or plastic glasses whenever you are working with tools or chemicals... period. Make sure that your eye protection conforms to those requirements set by either the American National Standards Institute (ANSI) or Canadian Standards Association (CSA). Products that meet these requirements will indicate that fact with a stamp. It's a good idea to purchase an extra pair for those times when a neighbor volunteers to lend a hand, or when you misplace your own pair.

The U.S. Occupational Safety and Health Administration (OSHA) recommends that hearing protection be worn whenever the noise level exceeds 85 decibels (dB) for an 8-hour workday. Considering that a circular saw emits 110 dB, even shorter exposure times can eventually lead to hearing loss. Insert and muff-type protectors are available; make sure that the model you choose has a noise reduction rating (NNR) of at least 20 dB.

Since sawdust is an inevitable by-product of any project, it's a good idea to wear a dust mask. Two types of masks are available, disposable dust masks and cartridge-type respirators. A dust mask is good for protecting you from most fine particles. Respirators generally offer superior protection, but also have certain disadvantages. With a respirator, breathing is more labored and it can get warm inside the mask. Whichever you purchase, be sure that it has been stamped by the National Institute for Occupational Safety & Health/Mine Safety and Health Administration (NIOSH/MSHA) and is approved for your specific operation. If you can taste or smell the contaminate, or if the mask starts to interfere with normal breathing, it's time for a replacement.

One type of dado cutter blade is often called a wobbler or wobble saw. When this single-blade cutter is installed in the table saw, its offset blade oscillates, or wobbles, creating a kerf that's wider than the usual 1/8 inch. A problem with this style cutter is that it tends to dish out the bottoms of the grooves.

Another type of cutter is called a stacked dado cutter set or simply dado set. This type consists of two cutters that resemble combination blades and a set of chippers and shims. The width of the cut is determined by installing different shims and chippers between the blades. Stacked cutters will not dish out the bottoms of dadoes and are less likely than a wobbler to splinter the wood. Stacked cutters are more expensive.

Table Saw, Blades, and Accessories

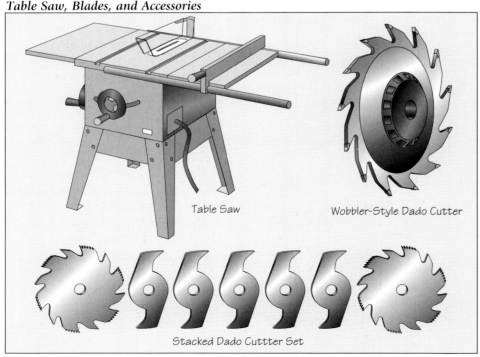

Table Saw

Wobbler-Style Dado Cutter

Stacked Dado Cuttter Set

MATERIALS

Building materials come in a dizzying array of types, species, grades, sizes, finishes, and configurations for an ever-growing variety of applications. There are hardwoods and softwoods, but some softwoods are actually harder than the softer hardwoods. There is some wood that's referred to by its nominal thickness and width instead of its actual dimensions, and other wood that's sold by its actual dimensions, which may or may not turn out to be true sizes. You can buy wood by the lineal or running foot or by the board foot. Hardboard comes tempered or not, perforated or not. There are interior and exterior grades of plywood, yet—you guessed it—we often use exterior plywood indoors.

Fortunately, you needn't know everything about everything all at once. It doesn't take long to gain a basic understanding of, and familiarity with, most of the materials you'll use in woodworking projects.

PLYWOOD

Plywood is made from thin veneers of wood glued together in a sandwich. Each veneer is oriented perpendicularly to the next to make plywood stronger and more resistant to warping than solid wood. Plywood is available with either softwood or hardwood surface veneers and is sold in 4x8-foot sheets, although many home centers also stock half and quarter sheets. Common thicknesses range from 1/8 to 3/4 inch. Because of its stability, its availability in wide panels, and because it is generally less expensive than comparable solid-wood panels,

plywood is used in all of the projects in this book.

Plywood Grades

Softwood plywood is graded by the American Plywood Association with a two-letter code. Each letter indicates the quality of one of the veneer faces. The best is "N" which stands for "natural" because the face veneer will look great with a clear finish that shows the grain. The remaining grades are "A" through "D" in descending order of quality. For example, a sheet graded A-A has two good face veneers and is an excellent choice if both sides of a finished project will show. However, two premium veneer faces make A-A an expensive choice. With one premium face and one utility-grade face, A-C plywood is the most economical option if one side of the panel will be against a wall or another cabinet.

Hardwood plywood is available with many different species of face veneers, such as red oak, white oak, mahogany, birch, and cherry. Most of the hardwood plywood sold in the United

States is imported, and as a result, grading isn't as standardized as it is for domestic softwood plywood. In general though, Grade A has clear wood surfaces with no visible defects and is well-matched in terms of grain patterns and color. Grade B also has clear surfaces free of defects, although its grain patterns won't be matched as well. Grade 2 is similar to A and B in wood quality, but is not well-matched in color and grain: It's fine for painting but not for clear finishes. Grade 3 will exhibit small knotholes, discoloration, spaces between veneer joints, and other minor defects easily hidden with a little filler and paint. Grade 4 is pretty rough, with splits up to an inch wide and knotholes up to 2 inches in diameter. Special A-quality sheets exhibiting unusual grain patterns, such as bird's eye or fiddleback, are graded SP.

As with softwood plywood, you can save money by buying hardwood plywood which is a better grade on one side than the other if only one side will show in the finished project.

Typical Backstamp

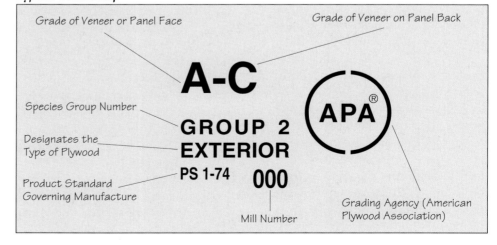

Plywood Veneer Face Grades

N- Smooth surface "natural finish" veneer is select, all heartwood or all sapwood. It is free of open defects and allows not more than six repairs, wood only, per 4x8-foot panel, made parallel to the grain and well-matched for grain and color.

A- This smooth paintable veneer allows not more than 18 neatly made repairs, parallel to the grain. It may be used as a natural finish in less demanding situations.

B- Solid-surface veneer permits shims, circular repair plugs, tight knots to 1 inch across the grain, and minor splits.

C-Plugged- Improved C veneer has splits limited to 1/8 inch wide and knotholes and borer holes limited to 1/4x1/2 inch. It permits some broken grain. Synthetic repairs also are permitted.

C- This veneer has tight knots to 1½ inches. It has knotholes to 1 inch across the grain with some to 1½ inches if the total width of knots and knotholes is within specified limits. Repairs are synthetic or wood. Discoloration and sanding defects that do not impair the strength are permitted. Limited splits and stitching are allowed.

D- Knots and knotholes to 2½ inches wide across the grain and 1/2 inch larger within specified limits are allowed. Limited splits are permitted.

Plywood Buying Tips. If you are planning to cover the edges of plywood with a matching solid wood, buy the plywood before the solid wood. This is the best way to ensure a match because in most areas, hardwood plywood is readily available only in a few commonly used domestic species. Of course, edging plywood with a contrasting wood is an excellent design option, too. You should be able to find a few species of hardwood with matching plywood that you can count on to be available most of the time.

Plywood that's damaged at the mill, en route, or at the lumberyard gets downgraded and sold at sale prices that are sometimes drastically reduced. Ask your supplier about shop grade plywood and blows. Most people are surprised to learn how much they can save on expensive plywood that exhibits only minor defects. A small dent on one side, or a little damage to one corner where the sheet was dropped or bumped can save you 30 to 50 percent.

PARTICLEBOARD

Particleboard is a term used to describe several different types of sheet materials made from ground-up bits of wood and glue. Admittedly, it's not much to look at, but because it is very stable and considerably cheaper than plywood, particleboard is typically used as an underlayment for plastic laminates and wood veneers when making countertops, cabinet doors, and shelving.

Some of the benefits of working with particleboard are that it doesn't warp, shrink, or swell with changes in humidity. On the downside, particleboard is heavy and tends to sag under a load more than plywood or solid wood, and interior grades of particleboard can disintegrate if placed in direct contact with water unless properly sealed. In addition, particleboard chips easily, and it doesn't hold fasteners well; it's best to use special particleboard fasteners instead of wood screws. Always use carbide-tipped blades when cutting particleboard,

because it will dull a tool-steel blade in a few passes.

Particleboard, like plywood, is available in 4x8-foot sheets. It also comes in a variety of board and panel widths up to 16 inches that are great for shelving. Thicknesses range from 1/4 to 3/4 inch.

HARDBOARD

Hardboard is made from wood fibers bonded with pressure and heat to form a thin, durable panel. It's normally used where it can't be seen, such as for drawer bottoms and rear panels for cabinets. Like particleboard, hardboard will dull your saw blades quickly, so always cut it with a carbide-tipped blade.

Perforated Hardboard. Also known as pegboard, perforated hardboard is often used as wall material in workshops and garages where it serves as a place to hang tools and other items. It also serves the same purpose in some specialized closets and cabinets. Because of its perforations, it's a good choice of back-panel material for hampers and other projects requiring ventilation.

Tempered Hardboard. Both plain and perforated hardboard are available as tempered products, which are impregnated with resin to make them stronger and more resistant to moisture. Hardboard is highly susceptible to humidity fluctuations, which can cause it to warp and buckle. So always buy tempered hardboard, which costs only a little more than the standard product.

LUMBER

Wood is classified as either softwood or hardwood. As the name implies, softwoods are usually softer than hardwoods, but that's not always the case. Balsa, for example, is a hardwood, but it's softer than Douglas fir, a softwood. Technically speaking, softwoods come from coniferous or cone-bearing trees, which include pine, redwood, cedar, and spruce. Hardwoods come from deciduous trees, such as oak, walnut, maple, cherry, and birch. Generally speaking, softwoods are less expensive and easier to work with than hardwoods, while hardwoods are more durable and are considered to have more attractive grain patterns.

Air-dried vs. Kiln-dried Wood

How lumber is dried after it is cut is almost as important as what it was cut from. Green, or unseasoned, lumber contains a lot of water—perhaps as much as 80 percent by weight. Drying to lower moisture levels increases the strength and stability of lumber.

Wood is either air-dried or kiln-dried. Air-dried lumber is stacked with spacers to allow air to circulate and is usually marked indicating its maximum moisture content at the time it leaves the mill; 19 percent lumber is stamped "S-dry" (semi-dry), 15 percent is marked "MC-15" (moisture content 15 percent). In a kiln, temperature and humidity can be controlled more carefully; the kiln-dried lumber typically has a moisture content of 10-12 percent. Kiln-dried wood is more expensive, but it has less tendency to shrink after it's been installed.

It is important to realize that no matter how wood is dried, it continues to contract and expand with changes in humidity. Air-dried wood will continue to shrink and dry if placed in a heated room. Likewise, kiln-dried wood will absorb moisture and expand if left outdoors or in a damp garage. It is a good idea to give lumber a sufficient amount of time to acclimate itself to its environment. If possible, you should try to buy wood products several weeks before you need them and store them in a dry (preferably heated) place.

No matter where you store lumber and wood products, or for how long, don't just lean it haphazardly against a wall until you need it. Take measures to protect it from damage and warping. To get an idea of how to store wood at home, pay attention to how it's stored where you buy it. If you bring home kiln-dried lumber that was stored indoors at a home center, stack it neatly indoors to prevent warping. If it's air-dried wood that was stored outdoors at a lumberyard, chances are it was stacked with spacers between the boards, placed about every 12 inches, to facilitate air circulation; do the same at home, using strips of one-by scrap.

Although you'll often find particleboard and lower grades of plywood stacked horizontally in racks, the higher grades are usually stored vertically to protect fine-face veneers. That's

Wood

Category	Grade	Description
Select (Best appearance)	A	Practically flawless—takes any finish
	B	A few small defects—takes any finish
	C	Some defects—paint recommended
	D	More defects, but easily concealed with paint
Common (Lesser quality)	1	Tight knots and limited physical blemishes
	2	No warps or splits. A few checks at ends, knots, and other blemishes
	3	Defects which may cause some waste removal
	4	Numerous defects such as open knotholes
	5 (Rare)	Very low quality. Use as filler only
Structural (Framing lumber 2" or more thick)	Construction	High quality
	Standard	Good quality with some defects
	Utility	Poor structural quality, space more closely
	Economy	Lowest quality structural lumber

Hardwood

Grade	Description
Firsts	91⅔% clear on both sides—best material
Seconds	83⅓% clear on both sides—very good material
Firsts and Seconds	Mixture of firsts and seconds containing not less than 20% firsts
Selects	90% clear on one side only—can be used for cabinet work but with some waste
No. 1	66⅔% clear on one side only—use as inside pieces, paint
No. 2	50% clear on one side only—paint

the way you should store sheet stock at home, too, with the best veneers protected and out of harm's way. If possible, store it away from high-traffic areas to protect vulnerable edges and corners.

Lumber Grades

In North America, most softwood is sold for construction purposes. It is used by carpenters who will cut it to length and nail it in place. In some carpentry applications, such as trim work, appearance is important. In other applications, such as framing, only structural strength matters. Hardwood, on the other hand, is used mostly by woodworkers who purchase rough-sawn, random-width lumber, which they plane to thickness and cut to width and length. The grading systems for softwood and hardwood reflect the difference in the way the materials are used.

The hardwood grading system emphasizes the percentage of clear wood you can expect to get out of a given piece. This information can be very useful if you choose to use hardwood for the projects in this book. Because the projects are made of plywood, solid wood is used mostly as edging material to hide plywood edges. This calls for narrow pieces. As a result, you can obtain clear stock by purchasing lower grade wood and cutting around the knots.

If you have the ability to plane and joint your own hardwood to thickness and width, you'll find your best price and selection by shopping at a sawmill instead of a lumberyard. Some mills do plane wood to thickness while leaving length and width random. This is known as surfaced two sides (often denoted as S2S). The most common hardwood sold by many lumberyards and home centers that already has been surfaced on both faces and edges is oak. Wood sold this way is called surfaced four sides (S4S).

Lumber Size and Finish. Softwood lumber is available in lengths of 4 to 20 feet in two-foot increments. Most of the softwood lumber you will buy has already been surfaced on both sides and both edges. Softwood lumber is sold according to its *nominal* size: the dimensions of the board when it was cut at the mill. After surfacing and drying, the wood's actual dimensions are smaller. The chart *American Standard Softwood Lumber Sizes* shows the nominal and actual thicknesses and widths of lumber.

When you buy rough-sawn hardwood in random widths and lengths, the nominal length and the actual length are the same thing. The exception is the planed and jointed oak boards you'll find at the lumberyard or home center. For this material, nominal and actual sizes differ just as they do for softwood.

Defects. Inspect lumber for any defects. Watch for small cracks, called checks, at the ends of the boards, and

American Standard Softwood Lumber Sizes*

Item	Thickness Actual Size Minimum Dressed			Face Width Actual Size Minimum Dressed		
	Named Size	Dry	Green	Named Size	Dry	Green
	(in.)	(in.)	(in.)	(in.)	(in.)	(in.)
Board	1	3/4	25/32	2	1 1/2	1 9/16
	1 1/4	1	1 1/32	3	2 1/2	2 9/16
	1 1/2	1 1/4	1 9/32	4	3 1/2	3 9/16
				5	4 1/2	4 5/8
				6	5 1/2	5 5/8
				7	6 1/2	6 5/8
				8	7 1/4	7 1/2
				9	8 1/4	8 1/2
				10	9 1/4	9 1/2
				11	10 1/4	10 1/2
				12	11 1/4	11 1/2
				14	13 1/4	13 1/2
				16	15 1/4	15 1/2
Dimension	2	1 1/2	1 9/16	2	1 1/2	1 9/16
	2 1/2	2	2 1/16	3	2 1/2	2 9/16
	3	2 1/2	2 9/16	4	3 1/2	3 9/16
	3 1/2	3	3 1/16	5	4 1/2	4 5/8
	4	3 1/2	3 9/16	6	5 1/2	5 5/8
	4 1/2	4	4 1/16	8	7 1/4	7 1/2
				10	9 1/4	9 1/2
				12	11 1/4	11 1/2
				14	13 1/4	13 1/2
				16	15 1/4	15 1/2
Timber	5 and greater		1/2 less than named size	5 and greater		1/2 less than named size

*From American Softwood Lumber Standard PS 20.70.

Defects in Wood

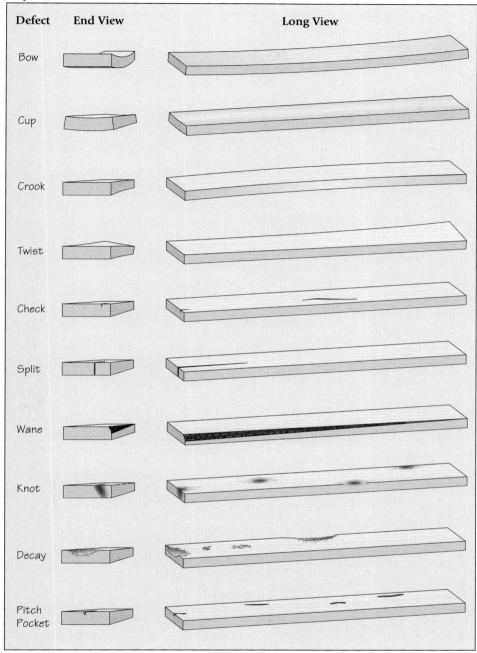

Defect	End View	Long View
Bow		
Cup		
Crook		
Twist		
Check		
Split		
Wane		
Knot		
Decay		
Pitch Pocket		

large cracks, called splits, that may extend through the entire board. Both are symptoms of uneven drying. The various manifestations of warp, also usually caused by improper drying or storage, include cup, twist, and bow.

Avoid warped boards because they're extremely difficult to work with. Pitch pockets are cavities in softwood that are filled with resin or pitch, which can ooze from the cavity, even through paint. Also be wary of stained wood where the discoloration penetrates the surface. Insect-damaged wood is obvious and unusable for most purposes.

Most lumber is sold by the board foot, lineal foot, or piece. Although prices on large quantities are usually quoted in board feet, most of the lumber you buy for the home workshop is priced by the lineal foot or by the piece, which eliminates the need for any complicated mathematical exercises. For wood that sells for $1.25 a lineal foot, for example, an 8-footer would cost you eight times $1.25, or $10.

Here is what you need to know to figure your cost with board-foot pricing. A board foot is simply one square foot of lumber, one (nominal) inch thick. An 8-foot 1x12 contains 8 board feet. The same size 2x12 contains 16 board feet. Other dimensions, however, don't translate so easily; for that operation you need a formula: thickness (nominal inches) times width (nominal inches) times length (actual feet) divided by 12 equals board feet. To determine how many board feet are in a 16-foot 2x8, for example, multiply 2 (thickness) times 8 (width) times 16 (length) for a product of 256. Dividing 256 by 12 tells you there are 21.333 board feet in that single piece.

It is good practice to buy lumber at least a few inches longer than needed, because the ends often contain flaws and are not squarely cut. If you're looking to salvage clear stock from large pieces of lower grade lumber, count on buying from 25 to 30 percent more stock than you might need for any project.

MOLDING

Molding can dress up many projects. Use it to tie a project in with the rest of the room, or simply to add some interesting detail. Practically speaking, molding is also handy for concealing seams, gaps, plywood edges, and other unsightly necessities of construction and assembly.

Both softwood and hardwood moldings are available. If you plan to finish any project with a clear or semi-transparent product, be sure to buy clear molding that matches the wood you're using. For painted projects, use paint-grade stock, sometimes called

Moldings

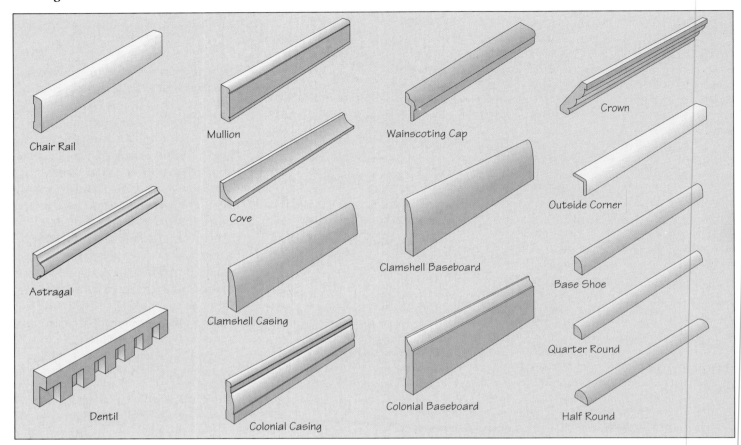

Chair Rail

Mullion

Wainscoting Cap

Crown

Astragal

Cove

Clamshell Baseboard

Outside Corner

Clamshell Casing

Base Shoe

Dentil

Colonial Casing

Colonial Baseboard

Quarter Round

Half Round

"finger-jointed" molding, which consists of short pieces of molding joined into longer strips by means of adhesive and interlocking joinery.

Molding is sold in standard lengths up to 16 feet, sometimes in increments of 2 feet. Most lumberyards will cut strips for you to specified lengths. Try to buy all the molding for any single project from the same mill run. Even within the same design, width and thickness can vary minutely, but nevertheless disastrously, if you end up with two sizes on the same project.

Most moldings are available only in softwood, usually pine. Hardwood moldings are also available, most commonly in oak. If you need another type of hardwood molding to match your project, you can always make it yourself with a router or with a table saw equipped with a molding head.

Grades of Molding

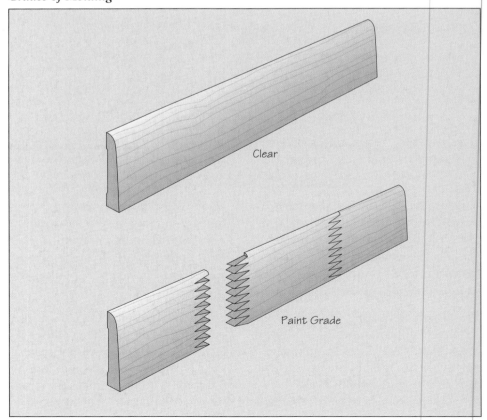

Clear

Paint Grade

HARDWARE AND ADHESIVES

Every home center and hardware store seems to have an endless variety of mechanical fasteners, dozens of different kinds of adhesives, and an overwhelming assortment of hardware for every imaginable purpose. The good news for woodworkers is that less can be more than enough. Two or three different adhesives will see to most of your joining needs; mechanical fasteners are mostly nails and screws; and the rest of the hardware you'll need to complete the projects in this book (knobs, hinges, and latches) is simple to understand and easy to install.

FASTENERS

The basic assembly system for all of the projects in this book is nails, or screws, and glue. Although screws are considerably stronger than nails, glue is the most important fastener in any wood joint. A good glue joint can be stronger than the wood itself.

For the projects in this book, nails and screws are most often used as clamps that hold the wood pieces together while the glue cures. There are, of course, instances in which you want to use screws without glue. One obvious instance is when you are fastening cabinets to walls. Another less obvious instance is when you need to allow a piece room for humidity changes. For example, the short bookcase project on page 135 is a plywood box with a solid wood top. The solid wood will expand and contract more than the plywood. If you glued it on, the top would crack or the glue joint would fail. Instead, the top is attached with

screws through oversized holes in the plywood.

Nails

Nail length is expressed in terms of the penny— at one time the price per hundred. Penny is designated by the small letter "d". A two-penny (2d) nail is 1 inch long. See the chart "Nail Sizes" to convert penny designations into inches. Nails longer than 6 inches are measured by the inch.

The five main types of nails are box nails, common nails, finishing nails, casing nails, and brads. Use box and common nails for rough work, and

Common Types of Nails

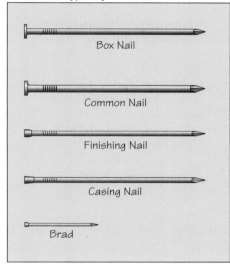

Nail Sizes

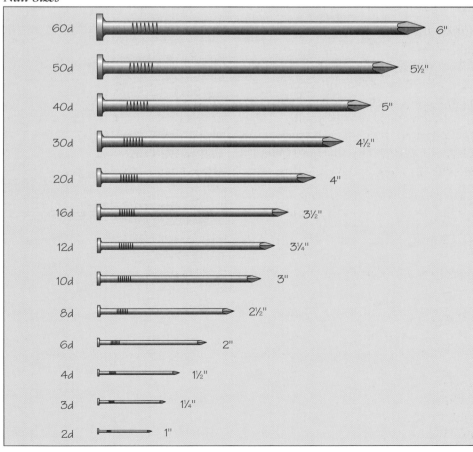

finishing and casing nails for cabinetry and trim, respectively. Casing nails have a slightly larger diameter than finishing nails and a more tapered head. Both finishing and casing nails come with either dimpled or smooth heads; the dimpled heads are easier to countersink with a nail set. Brads resemble finishing nails, except they are much smaller. Brads are used for attaching small moldings and other thin materials. They're sold in sizes from 3/8 inch to 1½ inches.

Screws

Screws come in a great variety of diameter and length combinations. They're identified by the thickness or gauge of their shafts and by their lengths, followed by head type. A flathead screw with a 10-gauge thickness and length of 3½ inches would be labeled as #10x3½-inch flathead. The two types of screws that you will need to complete the projects in this book are wood screws and drywall screws.

Wood screws. Wood screws are tapered so the threads bite into the wood, which makes a stronger bond than nails. Screws take longer to install, however, because most installations, especially in hardwood, require a pilot hole for each screw. Most screw holes also must be countersunk or counterbored.

The problem with using wood screws is that their heads remain visible after installation. Round-head screws are the most visible; use them where they won't show. Oval heads are less obvious, and are sometimes used for decorative purposes. Flathead screws are the most common for woodworking projects, because they are designed to be driven flush with the wood's surface. You can also counterbore holes to sink the screw heads beneath the wood's surface, and then conceal them with wood plugs.

Drywall Screws. One type of screw that has gained favor among carpenters, cabinetmakers, and other woodworkers is the drywall screw, also known as the all-purpose, or buglehead screw. These screws do not require a pilot hole in softwoods; their aggressive threads are designed to drive fast and hold tight. In addition,

Drywall Screw

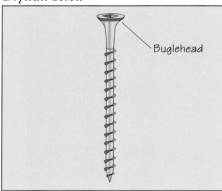

Buglehead

these screws are self-countersinking in most softwoods. The Phillips head is extra deep to prevent stripping and make driving easy with power drivers.

Specialty Fasteners

Some projects can't be installed with conventional nails and screws. For example, hollow plaster or drywall and solid masonry walls pose special problems that must be solved with specialty fasteners such as toggle bolts, hollow-wall anchors, and expansion shields.

Hollow-Wall Fasteners. Toggle bolts and hollow-wall anchors are designed for use in plaster or drywall walls. A toggle bolt has spring-loaded wings that open against the inside of the wall as the bolt is tightened. Instead of wings, a hollow-wall anchor bolt has a sleeve that expands against the inside of the wall.

It's best to attach cabinets and other built-ins to wall studs. When this is impossible, use hollow-wall fasteners, but even then, try to attach the unit to at least one stud; then use the hollow-wall fasteners where no studs are present. If there's no way to attach to even one stud, make sure you are using a fastener designed to support the weight of the object you are mounting.

Types of Wood Screws

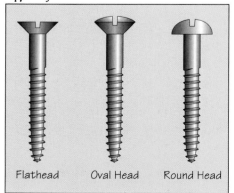

Flathead   Oval Head   Round Head

Hollow-Wall Fasteners

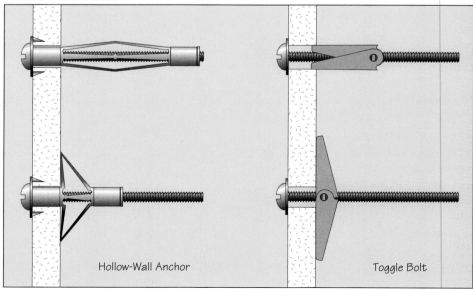

Hollow-Wall Anchor   Toggle Bolt

Solid-Wall Fasteners. Fasteners for use in brick or concrete walls usually take the form of bolts that fit into expansion shields or anchors of some kind, or plastic anchors used with wood screws. To attach a cabinet to a masonry wall using anchors, drill holes in the wall the same diameter as the anchors. Gently tap the anchors into the wall with a hammer. Rub chalk on the front of the anchors, set the cabinet in place, and tap it against the anchors. Drill holes in the cabinet back at the chalk locations, and install the cabinet with the anchor bolts or screws, which will cause the anchors to expand as they are tightened.

Solid-Wall Fasteners

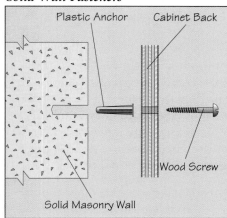

Plastic Anchor   Cabinet Back

Wood Screw

Solid Masonry Wall

ADHESIVES

Adhesives are available for all kinds of materials, from fabrics to ceramics, plastics to metals, and for porous and non-porous surfaces. For woodworking, you need only two or three adhesives for the bulk of your wood-joining tasks.

Carpenter's Wood Glue. Aliphatic resin glue, commonly called carpenter's glue or yellow glue, is the adhesive of choice for bonding wood to wood. It sets relatively quickly, can be cleaned up with water, and is sandable.

Aliphatic resin glues are available for both interior and exterior uses. Both versions are water soluble when wet, but after it has time to cure, the exterior formula is water resistant. This is the glue to use for outdoor projects and for projects used indoors around water, such as cutting boards and butcher-block countertops.

Contact Cement. This rubber-based liquid glue bonds on contact. Use it to join plastic laminate or other veneers to a wood, plywood, or particleboard underlayment. Apply contact cement to both surfaces, and allow it to dry for approximately 15 minutes before joining the parts. The parts will stick together immediately upon contact. Fumes given off by this adhesive can be dangerous, so look for the non-flammable type, and use it only in a well-ventilated area. Carefully read and follow the manufacturer's directions.

HARDWARE

Although the assortment of hardware available for cabinets and other woodworking projects might seem bewildering at first, much of it is repetitive in design and function. And some is highly specialized and rarely used. Fortunately, most of it is easy to understand and install.

Knobs and Pulls. Door and drawer knobs and pulls are made of plastic, metal, ceramic, and wood in hundreds of sizes, colors, and designs to fit any decor and serve any purpose. If your project calls for both knobs and pulls, you can buy matching sets. Most mount with screws driven from the back of the door or drawer front. You'll even find hardwood continuous-pull moldings that you can cut to length and finish to match your doors and drawers.

Hinges. Hardware for hanging cabinet doors is available in basic types for overlay, inset, and flush-fit (see "Installing Doors and Hinges," page 19), as well as designs for special purposes, such as concealed mounting and mounting on glass. There are plain hinges, and decorative hinges, and hinges that automatically close the

Knobs and Pulls

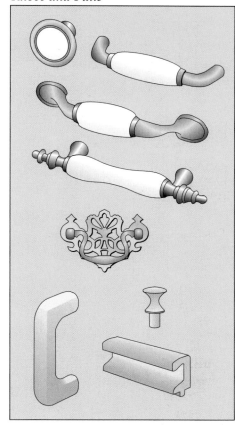

door. Several of the projects in this book use piano, or continuous hinges, which are available in lengths up to 72 inches, and can be cut with a hacksaw to any length you need.

Catches and Latches. If you don't use self-closing hinges, you'll need some kind of catch to keep your cabinet doors closed. Externally mounted catches and latches, usually made of brass or wrought iron, provide a rustic look. Mechanical or magnetic catches provide a cleaner, modern look. These catches consist of one part that attaches to the inside of the door and another that mounts inside the cabinet. Another choice is a called a push latch, or touch latch. It is a spring-loaded magnetic device that holds the door closed and pops it open when the door is pushed and released. This type is popular for use on cabinets with glass doors but is also useful with wooden doors.

Drawer Slides. For furniture projects such as the chest of drawers on

Hinges

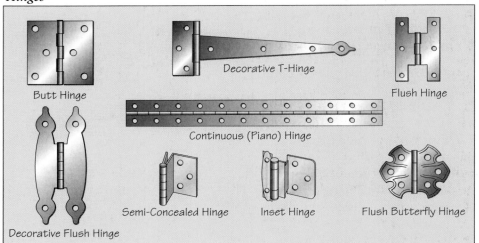

Butt Hinge

Decorative T-Hinge

Flush Hinge

Continuous (Piano) Hinge

Decorative Flush Hinge

Semi-Concealed Hinge

Inset Hinge

Flush Butterfly Hinge

Catches and Latches

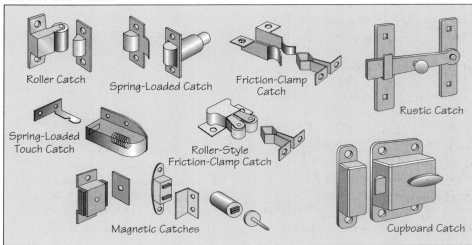

Roller Catch

Spring-Loaded Catch

Friction-Clamp Catch

Rustic Catch

Spring-Loaded Touch Catch

Roller-Style Friction-Clamp Catch

Magnetic Catches

Cupboard Catch

Drawer Slides

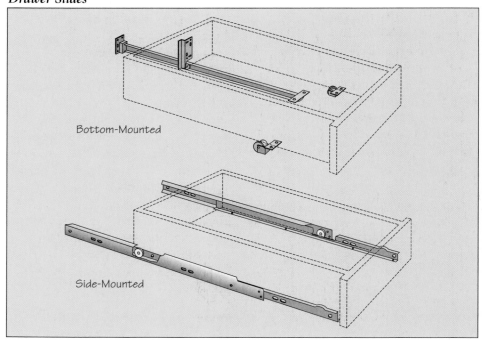

Bottom-Mounted

Side-Mounted

page 99, you'll want to make your own wooden drawer slides. For kitchen and bathroom cabinet drawers, however, which are subjected to heavier loads and more frequent use, you may opt for commercial slides. These metal slides come in dozens of designs for bottom, and side mounting. The smoothest operate on ball-bearing wheels or roller-bearing sleeves. For heavy-duty applications, you'll find slides rated for capacities of 75 to 100 pounds.

Shelf Standards and Supports. Metal shelf standards, also known as pilaster strips, are made of steel or aluminum and come in a variety of finishes. Standard lengths range from 12 to 144 inches and the standards can be cut with a hacksaw to fit any requirements. They are either surface or flush mounted with screws, nails, or staples. Clip-style shelf supports snap into holes located every 1/2 inch to allow shelves to be adjusted quickly and easily. This system is ideal for any cabinets or bookcase where you want shelves to be adjustable.

Even simpler are shelf support pins. These merely push into holes bored in pairs in cabinet and bookcase sides. Sometimes brass inserts go into the holes to give them a more finished look. Shelves are supported on four brass or plastic pins.

Shelf Standards and Support

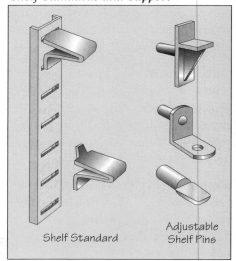

Shelf Standard

Adjustable Shelf Pins

WOOD FINISHING

Finishing is a simple craft that anyone can learn. The objective is nothing more complicated than to transfer a liquid stain, finish, or paint from a can, or other container, to the wood. There are only three tools used to do this: a rag, a brush, or a spray gun. Each tool is easy to use. Even a spray gun is no more difficult to use than a router. However, as discussed below, spray equipment is costly and the need for separate spraying space and special ventilation usually precludes its use in a home shop.

Stains, finishes, and paints are also easy to understand. There are only three main ingredients used to make up these products: colorant, binder, and thinner. Stains and paints are colorant, usually pigment, in a binder that is thinned with a thinner. The principal difference between a stain and a paint is the amount of thinner added. Stain has a lot of thinner; paint has just enough thinner to make it brushable. You want a stain to highlight the grain of the wood, not cover it. You use a paint to hide the wood.

Finishes are binder, usually with some thinner added. You can think of a clear finish as paint without the colorant. Finishes protect the wood, like paint does, but they don't color it.

FINISHING TOOLS

There are four key differences between rags, brushes, and spray guns.

Cost. Rags cost very little or nothing, especially if you make an effort to save old, worn-out cotton clothing. Brushes are also inexpensive. In contrast, even the cheapest spray guns cost $200 or more. So, if cost is a factor, choose a rag or brush.

Speed. You can apply stain, finish, or paint to a larger area faster with a rag or spray gun than you can with a brush. For example, if you want to apply stain to a set of cabinets and get all the excess wiped off before the stain begins to dry, you will be more successful if you use a rag or spray gun to apply the stain than if you use a brush.

Film Leveling. In cases where you are not wiping off the excess, leveling is important. The more flawed the film you apply, the less satisfied you will be with your work. It is nearly impossible to apply a stain, finish, or paint with a rag without leaving deep ridges in the film. Brushes perform better, but they leave brush marks. This is true even with sponge brushes which leave ridges at the edges. Spray guns produce the most level surface of the three tools. It is true that most spray guns leave a light pimply surface called "orange peel," but this defect is usually minor compared to ridges and brush marks.

Weather. If you live in a cold climate and can't finish outdoors for a large part of the year, you will have problems using a spray gun. Spray guns create a lot of overspray which floats around the room and lands on everything, including your work. You must exhaust this overspray, and this presents two problems: replacing the exhausted air with warm air, and trapping the overspray before it gets to the fan and builds up on it. In contrast, rags and brushes transfer all the liquid efficiently from the can to the wood. The only leftover is evaporating solvent as the coating cures.

Replacing air with warm air on cold days can be a strain on your heating system. Placing a heater in the room in which you are spraying can be a hazard, especially if there is an open flame in the heater. Never spray in a room where there is an open flame. It can cause an explosion.

To trap overspray arrange a bank of filters between you and the

(From left) Stains, paints, and finishes are each made with only three main ingredients. Stains and paints are colorant (usually pigment), binder, and solvent or thinner. Finishes are simply binder, with a solvent or thinner usually added.

exhaust fan. Don't allow finish or paint to build up on the fan. In addition, don't allow solvents from a solvent-based paint or finish to be drawn across a motor that is not explosion proof.

Rags

There's not much to say about rags except that cotton almost always works best, and rags can be a serious fire hazard when used with oil finishes and not disposed of properly. Oil finishes cure by absorbing oxygen from the air. The by-product of the reaction between the oil and oxygen is heat. If the heat can't dissipate from the rag, it will build up until it reaches the ignition temperature of the rag, and the rag will burst into flame.

The easiest and safest way to dispose of oily rags is to open them to air immediately after use. Spread the rags out on the floor or drape them over the edge of a table or trash can. As long as air can get to all parts of the rags so the heat can dissipate, there is no chance of a fire. When you have time, take the rags outside and hang them over a tree limb or fence. When the rags harden due to the oil curing, they can be safely thrown in the trash. Cured oil in rags is no more of a hazardous waste than cured oil in wood.

Brushes

There are four common types of brushes: natural bristle, synthetic bristle, sponge, and paint pads. All can be used to transfer stain, finish, or paint from the can to the wood.

Natural-bristle brushes are made from animal hair. The best are made from Chinese hog hairs. These hairs are tapered and have split ends which means that the parts of the hairs that are in contact with the wood are extremely thin. The thinner the bristles, or split ends, the

more level the applied film. Though China-bristle brushes are a little more expensive, the improved results are usually worth it.

Synthetic-bristle brushes are made from polyester and nylon. These brushes became popular for use with latex paint because natural bristles lose their shape in water. The better synthetic-bristle brushes also have split ends and perform almost as well as natural-bristle brushes. Use synthetic-bristle brushes with all water-based products. Use either type of brush with solvent-based products.

Sponge brushes are cheap and are usually considered to be disposable. They are very effective with all finishing products except lacquer which dissolves them. Sponge brushes deposit a very level film, but they leave ridges at the edges of each brush stroke which are usually quite pronounced.

Paint pads are flat sponge material with many tiny fibers attached. The pads are usually held in a plastic handle. Paint pads are effective for applying all finishing products except lacquer to a flat surface. They are particularly useful for floor finishing.

Cleaning Brushes

If you use a good-quality brush, you will want to clean it after each use. It is wise, in fact, to clean it before using it the first time in order to remove any loose bristles or dirt.

The procedure for cleaning brushes varies a little depending on the finish you are using. In all cases, however, the last step is to wash the brush in soap and water and store it in the cardboard holder it came in, or in a heavy-paper wrapping like that of a grocery-store bag. You can use any mild soap. A convenient one is dish-water soap. The idea is to wash the brush until it is clean enough so that the soap makes suds. Wrapping the brush is necessary so the bristles dry straight.

Variations in the cleaning procedure occur in the steps getting the brush ready to be washed with soap and water. The variations depend on the paint, stain, or finish you are using. For example, no prior steps are required for cleaning latex paint or water-based stains and finishes. Simply rinse the brush and then wash with soap and water. To clean shellac or lacquer, rinse the brush

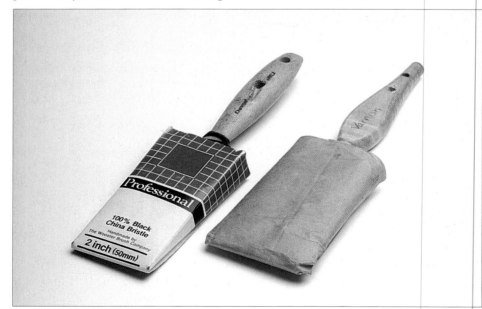

When you finish cleaning your brush, put it back in the cardboard holder it came in, or wrap it in heavy paper, so the bristles dry straight.

first in alcohol (for shellac) or lacquer thinner (for lacquer), or in a solution of half-and-half household ammonia and water, and then wash with a mild soap.

The most difficult paints, stains, and finishes to clean are oil-based. The easiest way to prepare a brush for the soap-and-water washing is to rinse it once or twice in paint thinner, then in lacquer thinner. Lacquer thinner removes the oiliness left by the paint thinner so that the soap succeeds in making suds after only one or two washings. Without the lacquer thinner wash, you will have to wash more times in soap and water. You could substitute lacquer thinner for the earlier paint-thinner steps, but lacquer thinner is more expensive.

You may find that you want to use the brush again in a finish like varnish before the brush has totally dried out from the water. To do so, rinse the brush in lacquer thinner first. The lacquer thinner will dry out the water and leave the brush ready for varnish.

If you think you may want to use the brush again within a day or two, and you'd rather not go to the trouble of cleaning it, you can store it in a can or jar containing the solvent or thinner for the finish you are using. Alcohol is the solvent for shellac. Lacquer thinner is the solvent for lacquer. Water is the thinner for latex paint and water-based stains and finishes. Paint thinner (mineral spirits) is the thinner for oil paints and stains, varnish, and polyurethane. Hang the brush in the container of liquid so that the liquid comes at least half way up the bristles. Don't let the brush rest on the bottom of the container or it will assume a permanent bent shape.

If you allow paint or finish to harden on the brush, you can often reclaim it by letting it soak in the solvent for the finish (this works with shellac

and lacquer) or in paint stripper (this sometimes works for water-based and oil-based coatings).

PREPARING WOOD

Of all the steps in finishing, preparing the wood is the most boring and labor intensive, but it is very important. You cannot achieve quality results if the wood has not been properly prepared.

Preparing wood for painting is easier than for finishing with a clear finish because paint covers flaws while clear finish highlights them. The following steps do not have to be done so well if you intend to paint the wood:

There are three steps to preparing wood for accepting a stain or finish:

• Sand the wood smooth.

• Remove all glue seepage.

• Make wood-putty patches blend in.

Sanding Wood

Sanding wood is a lot of work. It will help to make it easier if you understand why you have to do it. After all, before the invention of machine tools in the mid-nineteenth century, very little if any sanding was required once the boards were shaped and joined. Indeed, there was no sandpaper before the development of machine tools. Wood was smoothed and shaped with hand tools which left the surface of the wood almost perfectly smooth.

It is the machine tools, which you love because they make woodworking so much easier, that cause you to have to work so hard sanding before applying the stain and finish. Machine tools, no matter how sharp and how well tuned, leave marks in the wood that show up under a stain or finish. The price you pay for using machines to do woodworking is that you have to spend a lot of time sanding to remove the marks left by these machines.

The goal when sanding wood is to remove the flaws as quickly and efficiently as possible without leaving excessively deep scratches in the wood. In practice, this usually means beginning with either 80-grit or 100-grit sandpaper. There may be cases, however, when it would be more efficient to use a coarser grit, and there may be cases where you can get by beginning with 120- or 150-grit sandpaper. For paint, sanding to 100-grit usually is enough.

Always sand in the direction of the wood grain no matter which grit sandpaper you use. Sanding across the grain or at diagonals can damage wood fibers in a way that requires a great deal of sanding to remove.

Whichever grit sandpaper you begin with, you need to progressively sand out the scratches until you have all the wood sanded evenly to about 180 grit. There may be cases where you can stop at 150-grit or where you might want to continue to as fine as 220-grit, but until you gain some experience so

All power cutting and shaping tools leave marks in the wood that must be sanded out. The "washboarding" shown here is caused by a jointer or planer.

To see if you have sanded enough to remove washboarding and coarse sanding scratches, look at the wood in a raking light.

You can make a cork block by gluing 1/8-inch-thick gasket cork to the bottom of a soft-wood block about $2^3/4$ inches x $3^7/8$ inches. Chamfer the top edges.

you begin to notice differences, use 180-grit as your standard.

It is theoretically most efficient to sand through each grit of sandpaper until you reach 180-grit, but most people skip a grit when sanding. In other words, most people find they get good results jumping from, say, 80-grit to 120-grit to 180-grit, thus skipping 100-grit and 150-grit. Decisions like these are very individual because each of us uses varying pressures and sands more-or-less long with more-or-less worn sandpaper.

It's difficult to see what you are accomplishing with sandpaper on bare wood. A trick that will help is to look at the wood in a raking light. That is, arrange your work so there is a light or a window just above the plane of the wood. You will be able to see flaws or deep sanding scratches that you haven't yet removed in the reflection.

If you are hand sanding a flat surface, always back your sandpaper with a soft cork, rubber, or felt block. Otherwise, your fingers will cause the sandpaper to dig out the softer spring-growth wood creating a rippled effect that you may not notice until you make the surface shiny with a finish. You can make a cork block that fits snugly in your hand by gluing 1/8-inch gasket cork from an auto parts store to softwood that is chamfered on the top edges.

You can, of course, use hand-held machine sanders to make sanding easier. There are three common, hand-held, sanding machines: orbital, belt, and random orbit. Orbital or pad sanders are the cheapest and least efficient type. It is very difficult to do serious damage using these sanders, but they are very slow. Belt sanders are more expensive, and they are very efficient at removing a large amount of wood. But belt sanders are difficult to control. It is very difficult to sand with a belt sander without gouging

There are three commonly available hand-held machine sanders. (From left) An orbital sander, a belt sander, and a random-orbit sander.

the wood. It is even more risky using a belt sander to sand veneered plywood. You will most likely sand through in places.

The most effective hand-held sanding machine is the random-orbit sander. This sander is also relatively expensive. Random sanders remove a lot of wood without much risk of gouging. Only by setting the sander down on the wood while it is running are you likely to gouge the wood. It's best to place the sander on the wood before you turn it on.

No matter which sander you use, finish sanding by hand using your finest-grit sandpaper (usually 180-grit). Both the orbital and the random-orbit sanders leave squiggly marks in the wood that often show under a stain or finish. A light hand sanding removes these marks.

Sandpaper

There are four commonly available types of sandpaper. Two are best for sanding wood, and two are best for sanding finishes. All four types of sandpaper are identified by standard sandpaper grit numbers which run from a low of 36 grit to a high of 2000 grit. Grits are defined by the number of openings in a 1-inch-square mesh screen through which the abrasive stones are sifted. The smaller the openings, the higher the number describing the sandpaper, and the finer the sandpaper grit.

The sandpapers that are best for sanding wood are made with garnet and aluminum-oxide abrasives. Garnet sandpaper is usually orange in color. The abrasives break off at sharp angles, so garnet sandpaper continues to cut well until the abrasives are completely worn down. Garnet sandpaper is the least expensive of the four types and is the most popular sandpaper used for hand sanding wood. Grits range from 36 to 280.

Aluminum-oxide sandpaper is usually tan in color. The abrasives are more durable than garnet, but don't break off as sharply. Aluminum-oxide sandpaper is more expensive than garnet sandpaper, but it lasts longer. Because of this, aluminum-oxide abrasives are almost always used on sanding belts and disks which are expensive to make. Grits range from 36 to 280.

The sandpapers that are best for sanding finishes are made with silicon-carbide abrasives. There are two types. Black silicon-carbide sandpaper is made with a water-resistant glue to attach the abrasives to the paper. This sandpaper is often referred to as "wet-or-dry" sandpaper because it can be used with a water or oil lubricant, or no lubricant at all. In almost all cases, you should use this sandpaper together with some type of lubricant. Otherwise, it will clog up fast which makes sanding very expensive. Grits range up to 2000.

Gray silicone-carbide sandpaper contains a soap-like lubricant which makes it easier to sand finishes without using an additional lubricant. The lubricant is zinc stearate, the same one that is added to most sanding sealers. This type sandpaper is most often referred to as "lubricated," "no-fill," or "stearated" sandpaper. Grits range up to 400.

Black silicon-carbide sandpaper, used with a water or oil lubricant, is best for sanding after you have applied several coats of finish, enough so that you can be sure that you won't sand through. Gray silicon-carbide sandpaper, used dry, is best when sanding your first and second coats of finish. Damage will not be so great if you sand through in places.

Glue Seepage

Glue seepage at joints, or glue deposited on the wood by unclean hands, seals the wood and prevents the stain or finish from penetrating. The result is a lighter glue blotch. Glue blotching can be very frustrating.

On edge-to-edge glue-ups, whether solid-wood-to-solid-wood or solid-edging-to-veneered-plywood, you want glue seepage because it tells you that you have applied enough glue and enough pressure. You must remove all the seepage and then sand

An easy way to remove glue seepage is to lift it off in a strip with the help of a dull chisel or putty knife after the glue has begun to set.

Use masking tape to protect a stile from cross-grain scratching while you sand the rail.

the wood to below where the glue has penetrated.

There are two ways to remove the glue: wash it off immediately with a wet rag, or let the glue set up to the point where you can lift it off in a strip by getting under it with a putty knife or dull chisel. In both cases, you will have to sand to remove any remaining glue that has soaked into the wood.

If the glue dries solid before you remove it, you will have to scrape it off. This may tear up some of the wood. For this reason, it is best to remove the glue before it dries solid.

Glue seepage on perpendicular glue-ups, such as stiles and rails and legs and rails, is more difficult to deal with because sanding is more difficult. It is difficult to sand perpendicular joints without sanding cross grain on one of the pieces of wood. It's best, therefore, if you can keep the glue from seeping at all. This means don't apply more glue than necessary to make a strong bond. Unfortunately, this is not easy to do because you are moving too fast.

There is a trick that will help on dowel joints. Drill the dowel holes about 1/8 inch deeper than needed

and use dowels that are chamfered on the ends. This will create pockets at the bottom of the holes for excess glue that is squeezed deeper into the holes to collect. To create pockets for glue that is squeezed out the holes to collect, countersink the top of the dowel holes using a countersink bit.

Of course, you should not apply glue to the end-grain part of the glue up. Glue in this area adds no permanent strength, and it can't help but squeeze out when you clamp the parts together.

If glue does squeeze out of your cross-grain joints, and you catch it before it dries, wash it off with water. You will then need to sand the wood to remove the raised grain that the water causes. There are two ways to do this without leaving cross-grain scratches. Sand the short butted piece first, crossing over to the crossing piece. Then sand the crossing piece to remove the scratches left by the earlier sanding. Alternatively, place masking tape on each piece in turn, while you sand the other.

If the glue dries before you notice it, there are two ways to remove it: dissolve it off, or take it off mechanically by sanding or scraping.

You can dissolve white and yellow glue with water. By heating the water, or adding an acid such as vinegar to the water, you increase the effectiveness. Water raises grain, however, and stain will absorb more into this area making it darker. To even the stain penetration, you must re-sand this area to below the water damage after the wood has dried.

Toluene (sometimes called toluol) and xylene (sometimes called xylol) can also be used to remove cured white and yellow glue. These solvents soften the glue enough so it can be scrubbed off with a coarse cloth or soft-bristle brush, and they do this without raising the grain.

You can also sand or scrape off the glue to below where it has penetrated. Then, sand the area to the same grit as the rest of the wood so that the stain colors evenly.

If you have already applied stain before you notice the glue seepage, the correction is the same. You still have to dissolve or mechanically remove the glue. The problem you may experience here is that the stain acts as a lubricant for sandpaper causing the scratching to be a little less than it would be without the stain. The result is that more stain applied to the area you have sanded may not color quite as dark. If this happens, correct the problem by applying stain to the entire part—rail, stile, leg, etc.—and wet-sand this part with the same grit sandpaper or one grit lower than you have used elsewhere. Wipe off the excess stain.

If nothing you do evens the coloring, apply paint stripper to the entire project and strip out as much of the color as possible (paint stripper will also remove white and yellow glue). It's not necessary to remove all the color. Then re-sand the entire surface with your final grit sandpaper and re-stain. The stain should come out evenly as long as it's not the wood that is causing the blotching.

Wood Putty

You can use wood putty to patch gaps, gouges, large nailholes, and other flaws in your project. If you are going to paint the project, simply sand the putty patch flat. The paint will cover it. If you are going to stain the wood, the patch will show. This is because wood putty doesn't take stain like wood.

To make the wood putty blend in better to the stained wood, use a colored wood putty that matches the wood after it has been stained. You may need to apply a little stain to a piece of scrap to see what this color is.

Most commercial wood putties are made with wood flour (very fine sawdust) and some type of finish that cures and binds the wood flour particles to each other. Most homemade wood putties are made by mixing sawdust with glue, usually white glue

or epoxy. Since neither finish nor glue can absorb common stain, it's simply not possible to make a wood putty that takes stain like wood.

There are three common types of commercial wood putties: those based on lacquer, those based on water-based finish, and those based on gypsum (plaster-of-Paris). You can tell which kind you have by the instructions on the container. Lacquer-based wood putties will state that they can be thinned or cleaned up with acetone or lacquer thinner. Water-based wood putties will state that they can be cleaned up with water. Gypsum-based wood putties come in powder form which you are instructed to mix with water.

Applying wood putty. Each of these wood putties is applied in a similar manner. Take a little of the putty out of the container or tube with a putty knife (or screwdriver if the hole to be filled is small). Push the putty down in the hole or gouge, and if the depression is not very deep, smooth

off the top by pulling the putty knife across the surface towards you. You want the putty to form a very slight mound so that when it shrinks as it dries, it won't leave a depression.

It's best not to manipulate the putty any more than necessary since it becomes increasingly unworkable the longer it's exposed to air. Try to avoid sloppiness. Remember that the binder in the putty is finish, glue, or plaster. It will bond to any part of the wood it comes in contact with, prevent stain penetration, and cause a blotch.

For a nailhole, one or two coats usually does the job. If the depression is deep, it's best to apply several coats to build the putty level with the surface. One thick layer will take a long time to cure throughout and will probably crack due to uneven curing. Let each coat cure hard before applying the next. Once the putty is thoroughly cured, sand it level with the surrounding wood. If you're working on a flat surface, back the sandpaper with a flat cork, felt, or wood block.

Wood putty doesn't take stain like wood. A wood-putty patch stains a solid color without grain or figure.

To apply wood putty, press it into the hole with a putty knife or dull screwdriver, leaving a little excess so a hollow won't occur as the putty dries and shrinks.

Matching color

There are two ways to match the color of the wood putty to the surrounding wood. The easiest is to color the putty while it is still in paste form or use an already-colored commercial wood putty. The other is to color the patch after it has cured. You can combine the two by using a colored wood putty to approximate the lightest color in the surrounding wood, then continue coloring the wood putty after it has cured.

You can use universal tinting colors, available at most paint and art supply stores, to color any of the three commercial types of wood putty or your homemade glue-and-sawdust mixture. The color you want to match is the color the wood will be after it is stained and finished. It may take some experimentation to arrive at this color.

You should practice on some scrap wood. The trick is to judge the colors while they are still damp. At that stage they will give a fairly accurate approximation of the color you will get when the finish is applied. The color of the stain or putty when dry will not be accurate. Keep in mind that ready-made colored putties, usually identified by the names of the woods they are designed to imitate, are not meant to look like the wood after it has been stained. These putties can often be used successfully if you don't intend to stain the wood.

Coloring the putty before applying it is an easy way to approximate wood, but you can get better results by coloring the patch after it is dry and has been sanded smooth. Coloring the putty after application allows you to imitate the colors in the surrounding wood more exactly.

To color a patch, apply your first coat of finish (the sealer coat) to the entire surface in order see the correct colors you want to imitate. Once this sealer coat is dry, paint in the grain, figure, and the background color, that is, the lightest color visible in the surrounding wood. You may also want to scratch pores into the patch with the point of a knife to imitate deep-porous woods such as oak, mahogany, or walnut.

It's usually best to paint the grain and figure using an artists brush before painting the background color. Otherwise you will probably get the patch too dark. Once you have the grain and figure close, let it dry and protect it with a thin coat of finish. Then apply the background color.

For the coloring medium, it's best to use glaze or thinned varnish with some oil-pigment or Japan color added. The advantage of glaze and thinned varnish is that you can remove it if you don't like the result by wiping with paint thinner. The disadvantage is that it takes overnight to cure.

Drawing in grain and figure can be done only on film finishes, such as shellac, lacquer, varnish, polyurethane and water-based finishes. Oil finishes are too thin to color between coats.

STAINING WOOD

Stain is used to decorate wood. You can use or not use a stain depending on how you want the wood to look. Stain changes the color and highlights the grain of wood. But stain also highlights flaws in the wood. You have to prepare the wood extra well if you intend to apply stain to it, and you have to be aware that some woods, especially softwoods like fir and pine, and hardwoods like cherry, poplar, and birch, blotch when you stain them. These woods blotch no matter

The same stain looks different on different woods. Here the same stain was applied to mahogany (top left), maple (top right), poplar (bottom left), and oak (bottom right). The stain looks very red on mahogany because mahogany is red to begin with. The stain has only a slight effect on maple because maple is a dense, tight-grained wood that absorbs little stain. The stain darkens poplar because poplar is porous. The stain darkens and highlights the grain of oak because oak is porous with a pronounced grain.

how well you prepare them. Always test your stain on scrap pieces of the wood you are using for your project to be sure the stain produces the results you want.

There are several factors to consider in choosing a stain. First, the name of the color on the can is a manufacturer's interpretation. The same color name (English Oak, Red Mahogany, Fruitwood) from two manufacturers may be two very different colors. Pay more attention to the real color of the stain than the name on the can.

Second, the wood the stain is applied to plays a big part in how the stain will look. Woods vary in color, density, and grain pattern. The same stain applied to mahogany and maple will look redder on the mahogany because mahogany is redder than maple to start with. The same stain applied to poplar and maple will be darker on the poplar because poplar is more porous than maple. More stain is absorbed into the poplar. The same stain applied to oak and maple will look very different because oak has a very pronounced grain and maple doesn't.

Stains also often look different on solid wood and veneer of the same species. When you make a project using veneered plywood or medium density fiberboard with solid-wood edgings, there may be a color difference between the two parts. Usually, solid wood stains darker than veneer. The difference may be enough that you will want to even it by leaving a little more stain on some parts than on others.

Applying Stain

There are two ways to apply stain:

• Apply it and wipe off all the excess.

• Apply it and leave some or all of the excess.

When you intend to remove all the excess stain, it doesn't make any difference how you apply the stain or in what direction you apply it. You can wipe on the stain, brush it on, spray it on, or you can even pour on the stain and spread it around or dip the wood into the stain if the piece of wood is small enough. The trick is to wipe off all the excess stain before it dries.

Since stains dry at different rates, removing all the excess can sometimes be a problem when you are staining large surfaces. It's usually wise to divide large projects into parts and apply and remove the excess on each part before moving on. Once you get used to a brand of stain, you will get a feel for how large an area you can stain comfortably.

As a general rule, water-based and lacquer-based stains dry very quickly and oil- or varnish-based stains relatively slowly. Of course, the slower a stain dries, the longer you have to wait before applying a finish. Overnight is minimum for oil and varnish-based stains. A few hours is usually enough for water-based and lacquer-based stains.

Just as it doesn't make any difference in what direction you apply stain, it doesn't make any difference in what direction you remove the stain when you are removing all the excess. Since you're removing it all, you shouldn't leave any streaking. But, because of the possibility of missing some, it is good practice to make a final pass with your wiping cloth going with the grain. This will line up any remaining streaks of stain so they will be disguised by the grain.

If you want to make the color a little darker, you may need to leave some of the stain on the wood. In this case, you have to apply the stain with the grain of the wood or you will have cross-grain streaks that show badly.

All commonly available stains contain pigment, which is the same colorant used in paint. It's very difficult to wipe or brush pigment onto wood without leaving some streaking. You will find that the thinner the stain—that is, the less pigment contained in the stain—the easier it will be to brush or wipe successfully without leaving streaks. Of course, the less colorant, the lighter the resulting

As shown here, thin, lightly pigmented stains can usually be brushed and left to dry. With thicker, more heavily-pigmented stains, you usually need to wipe off all the excess to avoid leaving streaks.

color. But you can always brush or wipe on another coat.

If the stain you are using is too thick to brush or wipe without leaving streaks, thin it with the appropriate thinner. For oil and varnish stains, use paint thinner. For water-based stain, use water. Thinning will not damage the stain.

Staining Problems

Most staining problems can be fixed by applying more stain, the solvent or thinner for the stain, or paint stripper. For example, if the stain you are using dries before you get all the excess wiped off, or if brushing or wiping leaves streaks and you can't get rid of them, remove as much of the stain as you can and start again. You may want to work on a smaller area, work faster, or thin your stain the second time.

Pine is among the woods that commonly blotch when you apply a stain. The blotching is caused by uneven density or swirly grain in the wood.

To remove stain that has begun to dry, you may be able to just apply more stain, which will soften the existing stain. Then wipe off all the excess. If the stain has dried too much, try wiping with the solvent or thinner for the stain. If the stain is totally cured, you will probably need to use a paint stripper to remove it.

Paint stripper won't take all the color out of the wood, only some of it. There is no way to take out all the color short of sanding, scraping, or planing to below the depth the stain has penetrated. But, there is no reason to take out all of the color unless you decide that you would rather not stain the wood at all. Because of the work involved, this is not a decision that should be taken lightly.

Blotching. There is one staining problem that is not easy to correct. This is blotching. Woods often have swirly grain or uneven density which cause uneven stain absorption. The wood blotches darker in some places and lighter in others. On some woods, such as walnut and mahogany, this blotching is usually attractive. On other woods, though, especially fir, pine, poplar, birch, cherry, and sometimes maple, blotching is often quite ugly.

The problem with blotching is that it is not easy to fix once it has occurred because the only way to fix it is to sand, scrape, or plane to below the depth the stain has penetrated. On veneered plywoods this may not be possible without cutting through the veneer. Sometimes, the only practical way to fix the problem is to

paint the wood. It is therefore essential that you anticipate blotching before it occurs and take steps to prevent it. The most sure method for knowing in advance that blotching may occur is to test your stain on scrap pieces of the wood you are using for the project—both veneer and solid.

You can prevent blotching simply by keeping the stain from penetrating unevenly in the first place. In other words, keep all the stain very near the surface of the wood. There are two ways to do this.

• Use a gel stain which doesn't flow so it doesn't penetrate.

• Fill the pores first with a stain controller so the stain can't penetrate.

Gel Stains

Gel stains (also called gelled or paste stains) are commonly marketed as easy to use, but this is not their real value in finishing. Their real value is to reduce blotching.

Gel stains are thick. They resemble latex wall paint. When you roll latex wall paint onto a wall, the nap of the roller pulls the paint out into small nibs that remain just as the roller leaves them. The nibs don't flatten out and run down the wall as they would if you were using enamel paint.

In the same manner, a gel stain doesn't flow unless it is moved by your rag or brush. And, because it doesn't flow, it doesn't penetrate into the wood. The thicker the gel stain, the less it penetrates and the more effective it is at reducing or eliminating blotching. Keep in mind that the quality that works so well giving pine and cherry an even coloring works to a disadvantage on woods like mahogany and bird's eye maple where you usually want deeper stain penetration to bring out the beautiful figure.

Stain Controllers

Stain controllers can be used before applying a liquid stain to keep the stain from penetrating unevenly. Stain controllers (also called wood conditioner, pre-stain, and grain tamer) are composed primarily of slow-evaporating, petroleum-distillate solvents. They work by filling up the pores and less-dense parts of the wood so the stain can't penetrate. The stain just mixes with the solvent near the surface.

To use a stain controller successfully, apply it to the wood with a brush or rag until all parts of the wood stay wet and no more of the liquid is absorbing into the wood. This usually takes successive applications for five to ten minutes, but the number of applications needed will vary depending on the wood and the ingredients used in the stain controller.

When no more dry spots appear on the wood, wipe off all the excess stain controller and apply the stain as quickly as possible—within thirty minutes is best. If you wait too long, enough of the stain controller will have evaporated, or absorbed deeper into the wood, so that the stain will again penetrate and blotch the wood.

Pickling

In recent years, pickling, which means giving the wood a whitish cast, has become very popular. Pickling is very easy to do. There are two methods. One way is to apply a white or slightly off-white stain or paint to the wood and wipe off all or nearly all the excess before it dries. In other words, simply stain the wood white. The other way is to seal the wood first with your first coat of finish, then apply the stain. Again, the stain can be a regular white or off-white stain, or it can be paint. And, again, you can wipe off all the excess, leaving the colorant only in the grain, or you can leave some of the excess. Oil paint is easier to work with just like oil stains are easier because they give you more working time. However, when you're working on large surfaces in closed rooms, oil-based products can cause breathing problems because of the large amount of solvent that is released into the air. For this reason, painters often use latex paint when they are pickling built-in cabinets or paneling.

PRIMING AND SEALING WOOD

There is a great deal of confusion about primers and sealers. Because primers are necessary when applying paint to bare wood, it is commonly thought that it's necessary to use a special sealer under a clear finish. This is not the case. Primers and sealers perform entirely different functions.

Primers are necessary on bare wood because paint won't bond well by itself. Paint contains a high percentage of pigment (in order to cover bet-

Pickling can be done by wiping a white stain or paint on bare wood (left) or on sealed wood (right). Then wipe off all or most of the excess. More color will be left on the areas between the grain when you apply the colorant to bare wood.

ter) and only enough binder to glue the pigment particles to each other and to an underlying level surface. Since wood is porous, and thus not level, more binder is required to achieve a good bond. Paint primer

Sanding sealer contains a lubricant which causes the finish to powder easily when you sand it.

contains a higher binder-to-pigment ratio than does paint. Primer provides a level surface to which subsequent coats of paint will bond.

Sealers, on the other hand, do nothing to make finishes bond better. Finishes are 100 percent binder already. Sealers make sanding easier so production can be speeded up.

The first coat of any finish locks raised wood fibers in place causing the surface to feel rough after the finish cures. This roughness telegraphs through each subsequent coat of finish. It's easiest to sand off the roughness after the first coat of finish because the finish is thin and easier to sand at this point. Once the roughness has been removed, each additional coat will cure smooth.

The problem is that most finishes are difficult to sand even when thin. They gum up the sandpaper. So, manufacturers provide special easy-to-sand finishes to be used for the first coat. These finishes are usually the regular finish, varnish or lacquer, with zinc stearate, the same soap-like lubricant used in some sandpapers, added. These finishes are properly called "sanding sealers" because they are designed for easy sanding. But they are commonly referred to, and sometimes labeled "sealers," and this causes confusion.

Sanding sealers are useful in production situations where a large surface area must be sanded after the first coat. Sanding sealers speed production. You can achieve almost the same degree of easy sanding by thinning the first coat of finish about half with the appropriate thinner. Because this makes the resulting film thinner, it will cure harder faster, making sanding easier sooner. (This is the reason for thinning the first coat of finish, not to achieve a better bond to the wood as is sometimes claimed.)

The exception is water-based finish which looses its ability to flow out smoothly if it is thinned too much with water. Most water-based finishes sand fairly easily, though, without thinning.

CHOOSING A CLEAR FINISH

When you look at all the finishes on paint-store shelves, it's easy to feel overwhelmed by the number of choices. To aid in choosing a finish it helps to have an idea of the qualities you are looking for. The qualities that make the biggest difference are the following:

- Protection for the wood.
- Durability.
- Ease of Application.

Protection

The primary protective purpose of a finish is to reduce stresses by slowing moisture-vapor exchange in and out of the wood. When the air around wood is humid, moisture is absorbed into the wood and it expands. When the air around wood is dry, moisture is released from the wood and it shrinks. Most materials expand and shrink with humidity changes. But, with wood this expansion and shrinkage occurs only in one direction, across the grain. Wood doesn't expand or shrink significantly along the grain. Thus, when you cross the grain of wood, as you almost always do when making useful objects, you build in stresses that will eventually destroy the object.

All plywoods have built-in stresses because the plies run in opposite directions. Particleboard and medium density fiberboard with veneered faces are more stable, but there are still some stresses because the veneer expands and shrinks more than the substrate. All solid-wood boards glued cross grain, rather than edge to edge, also have built-in stresses.

If you want your project to have the greatest chance for long life, choose a finish that offers maximum resistance to moisture-vapor exchange. Within each finish type (oil, varnish, shellac, lacquer, water-based finish), the thicker the finish, the better it slows this exchange.

Don't make the finish too thick though. Film thicknesses greater than about .006 inch (about four or five coats of polyurethane) have a tendency to crack, especially if the weather goes through sudden radical changes. Cracks allow more moisture-vapor exchange.

Durability

Durability is the degree to which the finish film itself resists damage. Some finishes are more resistant to scratches, water, and heat than others. For a decorative object that will sit on a fireplace mantle all its life, finish durability is not very important. But for a vanity, table top, or set of kitchen cabinets, finish durability is very important. The finish will probably be subjected to a great deal of abuse. Just as with protection, a thicker finish film is more durable, but thickness is less important for durability than for protection. For durability, the type of finish is more important than the thickness.

Ease of Application

Assuming you have access to all three finish-application tools—rag, brush and spray gun—the quality that is most important for making finishes easy to apply is fast drying. This may surprise you until you recall the problems you have with dust getting into slow-drying finishes like polyurethane.

The problem with choosing a fast-drying finish is that it is very difficult to apply without a spray gun. If you don't have a spray gun, you will have to choose a slower-drying finish and learn ways to deal with dust. The exception is when you wipe off all the excess finish after each coat. In this case, fast drying is not important for reducing dust. There isn't enough finish left on the surface for dust to stick to.

TYPES OF FINISH

There are many types of finishes, but only a few are used for wood. It's more helpful to concentrate on types than on brands because brand differences within each type are small. You probably won't even notice differences between brands, but differences between types are significant.

There are five common types of finishes used on wood:

- Oil
- Varnish and polyurethane (polyurethane is a type of varnish)
- Shellac
- Lacquer
- Water-based finish

Oil finishes are easy to differentiate from the other four types because they don't cure hard, and as a result can not be built up into a hard film finish. Varnish, shellac, lacquer, and water-based finishes do cure hard and can build up into a hard film as you add coats. Oil finishes generally are easier to apply than film finishes, while film finishes offer more protection.

Oil

There are two types of oils: those that cure, and those that don't cure. Oils that cure can be used as finishes since they seal the wood and produce a fairly permanent sheen. Oils that don't cure don't perform well as finishes because they continue to soak deeper into the wood leaving the surface unprotected, or they remain sticky on the surface.

Common examples of oils that don't cure are mineral oil, vegetable oil, and motor oil. There are two commonly available oils that cure and thus perform well as finishes: linseed oil and tung oil.

Linseed oil is pressed from the seeds of the flax plant. In its raw form linseed oil takes a week or longer to cure. This slow curing makes raw linseed oil very impractical to use as a finish. To speed the curing, manufacturers add metallic driers which make the oil cure in about a day. With these driers added the oil is called "boiled linseed oil," but it is not actually boiled.

Tung oil is pressed from the nuts of the tung tree which is native to China. Pure tung oil sold in the United States as a wood finish does not have driers added. It takes two to three days for pure tung oil to cure when all the excess is wiped off of wood. Pure tung oil thus cures faster than raw linseed oil, but slower than boiled linseed oil.

Neither type of oil is very protective or durable, but tung oil is more so than boiled linseed oil. Both oils are easy to apply, and that is the main reason for their popularity.

Applying Oil Finishes

All that is required to apply an oil finish is to wipe or brush the oil onto the wood, let the oil soak in for five to ten minutes during which time you re-wet any places that dry out, and then wipe off all the excess. Allow boiled linseed oil to cure overnight; tung oil about three days. Then sand or steel wool lightly to make the wood feel smooth, and apply another coat in the same way as the first. Use 220-grit or finer sandpaper and 000 or 0000 steel wool.

Two or three coats of linseed oil will produce an attractive "rubbed" sheen. You don't need to actually rub the oil. It penetrates into the wood perfectly well without rubbing. In contrast to linseed oil, it may take as many as five or six coats of tung oil to produce a nice sheen. Tung oil cures dull and rough to the touch for the first several coats. Continue to sand lightly between coats with very fine sandpaper (220-grit or finer) until the coats begin to cure smooth.

Though oil finishes are not very protective or durable compared to other finishes, they are easy to repair if they become scratched or dull. Simply wipe on another coat of oil (you don't have to use the same oil you used originally), and wipe off the excess. If the surface feels a little rough to the touch, sand it lightly with very fine sandpaper before applying the oil.

Varnish

Varnish is made by cooking an oil, such as linseed oil, tung oil, or modified soybean oil, with a resin. The resins used in varnishes today are synthetic alkyds, phenolics, and polyurethanes. The product called "polyurethane" is simply a varnish that has been made with polyurethane resins. The polyurethane resins make this type of varnish a little more protective and durable than other types of varnish.

When more oil and less resin is used in the manufacture, the resulting varnish is softer and more flexible. This type of varnish, called "spar" varnish, is best for outdoor use because it flexes better with the greater wood movement outdoors.

Varnish comes in sheens that range from gloss to flat. Satin is probably the most popular sheen because it imitates a steel-wool rubbed appearance. Since the flatting agent that creates the sheen settles to the bottom of the can, stir the varnish before using.

Varnish is one of the most protective and durable of all finishes. Of course, three or four coats is more protective and durable than one or two. But varnish causes problems in application because it cures so slowly. Dust has a lot of time to settle and stick to the finish.

Applying Varnish

Varnish usually is applied with a brush. It is too thick to wipe on easily, and it is not pleasant to spray because small particles settle and stick to everything, including you.

Brushing varnish is just like brushing paint. The only real difference is that cleanliness is more important because dust and dirt show more in a clear varnish finish than they do in paint. Therefore, make an extra effort to make your work room as dust-free as possible. Use a clean brush, transfer the varnish to a separate container if you don't expect to use it all (so you don't contaminate the remaining varnish with dust), and dust the wood surface well before beginning. If the varnish you are using has dust or cured varnish particles in it, strain the varnish through a paint strainer or cheese cloth before beginning.

To remove dust from the wood, begin by vacuuming or wiping with a tack cloth—a sticky cloth you can buy at paint stores. Don't brush or blow the dust off the wood, or it will simply settle back onto your finish while it is wet. Just before you are ready to begin brushing, wipe over the wood with you hand. You will feel if any dust remains. If it does, your hand will pick it up and you can remove it by brushing your hand against your pant leg. When the surface is dust-free, you can begin brushing the varnish.

Begin spreading the varnish onto the wood in any direction. As you move

To line up your brush strokes so they are disguised by the grain of the wood, hold your brush almost perpendicular and drag it lightly across the surface in the direction of the grain.

from section to section, or across a large surface, tip off the varnish in the direction of the wood grain. To tip off, hold the brush almost vertical, and use a light touch. The purpose is to line up the brush strokes with the wood grain so they are less noticeable. On horizontal surfaces begin at the far edge and brush from left to right back towards you so that dust

doesn't fall off your arm onto already applied varnish.

Always work with lights set to reflect off the surface of the wood. If you don't have a reflection, you might as well be blindfolded because you can't see what is happening. A reflection is especially critical on vertical surfaces where the varnish is likely to run and

To remove runs and sags when brushing finish on a vertical surface, you have to view your work in reflected light.

sag. It is very difficult to apply varnish so that it doesn't run and sag on vertical surfaces. The trick is to see the runs and sags when they occur and remove the excess varnish until the running and sagging stop.

To remove runs and sags before they cure, drag your brush over a clean jar edge to remove excess varnish. Then re-brush the varnish while continuing to remove the excess from the brush. Work a section at a time until running and sagging stops.

To lessen brush marking and air bubbles curing in the finish, add 5 to 10 percent paint thinner to the varnish. The added thinner gives the varnish more time to flatten out. It also gives bubbles more time to pop out and the varnish to flow back level. Bubbles are caused by turbulence created by your brush, not by shaking or stirring the can as is often claimed. You can't avoid bubbles. The trick is to get them to pop out before the varnish skins over and traps them.

There is no way to totally eliminate dust settling on your varnish finish. If the dust nibs are worse than you can tolerate, you will need to sand them out. Sand between coats with 220 or finer-grit sandpaper (gray, lubricated sandpaper works best), and after the last coat with 600-grit, wet-or-dry sandpaper. You can use water or mineral oil as a lubricant with this sandpaper. Then rub the surface with 0000 steel wool to produce an even satin sheen.

Wiping Varnish

Varnish can be thinned with any amount of paint thinner and still be used as a finish. When varnish is thinned about half with paint thinner it is easy to wipe on wood, so it is called "wiping varnish." Unfortunately, many manufacturers label their wiping varnish "tung oil," and this causes confusion.

Varnish and tung oil are two entirely different finishes. Varnish, whether thinned or full-strength, cures overnight to a hard, smooth film if left thick on a surface. Tung oil takes months to cure, and then it cures soft and wrinkled. Because of the confused naming, you will need to test your finish in order to learn which you have. To test, pour some of your finish onto a nonporous surface like glass or plastic laminate and leave it overnight in a warm room. If the puddle cures hard and smooth, the product is varnish or wiping varnish. If the puddle cures soft and wrinkled, or it doesn't cure at all, the product is tung oil or a mixture of some type of oil and varnish.

You can apply wiping varnish just like full-strength varnish by brushing it on the wood and leaving it to cure. Or, you can apply it like an oil finish, by wiping or brushing it onto the wood and wiping off the excess. You won't have as much time as you do with an oil finish, however, because varnish cures much faster than oil. But, you can leave a little of the varnish on the wood to achieve a build up and, thus, more protection. This is not possible with an oil finish.

Wiping varnish provides excellent protection and durability, just like full-strength varnish, it just takes many more coats to achieve the same thickness. You can make your own wiping varnish by thinning any varnish or polyurethane about half with paint thinner.

Oil/Varnish Blend

Varnish can also be mixed with linseed oil or tung oil in any proportion. When this is done the product is a little more protective and durable than oil alone, but it still cures slowly to a soft, wrinkled film. Wipe off all the excess finish after each coat. When varnish and oil are mixed, they are called "oil/varnish blend."

Oil/varnish blends are very popular finishes because they are so easy to use. Most are sold under names like "Danish oil" and "teak oil" to suggest a supposed relationship with the finish used on imported Scandinavian furniture. (This furniture is actually finished with two-part, catalyzed lacquer, however, not oil.)

You apply oil/varnish-blend finishes just like boiled linseed oil. Let the first coat soak in for five to ten minutes. Sand or steel wool lightly the next day to make the surface feel smooth. Then apply one or two more coats.

Many formulas circulate for making your own oil/varnish-blend finish. The most common suggest mixing equal parts of varnish, boiled linseed oil, and turpentine or paint thinner. Turpentine differs from paint thinner in its source, not its qualities. Turpentine is distilled sap from pine trees. Mineral spirits is distilled petroleum. Before the twentieth century, mineral spirits was not available.

You can vary this formula in any way you like. For example, you can substitute tung oil for linseed oil, or you can use some of both oils. You can substitute polyurethane for other types of varnish. You can vary the ratio of oil and varnish, and you can add more or less thinner to achieve the working qualities you like best. Whatever changes you make, the results in protection, durability, and shine will be about the same.

Shellac

Shellac is the only natural resin still widely used to make a finish. The resin is secreted from the lac bug which inhabits certain trees native to India and Thailand. Shellac was once the premier wood finish. Almost all furniture and woodwork made between 1830 and 1930 was finished with shellac. During the 1920s lacquer replaced shellac in factories because lacquer is a little more durable and it is more versatile to apply when sprayed. Shellac continued to be used on woodwork in houses until the 1940s.

Unfortunately, shellac has gotten an undeserved reputation for poor water resistance and imperfect hardening. Neither are legitimate problems once you understand the finish.

Shellac is actually quite water resistant. It is just not as much so as varnish, lacquer, and water-based finishes. Water rings you often see on old furniture that was finished with shellac are due more to the aging of the finish than to the type of finish. All finishes become more porous as they age and, thus, become more susceptible to water damage. So, shellac is still fine for most types of furniture and woodwork. It is not the best choice, however, for surfaces that take a lot of abuse, like dining-table tops and kitchen cabinets.

Imperfect drying is caused by the shellac deteriorating in the can before it was applied. Shellac begins deteriorating as soon as it is dissolved in its alcohol solvent. The deterioration is slow, but over a period of a year or two you can tell that the shellac takes longer to dry and it never gets as hard. Always buy the freshest shellac you can find. Most cans of shellac are stamped with the date of manufacture. Try to find shellac that is not more than six months to a year old. If the container of shellac is not dated, don't buy it.

Shellac varies in color between orange (amber) and clear. Orange shellac adds warmth to woods like walnut, pine, maple, and oak. Pine, maple, and oak woodwork in old buildings was almost always finished with orange shellac. Clear shellac is best if you don't want to add color to the wood.

Shellac's fast drying property is a real advantage for reducing dust problems. Shellac dries as fast as its alcohol solvent evaporates. In most cases, this is fast enough so that dust doesn't have time to settle and become embedded. The disadvantage of fast drying, of course, is that it makes shellac a little difficult to apply with a brush.

Applying Shellac

Shellac is difficult to brush straight out of the can. It is too thick, it doesn't flow out well, and it dries too quickly. Thin the shellac about half-and-half with denatured alcohol (sometimes sold as shellac thinner). The more you thin shellac the easier it is to brush without leaving brush marks, but the thinner each coat becomes.

Because shellac dries much faster than varnish, you have to follow a different brushing procedure. Begin brushing shellac close to the way you want the brush strokes to line up. You won't have as much time to come back and line them up as you do with varnish. The trick is to move fast enough so that each new brush stroke overlaps a stroke that is still wet. If the previous stroke has begun to set up, your brush will drag it resulting in ridges curing in the finish. To get ridges out, if they do occur, let the shellac cure. Then sand the surface until it is level, and apply another coat of shellac.

You can apply three or four coats of shellac in a day if the weather is dry and warm. Just like all finishes, shellac dries slower in cool, damp conditions.

Lacquer

Lacquer is the primary finish used in factories and by professional finishers and refinishers. This is because lacquer dries very fast, reducing dust problems, and lacquer is easy and very versatile to apply using a spray gun. But the solvent fumes left by spraying lacquer are bad for your health, so it's not wise to spray lacquer unless you have a means of exhausting these fumes. As a result, few home woodworkers use lacquer.

Shellac dries fast so you must move fast and not continue to brush back over already-brushed parts.

There are lacquers, however, that are made to cure slowly enough so they can be brushed. Though the solvent smell in these lacquers is pretty strong, brushing a "brushing lacquer" is no more difficult than brushing shellac. In fact, the procedure for brushing a brushing lacquer is the same as for brushing shellac. If you can tolerate the increased solvent smell and want the added durability of lacquer, a brushing lacquer is a good choice.

Though it is a bit more expensive, you can purchase lacquer in aerosol spray cans. You might find this convenient for finishing small projects.

Water-based Finish

Because of stricter air-quality laws in some parts of the country, a market has been created for water-based finishes. These finishes are often marketed as "varnish," "polyurethane," and "lacquer" which confuses them with like-named solvent-based products. However, water-based finishes are always identifiable by some mention of water cleanup on the can. Though water-based finishes still do contain organic solvents, they contain less than most other finishes.

The easiest way to understand water-based finishes is to think of them as latex paint without the pigment—because that is essentially what they are. It makes little difference whether the resin in the finish is polyurethane or acrylic. Just as in comparing oil paint and latex paint, the significant difference is finish type rather than the particular resins used.

Water-based finishes have many of the same good and bad qualities of latex paint. The most important good qualities are reduced solvent smell and easy brush clean up. The significant limitations are pronounced brush marking and reduced durability. Compared to oil-based varnishes, water-based finishes level poorly and

are much less resistant to heat, solvent, acid, and alkali damage.

In addition, water-based finishes bubble at least as bad as oil-based varnishes, and the bubbles are less likely to pop out. Adding water to the finish seldom helps. Some manufacturers supply a solvent that reduces bubbling and improves flow out, but few stores stock it. Adding solvent to the finish, though, defeats one of the primary purposes of using a water-based finish in the first place.

Applying Water-Based Finishes

Weather conditions are critical to achieving good results when brushing water-based finishes. Work in conditions as close as possible to 70 degrees Fahrenheit and 40 percent humidity. Use a synthetic-bristle brush and don't over-brush the finish. Continuing to brush a water-based finish raises more bubbles. The best procedure is to try to lay down a level coat without having to go back over it. It also helps to keep the coats as thin as possible. Bubbles pop out of thin coats easier than thick coats.

Beyond this, brushing a water-based finish is similar to brushing shellac. Try to brush only in the direction of the wood grain because you won't have much time to line up your brush strokes after they are applied. And, apply each brush stroke rapidly enough so that the previous stroke is still wet when you overlap it.

Finishing the Finish

All finishes can be improved in appearance and feel by rubbing them with an abrasive after they have cured. It is wise to practice this step on a scrap before doing it on a project because you need to experience how much you can rub before cutting through. Not only does rubbing through a finish cause added work repairing the damage, especially when you have stained the wood, but

sometimes the repair is very difficult or impossible to do.

The easiest way to rub a finish is with 0000 steel wool or synthetic steel wool. Using one or both hands and medium to heavy pressure, rub in long straight strokes in the direction of the wood grain. Avoid making arcs with your strokes. Keep the pressure even over the entire surface, and overlap each stroke by 80 to 90 percent. Be very careful not to rub over the edge, or you will cut through the finish and expose bare wood.

To avoid cutting through edges at the ends of your strokes, rub right up to the edge first, using short strokes. Then rub the entire length using long strokes, stopping just short of the edge.

When you've gone over the entire surface once, remove the dust to see what you've done. It's best to blow the dust off using compressed air, or suck the dust off with a vacuum. Then wipe lightly with the grain using your hand to be sure no dust remains. If you don't have compressed air or a vacuum, wipe with a dampened cloth going with the grain. If you wipe across the grain, you may put noticeable cross-scratches in the finish.

Look at the surface in reflected light. If you're not happy with it, determine what is wrong and begin rubbing again to correct the problem. Common problems are incomplete rubbing and irregular scratch patterns caused by uneven pressure or arcing strokes.

The Ultimate Fix. Any number of problems can occur applying finishes, including runs and sags, dust and dirt getting into the finish, severe brush marking or streaking, blisters or bubbles, too-slow or too-fast curing, and rubbing through the finish. No matter what goes wrong you can always fix it by stripping off the finish and starting over.

TYPES OF PAINT

The first rule of buying paint is: Never buy cheap paint because it is never good. Among top-of-the-line paints, there are variations in quality. Reputable paint suppliers usually sell top-of-the-line paint that is very good. One way to save money on brand-name paint is to buy premixed standard colors. They are less expensive than colors that have to be mixed at the store.

Read the can labels to compare paint ingredients. And remember, the heavier the can, the better the paint.

Latex Versus Oil-Based Paints

Paint is composed of pigment, a vehicle, solvents and additives, all of which affect the flow and drying characteristics of the paint. With latex paint, the vehicle is a water-based emulsion. With oil-based paint, the vehicle is natural or synthetic (alkyd) oil. A third, new type of paint is latex paint that has some alkyd resins.

Choosing Latex Paint. Homeowners and professional painters like latex paint because it dries in just a few hours and because cleanup is easy. Quick drying allows the application of two coats in one day. When the job is done, everything can be cleaned with soap and warm water.

Latex paint is environmentally friendlier than its oil-based cousin. Unlike oil-based paint, latex does not emit volatile organic compounds (VOCs), which have been virtually outlawed in some states. Also latex paint does not require toxic solvents such as mineral spirits for cleanup. Compared to oil-based paint, latex paint is easier on the eyes, nose, lungs and skin.

In the past, however, many professional painters have resisted using latex paint. They preferred oil-based paint, especially for woodwork and areas where the paint has to hold up to a lot of scrubbing, such as the kitchen and bathroom. The truth was, that even the best latex enamel did not dry quite as hard, smooth or shiny as a good oil-based paint. Some painters complained that latex paint did not flow off the brush as smoothly as oil-based paint.

Recently however, as more states pass laws restricting the use of VOCs, paint manufacturers have put all their research dollars into improving latex paints. Today, many professional painters use oil-based paint only to prime or recoat old oil-based paint.

Choosing Oil-Based Paint. If you do choose to use oil-based paint, mineral spirits or turpentine are necessary to clean brushes, rollers, drips and yourself. These solvents are relatively costly (especially compared to water); they smell bad (do not be fooled by labels that say "odorless"); and can be irritating to eyes, nose, lungs and skin. In addition, after you have cleaned tools and skin with mineral spirits, a final cleanup with soap and water is necessary as well.

Usually you have to wait at least overnight before recoating oil-based paint. This can be inconvenient, especially if you can only work on weekends. If the first coat isn't dry on Sunday, you'll wind up waiting a week to finish the job.

Most municipalities have strict rules regarding the disposal of leftover solvents and oil-based paints which means you may find yourself stuck with half-empty containers. In addition, you may end up paying to dispose of excess paint products the same way you would pay to dispose of toxic waste.

Choosing a Sheen

In addition to choosing the color and whether you want latex or oil-based paint, you also need to choose the degree of sheen you want. The range runs from flat to gloss. Most sheens are available in interior or exterior as well as latex or oil-based formulations.

The degree of sheen is determined by the proportion of resin in the paint. The resin determines the degree to which the paint is absorbed into the painted surface and how much pigment is left to form a film on the surface. In short, the more resin, the less the absorption, and thus the glossier the paint.

Flat or Matte. A low-gloss finish hides surface flaws and flaws in pre-paint preparation. Because the paint is slightly rough, flat paints do not take scrubbing as well as glossier finishes. Scrubbing flat paint tends to spread out the dirt, leaving a larger dirty spot.

Eggshell and Satin. This is glossier than flat paint, with slightly better abrasion resistance. Satin is glossier than eggshell.

Semi-Gloss. Semi-gloss paints take scrubbing moderately well. They are available in latex or oil-based.

Gloss. This is the highest gloss classification. It is highest in resin and lowest in absorption. Gloss paints take scrubbing well, and are easiest to clean. However, the glossier the paint, the more obvious the surface flaws.

Enamel. Years ago, this term was synonymous with oil-based paint. These days, it is a loose term that refers to the glossiness of paint. The term is reliable only in that you can be reasonably sure that a paint labeled "enamel" is a semi-gloss or gloss paint. One manufacturer's enamel may be glossier than others.

for the kitchen...
Base Cabinet

This finely crafted base cabinet could easily be the basic building block of any kitchen remodel. It is designed to go with the wall cabinet featured on page 71. As with that project, you may decide to use a different style of cabinet door rather than the overlay frame-and-raised-panel door shown.

The Materials List provided is for a cabinet that is 18 inches wide, a standard cabinet width. You'll probably want to gang several cabinets together for the counter length you need. Size the cabinets to fit your space exactly.

Make the cabinets from plywood. Use hardwood plywood for side panels that will show and AC grade fir plywood for side panels that abut other cabinets or walls. Make the face frames, doors, drawer front, and edge trim from hardwood to match the hardwood plywood. The kick-plate can be solid wood or plywood. The drawer sides and backs can be matching hardwood or clear pine.

The plans presented here call for a countertop of particleboard covered with plastic laminate. The counter edging and backsplash are solid wood. Make the countertop as long as you need to cover a run of cabinets. For other countertop options, refer to "Countertops," page 26.

Base Cabinet Materials List

Difficulty Level 🔨🔨

Qty	Part	Dimensions
Carcase and face frame		
2	Plywood sides	3/4" x 23¼" x 35¼"
1	Plywood bottom	3/4" x 22⅞" x 17"
1	Plywood back	1/4" x 17¼" x 35¼"
1	Plywood shelf	3/4" x 21¼" x 16"
1	Kickplate	3/4" x 5" x 18"
1	Nailing cleat	3/4" x 1½" x 16½"
3	Plywood crosspieces	3/4" x 5" x 16¼"
2	Solid-wood guide hangers	3/4" x 3¼" x 22⅞"
1	Solid-wood shelf edge	3/4" x 3/4" x 16"
2	Stiles	3/4" x 1½" x 31"
3	Rails	3/4" x 1½" x 15"
Door		
1		3/4" x 15¾" x 23¼" (with 3/8" overlay)
Drawer		
2	Plywood sides	1/2" x 3" x 23½"
1	Front	3/4" x 3" x 13½"
1	Back	3/4" x 2½" x 13½"

Qty	Part	Dimensions
1	Plywood bottom	1/4" x 13½" x 23⅛"
1	False front	3/4" x 4¾" x 15¾"
Countertop		
1	Particleboard panel	3/4" x 23⅜" x as needed
1	Sheet plastic laminate (rough size)	25" x as needed
1	Front edge strip	3/4" x 1½" x as needed
2	Side edge strips	3/4" x 1½" x 24⅞"
1	Solid-wood backsplash	3/4" x 5" x as needed
Hardware		
	4d Finishing nails	
	6d Finishing nails	
4	Adjustable shelf pins	
1 pair	Side-mounted drawer slides	
	7/8" Brads	
1 pair	Overlay hinges	
2	Door/drawer pulls	
	#6x2" Flathead wood screws	
	#6x1¼" Flathead wood screws	

BUILDING THE CARCASE

1. Cut the plywood. Cut the sides, bottom, back, shelf, and kickplate to the dimensions in the Materials List. Cut a notch for the kickplate in each side panel as shown in *Side Panel Details*. Drill holes in the inside faces of both side panels as shown for the adjustable shelf pins. See "Installing Shelf Pins", page 22, for instructions on making and using a shelf pin drilling template.

2. Dado and rabbet the sides. Dado and rabbet the side panels as shown in *Side Panel Details*. The rabbet for the back is 1/8 inch deeper than the plywood thickness to create a fitting allowance for a less-than-perfect wall. Note that the drawing shows one cabinet side. Don't forget to make the other side in a mirror image. For more information on cutting rabbets and dadoes, refer to "Dadoes, Grooves, and Rabbets", page 10.

Side Panel Details

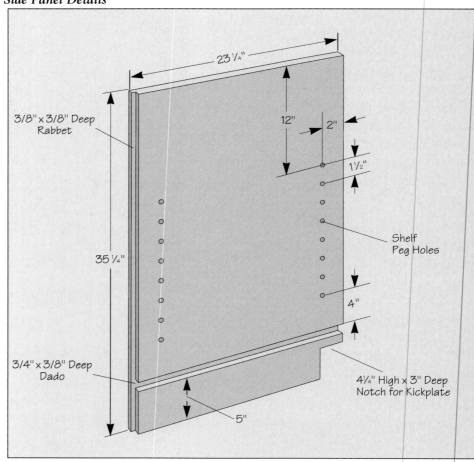

3/8" x 3/8" Deep Rabbet

23 ¼"

12"

2"

1½"

35 ¼"

Shelf Peg Holes

4"

3/4" x 3/8" Deep Dado

4¼" High x 3" Deep Notch for Kickplate

5"

Overall View

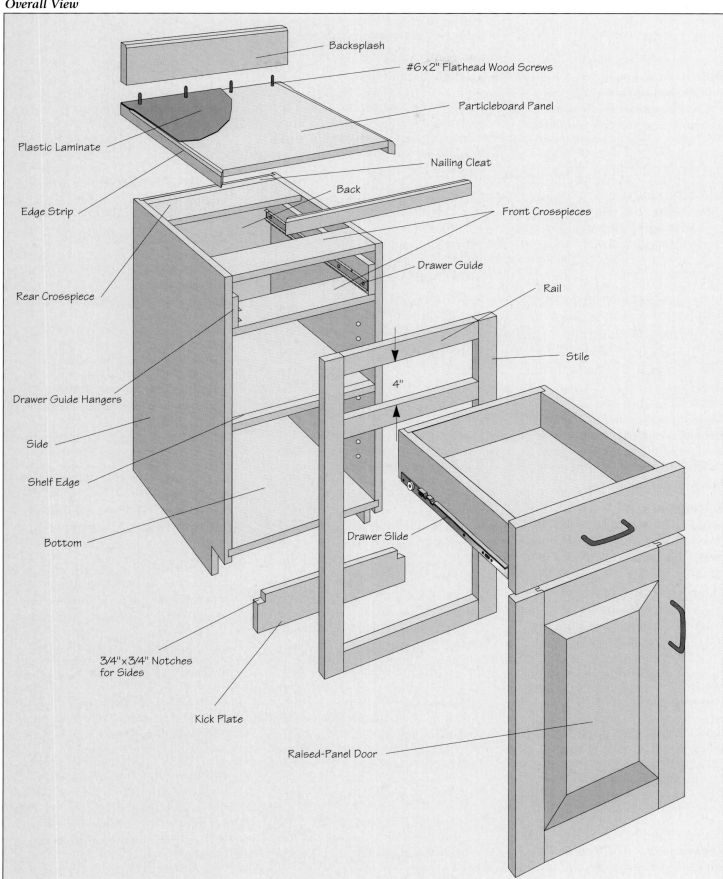

Backsplash

#6x2" Flathead Wood Screws

Particleboard Panel

Plastic Laminate

Nailing Cleat

Edge Strip

Back

Front Crosspieces

Rear Crosspiece

Drawer Guide

Rail

Stile

Drawer Guide Hangers

4"

Side

Shelf Edge

Bottom

Drawer Slide

3/4"x3/4" Notches for Sides

Kick Plate

Raised-Panel Door

3. **Assemble the carcase.** Use glue and 6d finishing nails to join the sides to the bottom shelf. Cut the nailing cleat and crosspieces to the dimensions in the Materials List. Glue and nail the nailing cleat to the sides. Glue the rear crosspiece to the nailing cleat and nail it to the sides. Install the remaining crosspieces as shown in the *Overall View*. Note that the lower crosspiece is 4³/₄ inches below the top crosspiece. This will give you a 4-inch high drawer opening.

4. **Notch and install the kickplate.** Notch the kickplate to fit around the sides as shown in the *Overall View*. Install the kickplate at the bottom front of the carcase with glue and 4d finishing nails.

5. **Install the Drawer Guide Hangers.** The drawer guide hangers are necessary only if you plan to use side-mounted metal drawer slides. You won't need them for bottom-mounted slides, but for bottom mounts you may have to shorten the drawer to make room for the hardware behind the drawer. Purchase your slide hardware before you build the drawer.

Cut the drawer guide hangers to the dimensions in the Materials List. The top of the hangers will fit under the nailing cleat while the bottom of the hangers will rest on the lower front crosspiece. Glue and screw the hangers to the cabinet sides. Use #6x1¹/₄-inch flathead wood screws.

6. **Install the back.** Use a framing square to make sure the sides are square with the upper crosspiece. Apply glue to the rabbets in the side panels, lay the back in place, and secure it with 7/8-inch brads.

7. **Make the shelf.** Cut the shelf edge to the dimensions in the Materials List. Glue and clamp it to the front edge of the shelf. Install the shelf.

8. **Cut and attach the stiles and rails.** The rail dimensions in the Materials List will make the stiles flush to the sides of the cabinet. This looks best for a freestanding cabinet. However, if you are building a run of cabinets you may want to add 1/4 inch to the rail lengths. This way the stiles will extend 1/8 inch past each side of the cabinet. This will allow for warped cabinet sides or irregular walls. If you do this, you'll need to adjust the door widths accordingly. Cut the stiles and fasten them with glue and 6d finishing nails. Then cut the rails to fit between and fasten them the same way.

9. **Make and hang the door.** The door dimensions in the Materials List are for a door that overlays the stiles and rails by 3/8 inch on all sides. See "Making Cabinet Doors," page 15.

To hang the door, fasten a pair of overlay hinges 2 inches from each end of a stile. See "Installing Overlay Doors," page 20. Hold the door over the face frame, aligning door edges squarely and evenly with the face frame. Use an awl to mark centers for hinge screws. Drill pilot holes, and attach the door with the screws provided.

10. **Make the drawer.** The drawer shown is a simple box with a false front that overlays the drawer opening by 3/8 inch on all sides. Cut the parts to the dimensions in the Materials List. Make the drawer as described in "Drawer Construction," page 23.

11. **Finish and install the cabinet or cabinets.** Apply finish to the cabinets (polyurethane is a good, durable choice for kitchen cabinets). Install drawer pulls with screws provided. See "Installing Cabinets and Built-ins," page 28.

MAKING AND INSTALLING THE COUNTERTOP

1. **Cut the particleboard.** Cut particleboard to the width in the Materials List and 1/8 inch longer than the run of cabinets. For a single cabinet, cut it 18¹/₈ inches long.

2. **Cut and attach the hardwood edging.** Cut edging strips to the thickness and width in the Materials List and to length as needed (18³/₄ inches for a single cabinet). Cut pieces to length with mitered joints at the corner and square cuts to meet the walls. Attach the edging with glue and 6d finishing nails.

3. **Install the laminate top.** Install the laminate with contact adhesive. See "Countertops," page 26. Use a router and flush-trimming bit to trim all four edges of the laminate flush with the sides of the solid-wood edging. The laminate will cover the top of the edging.

4. **Chamfer the side and front edges.** Use a chamfering bit in the router to complete the countertop's edge detail. Stop the chamfer 1¹/₂ inches from each back corner of the countertop.

5. **Install the backsplash.** Cut the backsplash to the dimensions in the Materials List and to length as needed for your run of cabinets. Drill four equally-spaced countersunk pilot holes from the underside of the countertop for the installation screws. Attach the backsplash with four 2-inch flathead wood screws in countersunk holes.

6. **Install the countertop.** Lay the finished countertop in place, and secure it to the cabinet with four 1¹/₄-inch flathead wood screws, driven up through the top crosspieces into the underside of the particleboard.

Base cabinets are the foundation of a kitchen re-model, but well-designed wall cabinets make the first impression. Because they are at eye level, wall cabinets are often the first thing people see in a kitchen. This wall cabinet is designed to go with the base cabinet on page 67. Both cabinets feature overlay frame-and-raised-panel doors, but you may decide on a different style.

Like the base cabinet it matches, this cabinet is 18 inches wide, a standard cabinet width, and the Materials List reflects this. However, you can modify the dimensions. For example, you can re-size upper cabinets to fit around a range hood or over a refrigerator. Because

this cabinet has no fixed shelves, it is particularly easy to modify for height; simply shorten the sides, face frame, and door by the same amount.

Similarly, if you have a wider expanse to cover, you can widen the cabinets and install double doors. If you do this, you'll need to add a center stile to the face frame. Make the center stile twice as wide as the side stiles.

To make the basic wall cabinet, use hardwood plywood for the side panels that will show and AC grade fir plywood for the side panels that abut other cabinets or walls. Face frames, doors, and edge trim should all be hardwood to match the hardwood plywood you use.

Overall View

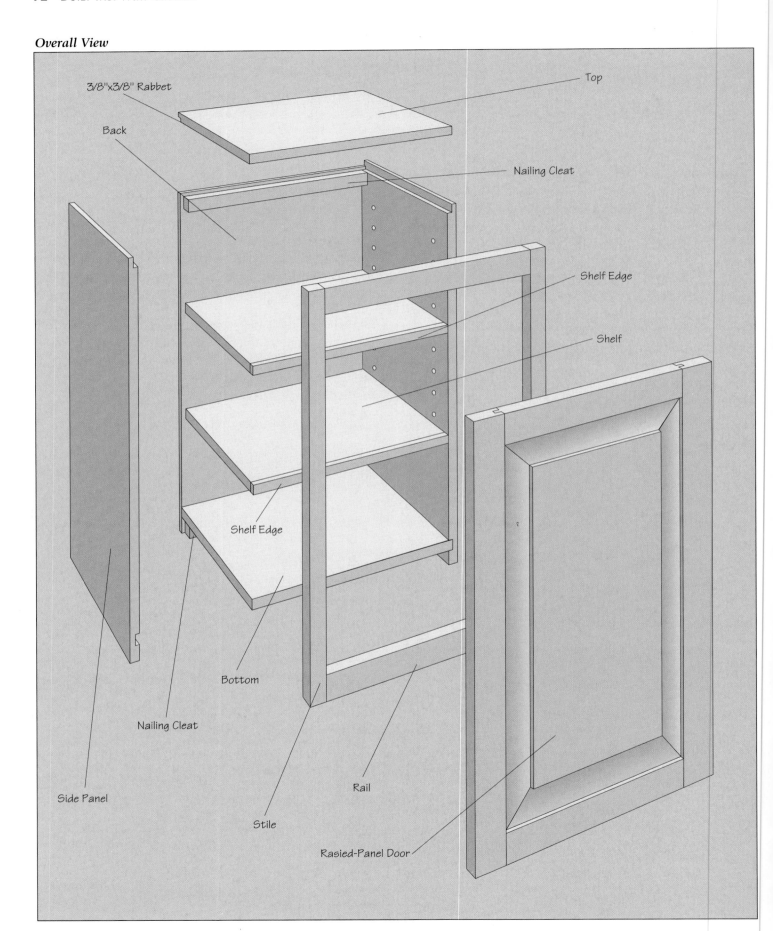

3/8"x3/8" Rabbet

Back

Top

Nailing Cleat

Shelf Edge

Shelf

Shelf Edge

Bottom

Nailing Cleat

Side Panel

Stile

Rail

Rasied-Panel Door

Wall Cabinet Materials List

Difficulty Level

Qty	Part	Dimensions	Qty	Part	Dimensions
Carcase and face frame			**Door**		
1	Plywood top	3/4" x 11¼" x 17¼"	1		3/4" x 15¾" x 26¼" (with 3/8" overlay)
2	Plywood sides	3/4" x 11¼" x 30"			
1	Plywood bottom	3/4" x 11" x 17¼"	**Hardware**		
2	Plywood shelves	3/4" x 10¼" x 16¼"	12	Adjustable shelf pins	
1	Plywood back	1/4" x 17¼" x 29⅝"		6d Finishing nails	
2	Nailing cleats	3/4" x 1½" x 16½"		7/8" Brads	
2	Stiles	3/4" x 1½" x 30"	1 pair	Overlay hinges	
2	Rails	3/4" x 2¼" x 15"	1	Door pull	
2	Solid-wood shelf edges	3/4" x 3/4" x 16¼"		3" Drywall screws	

BUILDING THE CARCASE

1. Cut the plywood. Cut the top, sides, bottom, shelves, back, and nailing cleats to the dimensions in the Materials List. Drill holes for the adjustable shelf pins in the inside faces of both side panels as shown in *Side Panel Details*. See "Installing Shelf Pins," page 22, for instructions on making and using a shelf pin drilling template.

2. Dado and rabbet the sides and top. Dado and rabbet the side panels as shown in *Side Panel Details*. The rabbets for the back are 1/8 inch deeper than the thickness of the back to create a fitting allowance for less-than-perfect walls. Note that the drawing shows one cabinet side. Don't forget to make the other side in a mirror image. See "Dadoes, Grooves, and Rabbets," page 10.

3. Assemble the carcase. Use glue and 6d finishing nails to join the sides to the bottom and top. Glue and nail the nailing cleats in place as shown in the *Overall View*.

4. Install the back. Use a framing square to make sure the sides are square with the top and bottom. Apply glue to the rabbets in the side panels and top panel, lay the back in place and secure it with 7/8-inch brads.

5. Cut and attach the stiles and rails. The rail dimensions in the Materials List will make the stiles flush to the sides of the cabinet. This looks best for an individual cabinet. However if you are building a run of cabinets you may want to add 1/4 inch to the rail lengths to allow for warped cabinet sides or irregular walls. Cut the stiles and fasten them with glue and 6d finishing nails. Then cut the rails to fit between and fasten them the same way.

SHELVES, DOOR, AND INSTALLATION

1. Make the shelves. Cut the shelf edges to the dimensions in the Materials List. Glue and clamp them to the front edges of the shelves.

2. Make and hang the door. The door dimensions in the Materials List are for a door that overlays the stiles and rails by 3/8 inch on all sides. See "Making Cabinet Doors," page 15. To hang the door, fasten a pair of overlay hinges 2 inches from each end of a stile. See "Installing Doors and Hinges," page 19. Fasten the hinges to the stiles and hang the door, making sure it is square with the face frame.

3. Finish and install the cabinet or cabinets. Apply finish to the cabinet (polyurethane is a good, durable choice). Install the door pull with screws provided. Use 3-inch drywall screws through the top and bottom nailing cleats to hang the cabinet. Hanging a wall cabinet can be tricky since it must be supported until it is secured. See "Installing Cabinets and Built-ins," page 28.

Side Panel Details

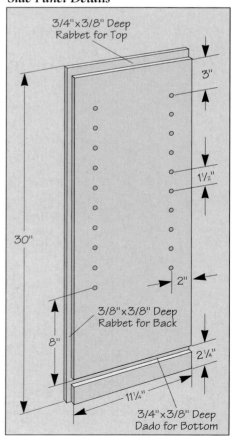

3/4"x 3/8" Deep Rabbet for Top

3"

1½"

2"

30"

3/8"x3/8" Deep Rabbet for Back

8"

2¼"

11¼"

3/4"x3/8" Deep Dado for Bottom

for the kitchen...

Pantry Cabinet

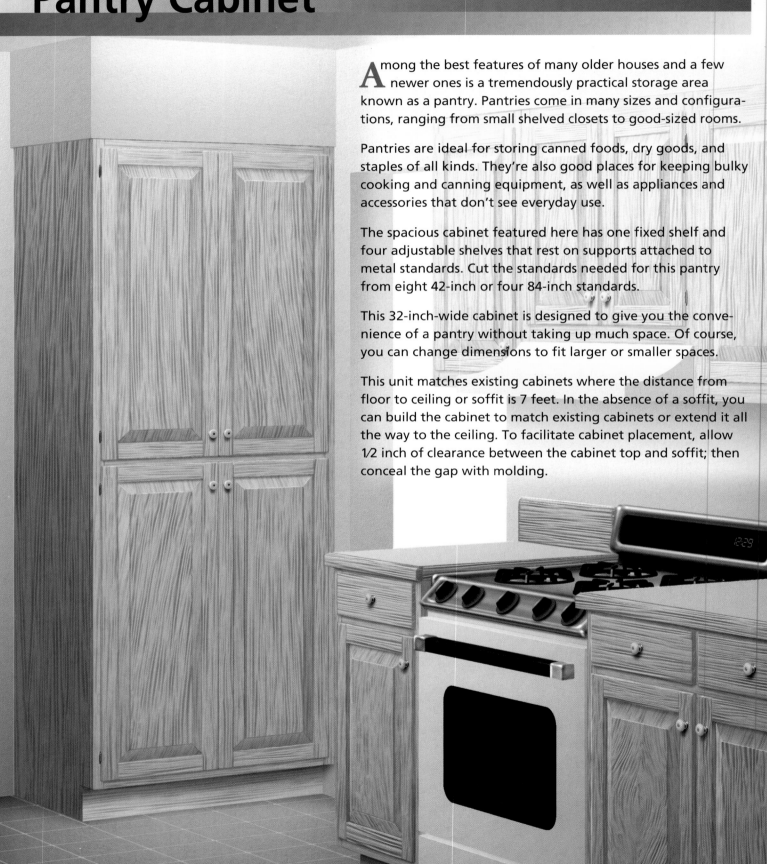

Among the best features of many older houses and a few newer ones is a tremendously practical storage area known as a pantry. Pantries come in many sizes and configurations, ranging from small shelved closets to good-sized rooms.

Pantries are ideal for storing canned foods, dry goods, and staples of all kinds. They're also good places for keeping bulky cooking and canning equipment, as well as appliances and accessories that don't see everyday use.

The spacious cabinet featured here has one fixed shelf and four adjustable shelves that rest on supports attached to metal standards. Cut the standards needed for this pantry from eight 42-inch or four 84-inch standards.

This 32-inch-wide cabinet is designed to give you the convenience of a pantry without taking up much space. Of course, you can change dimensions to fit larger or smaller spaces.

This unit matches existing cabinets where the distance from floor to ceiling or soffit is 7 feet. In the absence of a soffit, you can build the cabinet to match existing cabinets or extend it all the way to the ceiling. To facilitate cabinet placement, allow 1/2 inch of clearance between the cabinet top and soffit; then conceal the gap with molding.

Pantry Cabinet Materials List

Qty	Part	Dimensions		Qty	Part
Carcase, shelves, and doors				**Hardware**	
2	Plywood side panels	3/4" x 23¼" x 83½"			4d Finishing nails
3	Plywood top, bottom, and fixed shelf	3/4" x 23" x 31¼"			7/8" Brads
					6d Finishing nails
4	Plywood shelves	3/4" x 22⅛" x 30¼"			#10 x 3½" Wood screws
1	Plywood back	1/4" x 31¼" x 76¾"		4	37⅞" Metal shelf standards
2	Solid-wood nailing cleats	3/4" x 3½" x 31¼"		4	38⅛" Metal shelf standards
1	Solid-wood kickplate	3/4" x 5" x 32"		16	Metal shelf supports
2	Solid-wood face frame stiles	3/4" x 1½" x 79¼"		4	Door pulls
3	Solid-wood face frame rails	3/4" x 1½" x 29"		8	Self-closing hinges
4	Solid-wood shelf edges	3/4" x 3/4" x 30¼"			
4	Doors (with 3/8" overlay)	3/4" x 15" x 38⅛"			

BUILDING THE CARCASE

1. Cut the parts. Cut the sides, top, bottom, shelves, back, nailing cleats, and kickplate to the dimensions in the Materials List. Then cut the kickplate notches in the bottom edge of each side panel, as shown in *Side Panel Details*.

2. Cut the dadoes. Cut dadoes across the inside surfaces of the side panels positioned as shown in *Side Panel Details*. See "Dadoes, Grooves, and Rabbets," page 10.

3. Cut grooves for the standards. Rout 3/16-inch-deep and 5/8-inch-wide grooves in the side panels. Locate these grooves as shown in *Side Panel Details*. Note that the drawing shows one cabinet side. Don't forget to make the other side in a mirror image. See "Making Dadoes and Grooves with the Table Saw," page 11.

4. Cut the rabbets. Cut a 3/8x3/8-inch rabbet along the rear inside edge of each side panel as shown in *Side Panel Details*. These rabbets are 1/8 inch deeper than the back panel thickness to create a fitting allowance for less-than-perfect walls. Then use a straight bit to widen the rabbet to 1 inch for 3½ inches below the top dado and 3½ inches above the bottom dado.

Side Panel Details

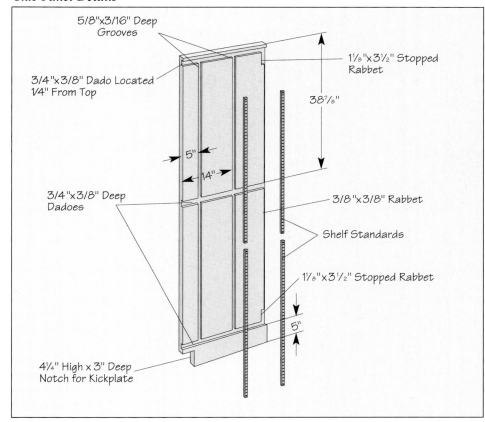

5/8"x3/16" Deep Grooves

3/4"x3/8" Dado Located 1/4" From Top

1⅛"x3½" Stopped Rabbet

38⅞"

5"

14"

3/4"x3/8" Deep Dadoes

3/8"x3/8" Rabbet

Shelf Standards

1⅛"x3½" Stopped Rabbet

5"

4¼" High x 3" Deep Notch for Kickplate

This accommodates the 1x4 nailers. Square off these widened areas with a chisel.

5. Assemble the cabinet. Assemble the top, bottom, and fixed shelf to the sides with glue and four 4d finishing nails into each dado. See "Squaring a Carcase," page 14.

6. Notch and attach the kickplate. Notch the kickplate to fit around the sides as shown in the *Overall View*. Attach the kickplate to the sides with glue and two 4d finishing nails at each end.

7. Attach the nailing cleats. Apply glue to the widened rabbets in the rear of the side panels, position

Overall View

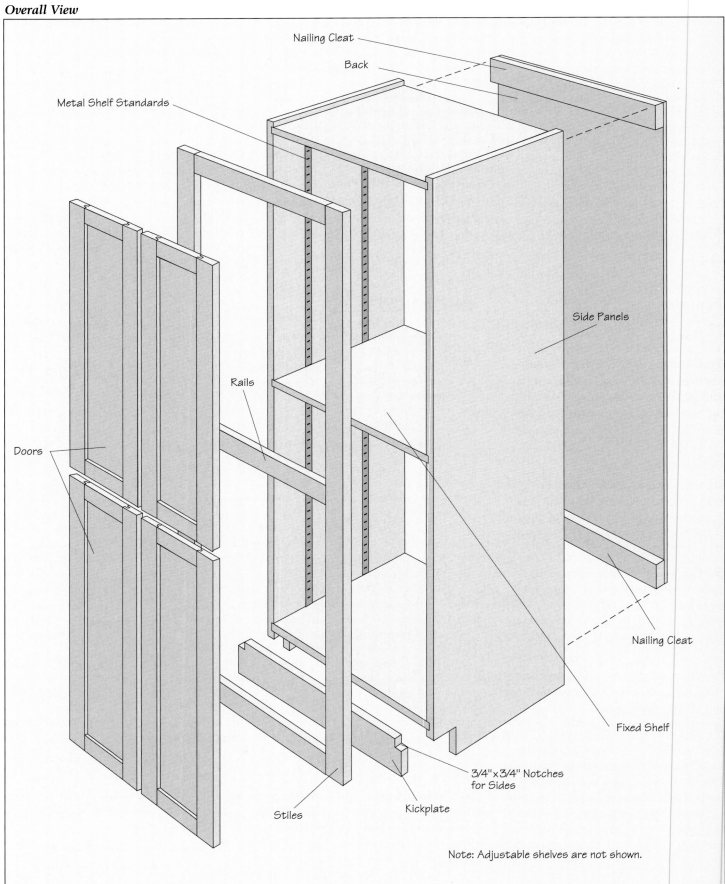

Nailing Cleat

Back

Metal Shelf Standards

Side Panels

Rails

Doors

Nailing Cleat

Fixed Shelf

3/4"x3/4" Notches for Sides

Stiles

Kickplate

Note: Adjustable shelves are not shown.

the nailing cleats between the rabbets, and drive two 4d finishing nails through the side panels into each end of each nailing cleat.

8. **Attach the back panel.** Apply glue to the rabbets in the rear edges of the side panels, the rear edges of the horizontal panels, and the rear surfaces of the nailers. Lay the back panel in place with its top edge flush to the top of the top panel. Secure the back with 7/8-inch brads.

BUILDING AND INSTALLING THE FACE FRAME AND SHELVES

1. **Cut and attach the stiles and rails.** Cut the face frame stiles to the dimensions in the Materials List and fasten them to the cabinet with glue and 6d finishing nails. Cut the rails to

fit between, and then glue and nail them with their tops flush to the tops of the sides, fixed shelf, and bottom.

2. **Complete the adjustable shelves.** Cut the solid-wood shelf edges to the dimensions in the Materials List. Glue and clamp the edges to the front of the adjustable shelves.

3. **Install the cabinet.** Before installation, sand the solid-wood parts and apply the finish of your choice. Set the cabinet in place against the wall. Make sure the unit is plumb and level, and shim it as necessary beneath the side panels and kickplate. Then attach the cabinet to the wall by driving two #10x3$\frac{1}{2}$-inch wood screws through each nailer into each stud (four screws per nailer). For more on installation techniques, see "Installing Cabinets and Built-ins," page 28.

4. **Install the shelves.** Use a hacksaw to trim the metal shelf standards to length. Make all the cuts from the top ends of the standards to keep

them in perfect register. Then set the standards in place inside the grooves in the side panels, and secure them with the nails provided. Snap a metal shelf support into each standard for each shelf; then lay the shelves atop the supports.

BUILDING AND FINISHING THE DOORS

1. **Build the doors.** The dimensions in the Materials List are for doors that overlay the cabinet by 3/8 inch all around. See "Making Cabinet Doors," page 15.

2. **Finish the doors.** Finish the doors to match the cabinet carcase. Attach door pulls and self-closing hinges with screws provided. Then hang the doors on the cabinet. See "Installing Doors and Hinges," page 19.

for the kitchen...

Door-Mounted Shelves

Most homes have an abundance of potential storage space that goes to waste, some of which is no farther than the nearest cabinet door. Wherever cabinet doors have no shelves behind them or have shelves that lie at least four inches from the door, you can add shallow shelving to the doors themselves.

Door-mounted shelves are ideal for under-sink cabinets in kitchens, bathrooms, and utility rooms, where they store and organize soaps, cleansers, and cleaning paraphernalia. Other good prospects for this project are pantry, workshop, and hobby-room cabinets.

This plan is for a shelf unit designed to fit on the door of a standard 18-inch-wide single-door cabinet or 36-inch-wide two-door cabinet. Adjust the dimensions to fit your needs, but make sure the shelf unit is mounted at least 1/2 inch inside all door edges to allow adequate clearance of the face frame.

Door-Mounted Shelves Materials List

Difficulty Level

Qty	Part	Dimensions	Part
			Hardware
1	Plywood support panel	3/4" x 12½" x 19¼"	
3	Solid-wood shelves	1/2" x 3" x 13"	4d Finishing nails
2	Solid-wood sides	3/4" x 3½" x 19¼"	#8 x 1¼" Wood screws
3	Shelf stops	1/4" x 1⅛" x 14"	

CONSTRUCTING SUPPORTS AND SIDE PANELS

1. **Cut and sand the parts.** Cut the support panel, shelves, sides, and shelf stops to the dimensions in the Materials List. Then cut off the top front corners of the sides at 45 degrees. Start the cuts 1 inch down from the top edge of the sides as shown in the *Overall View.* Lightly sand all parts.

2. **Dado support and side panels.** Cut dadoes in the support panel and sides as shown in the *Overall View.* You can use the shelf spacing shown or adjust the spacing to suit your needs. See "Dadoes, Grooves, and Rabbets," page 10.

3. **Assemble the shelf unit.** Put glue in the support panel dadoes. Affix the support panel to the shelves with 4d finishing nails through the back of the panel. Put glue in the side panel dadoes. Attach the side panels to the shelves with 4d finishing nails. Check that the assembly is square.

4. **Attach shelf unit to the cabinet door.** Center the unit on the inside surface of a cabinet door, and attach the panel to the door with four 1¼-inch wood screws.

5. **Attach shelf stops.** Apply a small amount of glue to each end of each shelf stop. Position each stop about an inch above its respective shelf and attach the stop with one 4d finishing nail at each end.

6. **Apply Finish.** Sink all nails with a nail set and fill holes with wood putty. Lightly sand as required and apply the finish of your choice.

Overall View

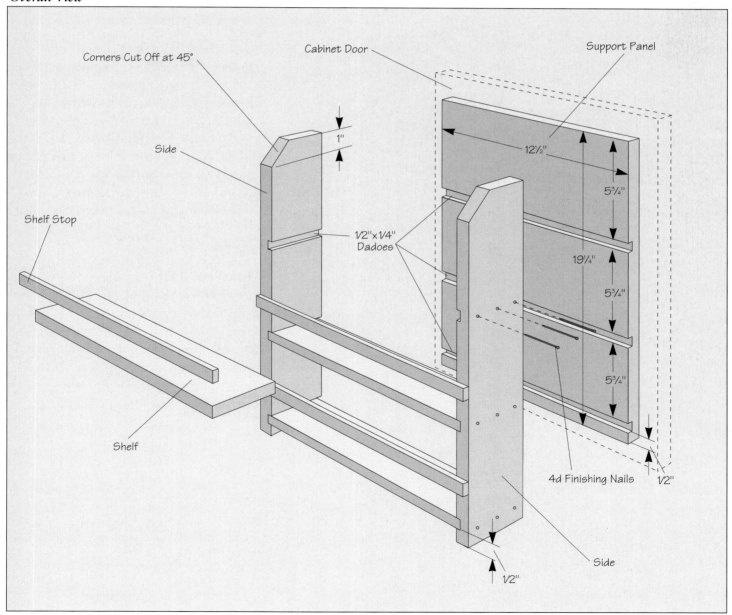

for the kitchen...
Roll-Out Shelf

Some base cabinets can be a pain in the back, especially when you try to reach pots, pans, or other items stored in them—invariably, whatever you're reaching for is at the very back of the cabinet. If you're tired of being a kitchen contortionist and unloading cabinets just to reach a sauce pan or to lift out a heavy food processor, this roll-out shelf is the prescription for your relief. You'll probably want to make and install several of them.

The shelf featured here is sized to fit into a cabinet that is 18 inches wide and 24 inches deep. It's designed to work with the base cabinet on page 67. The base cabinet is built of 3⁄4-inch-thick plywood with 1½-inch-wide face frames. As a result, the roll-out shelf uses 3⁄4-inch-thick wood slide hangers to allow the shelf to slide past the face frames. If you are installing the roll-out shelf in cabinets that have a 3⁄4-inch-wide face frame or no face frame at all, omit the slide hangers.

The roll-out shelf uses side-mounted metal drawer slides. Typically, these slides require 1⁄2 inch of clearance on each side. This leaves you with an overall shelf width of 20 inches. To accommodate wider or narrower openings and deeper or shallower cabinets, adjust shelf dimensions to suit your needs.

Roll-Out Shelf Materials List

Difficulty Level

Qty	Part	Dimensions	Qty	Part
2	Solid-wood sides	3/4" x 3" x 22½"	**Hardware**	
1	Solid-wood back	3/4" x 3" x 14"		3/4" Brads
1	Plywood bottom	1/2" x 13¼" x 22½"		#6 x 1¼" Wood screws
2	Guide hangers	3/4" x 4" x 22⅞"	1 set	22" Side-mounted metal drawer slides

Overall View

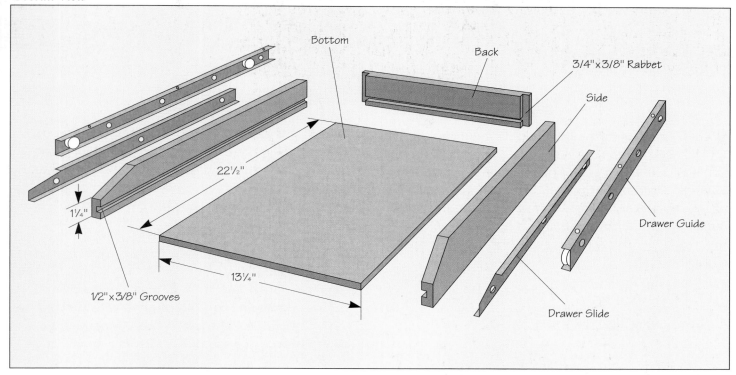

Bottom

Back

3/4"x3/8" Rabbet

Side

Drawer Guide

Drawer Slide

22½"

1¼"

13¼"

½"x3/8" Grooves

BUILDING THE SHELF

1. Cut the parts. Cut sides, back, bottom, and slide hangers to the dimensions in the Materials List. Then cut off the top front corner of each side. Make the cut at a 45-degree angle, 1¼ inches up from the bottom front corner.

2. Groove and rabbet sides and back. Cut grooves in the sides and back as shown in the *Overall View*. Then cut rabbets into the ends of the back panel. See "Making Dadoes and Grooves with a Table Saw," page 11; and "Making Rabbets with a Table Saw," page 12.

3. Assemble the shelf. Sand all parts before assembly. Assemble the shelf with glue and 3/4-inch brads. Clamp it with bar or pipe clamps, and let it stand until the glue sets.

4. Apply finish. Sand the shelf and apply the finish of your choice. Allow the finish to dry.

INSTALLING SLIDES AND SHELF

1. Install the guide hangers. If the roll-out shelf will be installed directly over an existing fixed shelf, simply attach the slide hangers directly on top of the shelf with glue and countersink 1¼-inch wood screws into the cabinet sides as shown in *Shelf Installation*. Otherwise draw level lines where you want the shelf to go and attach the hangers along those lines.

2. Attach slides and glides. Following the manufacturer's directions, attach drawer slides to the roll-out shelf with screws provided. Fasten the drawer guides to the cabinet side panels with the screws provided. Make sure the guides are level both front to back and with each other.

Shelf Installation

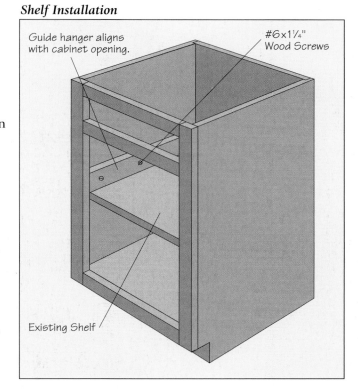

Guide hanger aligns with cabinet opening.

#6x1¼" Wood Screws

Existing Shelf

for the kitchen...

Cutting Board with Knife Storage

Why not store your knives right where you use them? If this reasoning makes sense to you, you'll enjoy making and using the project shown here. Beneath the hefty hardwood cutting board, there's a compartment that holds a drawer for storing your cutlery. Inasmuch as cutting boards need regular cleaning, this one is designed to separate easily from the storage compartment.

Maple is the hardwood most commonly used for cutting boards and butcher blocks because it is a particularly hard and tight-grained wood that stands up to use and washing. It's also widely available. Other good choices are birch, cherry, and myrtlewood (also known as California laurel).

Regardless of the species you choose, be sure to use a water-resistant glue when laminating the board. You can make the drawer front of matching hardwood, or choose another wood to correspond with the decor of your kitchen. The other solid-wood components can be hardwood, or a softwood, such as pine.

Kitchen cutting boards range in thickness from 3⁄4 inch to 2 inches or more. These plans call for a thickness of 1½ inches simply because you may be able to find maple or other suitable hardwood available in nominal 1x2 (3⁄4 by 1½ inches), finished on all four sides. If that stock isn't locally available, you can rip your own from any suitable 3⁄4-inch-thick stock, then run the sawn edges through a jointer. If you don't own a jointer, you can hand-plane the edges or use a portable belt sander to rough-sand the assembled board. In any event, for visual purposes, plan for the finished board to be between 1 and 1½ inches thick.

Cutting Board with Knife Storage Materials List

Difficulty Level

Qty	Part	Dimensions	Qty	Part	Dimensions
Cutting board			1	Solid-wood false front	3/4" x 2½" x 11"
16	Solid-wood strips	3/4" x 1½" x 18" (rough length)	2	Solid-wood runners	3/8" x 11/16" x 14⅜"
Compartment			**Hardware**		
2	Solid-wood sides	3/4" x 3" x 15"		6d Finishing nails	
1	Plywood back	1/2" x 2¼" x 10¼"		4d Finishing nails	
1	Solid-wood bottom	3/4" x 10¼" x 15"	4	1/4" x 1" Wooden dowels	
Drawer				3/4" Brads	
2	Solid-wood sides	3/4" x 2⅛" x 14⅜"		5/8" Drywall screws	
1	Plywood bottom	1/4" x 8⅝" x 14⅜"		1" Drywall screws	
2	Plywood front & back	1/2" x 1⅞" x 8⅝"	1	Wood knob	
			4	Self-adhesive, non-skid furniture cushions	

MAKING THE CUTTING BOARD

1. **Cut the strips.** If necessary, rip the solid-wood strips from 3/4-inch stock; then cut them to a rough length of 18 inches.

2. **Glue the strips.** Tape waxed paper or coated freezer paper to the top of your work surface. Use a small brush or roller applicator to apply an even coat of glue to all broad surfaces, except the outer ones, of all the strips. Clamp them together with a pair of bar or pipe clamps, keeping all the strips aligned as you slowly tighten the clamps. Let the strips stand overnight with the clamps in place.

3. **Trim and sand the cutting board.** After removing the clamps, scrape off the hardened glue. Trim one end of the board square and even; then cut the other end to the board's finished length of 16¾ inches. Use a router and roundover bit to roundover all edges and corners.

MAKING THE COMPARTMENT

1. **Cut the parts.** Cut the compartment sides, back, and bottom to the dimensions in the Materials List. (Note: This is also a good time to cut

Overall View

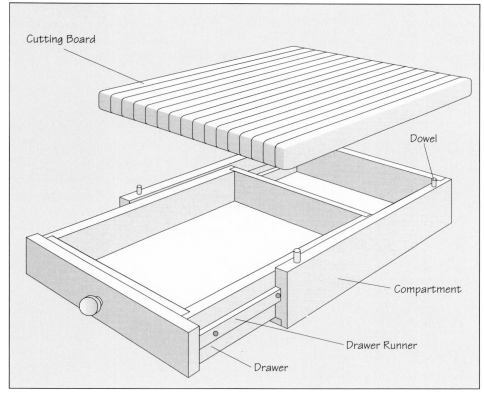

Cutting Board

Dowel

Compartment

Drawer Runner

Drawer

all the drawer parts to save the time and trouble of removing and then replacing the dado cutter later on.)

2. **Rabbet the sides.** Mill a 1/2-inch-wide, 3/8-inch-deep rabbet in the back end of each side panel as shown in *Compartment Construction*. Then mill a 3/4-inch-wide, 3/8-inch-deep rabbet along the bottom inside edge of each side panel. See "Dadoes, Grooves, and Rabbets" page 10.

3. **Groove the sides.** Mill a 3/4-inch-wide, 3/8-inch-deep groove in the inside surface of each side panel 3/4 inch from the top edge. See "Making Dadoes and Grooves with a Table Saw," page 11.

4. **Assemble the compartment.** Using 6d finishing nails and glue, attach the bottom to the sides with the back edges flush. Then attach the back panel with glue and 4d finishing nails, as shown in *Compartment Construction*.

5. **Install the dowels in the compartment sides.** Lay out the center points for the four dowels in the compartment sides as shown in *Compartment Construction*. Drill the 1/4-inch-diameter holes 1/2 inch deep, and glue a dowel in each.

6. **Locate the dowel centers on the cutting board.** Turn the compartment upside down and position it on the bottom of the cutting board, so that the board will overlap the sides and back by 1/2 inch and the front by 1¼ inches. Put a piece of scrap wood on the compartment and rap the scrap once with a hammer so that the dowels will mark the cutting board.

7. **Drill the dowel holes in the cutting board.** Drill 5/16-inch-diameter holes 5/8 inch deep at the marks on the cutting board.

MAKING THE DRAWER

1. **Cut the parts.** If you haven't already done so, cut the drawer sides, bottom, front, back, false front and runners to the dimensions in the Materials List. Rip down the solid-wood drawer runners so that they are slightly less than 3/4 inch wide.

2. **Rabbet the sides.** Mill a 1/2-inch-wide, 3/8-inch-deep rabbet in the ends of each side panel. Make a 1/4-inch-wide, 3/8-inch-deep rabbet in the bottom inside edge of each side panel.

3. **Assemble the drawer.** Use glue and 3/4-inch brads to fasten the sides to the back. Make sure the assembly is square, and attach the bottom with glue and 3/4-inch brads.

4. **Attach the solid-wood runners.** Center the runners along the sides as shown in *Drawer Construction*. Clamp each runner in position, and install it by driving three 5/8-inch drywall screws in holes that have been counterbored about 1/8 inch. This will keep the screw heads just below the wood surface. Use a block plane to chamfer the two long edges on each runner.

5. **Install the false front.** Clamp the false front against the plywood drawer front so that their top edges are flush and the front overlaps the drawer sides evenly. Install the front by driving four 1-inch drywall screws from inside the drawer. Soften the corners of the drawer front by chamfering or sanding.

6. **Install the knob.** Center the knob's installation hole in the front, and screw the knob in place.

FINISHING UP

The cutting board requires a non-toxic finish. Don't use corn oil or other vegetable oils that can soon turn to a rancid, sticky varnish. The best choices are mineral oil or products formulated specifically for wood surfaces that will come in contact with food.

Use a polyurethane varnish on the compartment and drawer. Apply two or three coats for maximum durability. Once the finish has dried, install the non-skid furniture cushions on the bottom corners of the compartment. These will give the unit a firm footing, preventing it from sliding around, even when you're doing vigorous cutting.

You may want to customize the inside of your drawer to hold particular knives. Kerfs cut with a backsaw in a length of wood will keep knives separated inside the drawer. Rub some candle wax or beeswax along the runners to ensure that the drawer runs smoothly.

Compartment Construction

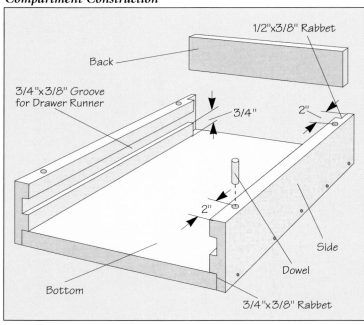

Drawer Construction

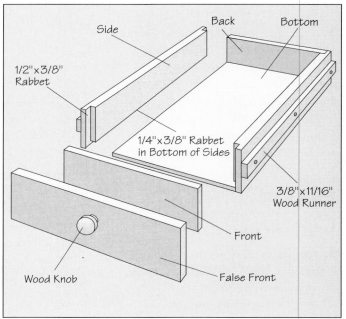

Spice Rack

Any cook who has tried storing jars of spices and herbs in a kitchen cabinet knows how difficult it can be to organize and locate the small jars. By simply adding a spice rack, this problem can be easily solved. However, the trouble with most commercially made spice racks is that they're too small and usually hold only one jar size.

This ample and handsome rack will provide all the room you need to store and organize your dried herbs and spices as well as jars and tins of pasta, grains, legumes, teas, flavored vinegars, salt and pepper shakers, and more.

Beyond its utilitarian value, the rack has been designed to complement any kitchen design. The use of picture–frame molding and the arrangement of shelves and partitions combine to create a shadow box with the appeal of a still–life painting. There's even a tall compartment that can house a small vase of fresh–cut or dried flowers.

Plans call for the rack to be made with 1/2 x 3½–inch stock, which you'll need to rip to a

3¼–inch width for the shelves and partitions. Nice clear 1/2–inch stock is available at most lumberyards as "door stop."

You can paint the rack or finish it naturally and choose picture-frame molding to complement any decor. The plans call for 1¼–inch–wide molding, but you can use any size molding as plain or ornate as you wish.

Attach the unit directly to studs. If you must mount it on a hollow or masonry wall, substitute the appropriate anchors for the ovalhead screws.

Spice Rack Materials List

Qty	Part	Dimensions
Carcase		
2	Solid–wood top and bottom	1/2" x 3½" x 45"
2	Solid–wood sides	1/2" x 3½" x 33½"
1	Plywood back	1/4" x 33½" x 44½"
Shelves and Partitions		
1	Solid–wood shelf (S–1)	1/2" x 3¼" x 44½"
2	Solid–wood shelves (S–2, S–4)	1/2" x 3¼" x 8½"
1	Solid–wood shelf (S–3)	1/2" x 3¼" x 29½"
1	Solid–wood shelf (S–5)	1/2" x 3¼" x 17½"
1	Solid–wood shelf (S–6)	1/2" x 3¼" x 32½"
1	Solid–wood shelf (S–7)	1/2" x 3¼" x 12"
2	Solid–wood partitions (P–1, P–2)	1/2" x 3¼" x 16½"
1	Solid–wood partition (P–3)	1/2" x 3¼" x 20½"

Qty	Part	Dimensions
Frame		
2	Picture-frame molding	3/4" x 1¼" x 36"
2	Picture-frame molding	3/4" x 1¼" x 47"
Hardware		
	1" Brads	
	4d Finishing nails	
4	1½" x #10 Ovalhead wood screws	
4	#10 Finishing washers	

Overall View

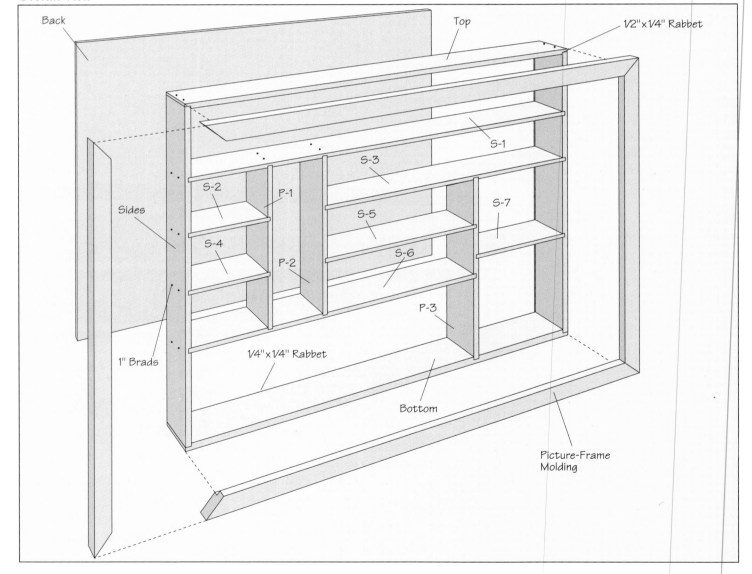

Back

Top

1/2" x 1/4" Rabbet

S-1

S-3

S-2

P-1

S-5

S-7

Sides

S-4

P-2

S-6

1" Brads

1/4" x 1/4" Rabbet

P-3

Bottom

Picture-Frame Molding

MAKING THE CARCASE PARTS

1. **Cut the outer parts.** Cut the top, bottom, and sides from clear stock to the dimensions in the Materials List. Cut the back panel from 1/4–inch plywood.

2. **Cut and label the shelves and partitions.** Rip enough clear stock to 3¼ inches to make the shelves and partitions. Cut the shelves and partitions to the lengths in the Materials List. As you make the length cuts, mark each piece with the designations in the Materials List –– S-1, S-2, P-1, P-2, and so on.

3. **Mill the rabbets.** Use a router to rabbet the ends of the top and bottom pieces as shown in the

Laying Out Dadoes

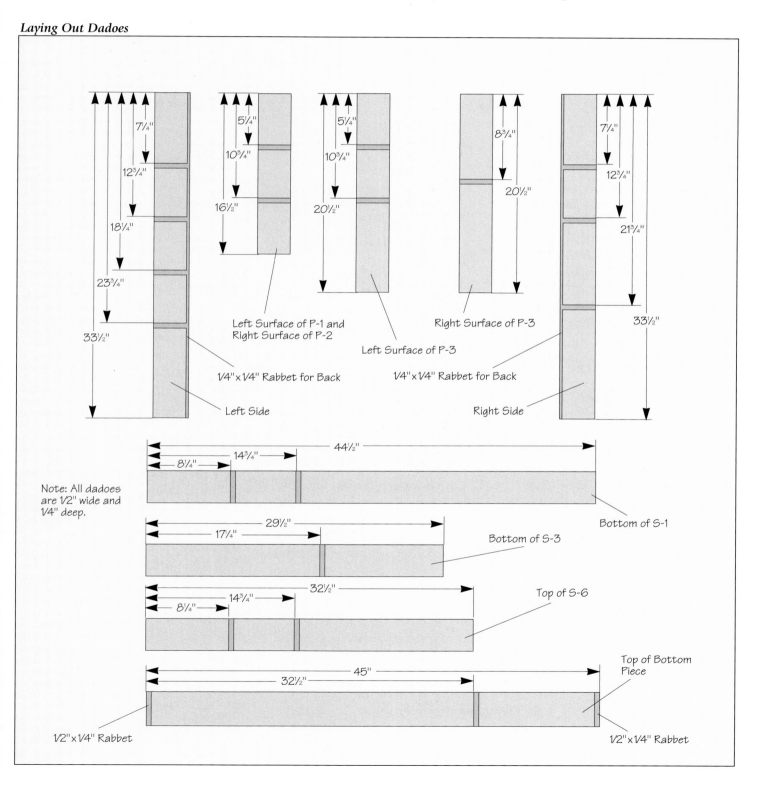

Left Surface of P-1 and Right Surface of P-2

Left Surface of P-3

Right Surface of P-3

1/4"x1/4" Rabbet for Back

1/4"x1/4" Rabbet for Back

Left Side

Right Side

Note: All dadoes are 1/2" wide and 1/4" deep.

Bottom of S-1

Bottom of S-3

Top of S-6

Top of Bottom Piece

1/2"x1/4" Rabbet

1/2"x1/4" Rabbet

Overall View. See "Making Rabbets with a Router," page 14.

Use the router or table saw to rabbet the rear inside edge of the top, bottom, and sides as shown in the *Overall View.* See "Making Rabbets with a Table Saw," page 12.

4. **Mill the Dadoes.** Lay out the 1/2-inch x 1/4-inch dadoes as shown in *Laying Out Dadoes.* Cut the dadoes. See "Making Dadoes with the Router," page 13.

ASSEMBLING THE SPICE RACK

1. **Assemble the Carcase.** Assemble the sides into the rabbets in the top and bottom with glue and two 1-inch brads at each joint as shown in the *Overall View.* Before the glue sets, install the back with glue and 1-inch brads every 8 inches. Check that the carcase is square. (Installing the back will help square the carcase.)

INSTALLING THE SHELVES AND PARTITIONS

1. **Make a subassembly.** If you have corner clamps, they'll be handy for assembling the partitions and shelves. Using glue and two 1-inch brads at each dado joint, assemble shelves S-1 and S-6 to partitions P-1 and P-2. Then attach shelf S–5 and partition P–3.

2. **Install the subassembly.** Apply glue to the rear edges of the subassembly and to the ends of shelf S–1, the left end of shelf S–6, the bottom end of partition P–3, and to the corresponding dadoes in the carcase. Slide the subassembly into the carcase and secure it with two 1–inch brads at each joint.

3. **Install the remaining shelves.** Glue the remaining shelves in place and secure the ends with brads wher-

Attaching the Picture-Frame Molding

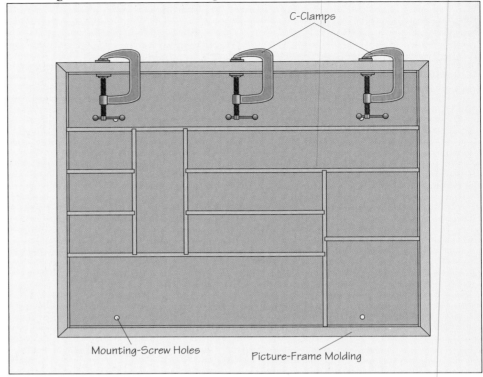

C-Clamps

Mounting-Screw Holes

Picture-Frame Molding

ever there's room to swing a hammer. Where there isn't sufficient space, use bar or pipe clamps to pull joints together. Wipe away seeping glue with a damp sponge.

ATTACHING THE PICTURE-FRAME MOLDING

1. **Cut and attach the top molding piece.** Picture-frame molding is used for this project because it comes with a rabbet in the back, which is usually used to contain a picture. Use a miter box and backsaw to miter–cut a piece of molding to the dimensions in the Materials List. Apply glue to the rabbet in the molding and hold the piece in place with several cushioned C–clamps as shown in *Attaching the Picture-Frame Molding.*

2. **Cut and attach the remaining molding pieces.** Miter-cut the right–side molding to the dimensions in the Materials List. Apply glue to the rabbet in the molding, to the top

mitered end, and the right mitered end of the top piece. Clamp the piece to the carcase side and secure the top right corner with a 4d finishing nail. Cut and attach the other two pieces the same way.

COMPLETING THE PROJECT

1. **Drill the mounting–screw holes.** Drill four 11/64–inch mounting–screw holes, locating them as shown in *Attaching the Picture-Frame Molding.*

2. **Apply the finish.** After filling nail-holes, scraping away any visible dried glue, and doing any necessary sanding, apply the finish of your choice.

3. **Hang the spice rack.** Find the studs you intend to hang the rack from. Place the rack against the wall, level it, and then use the holes in the rack as guides to mark for the screw holes. Drill 7/64-inch pilot holes into the studs and then secure the rack with four 1½-inch x #10 screws and finishing washers.

Medicine Cabinet

A medicine cabinet with mirror is a standard bathroom fixture, but it needn't be standard fare. This attractive built-in model will grace any bathroom and is a good project to consider if you're planning to add a bath or remodel an existing one. Depending on the decor of your bathroom, you can build the cabinet from hardwood and finish it with or without stain, or you can build it with pine and paint it.

The plans call for three adjustable shelves, which you can make from 1x4 stock if you wish, but shelves of 1/4-inch glass also add a nice touch and don't cost much. When you order your shelves cut to size, ask for used or reclaimed plate glass, which is salvaged from broken store windows and is usually available at about half the price of new glass. Have the glass shop seam or sand one of the edges of each shelf to remove the sharp edges.

This cabinet is designed to fit between studs that are on 16-inch centers, so you'll have to cut a hole in the wall where the cabinet will go. Use a stud finder to locate the studs. Then, use a level to scribe horizontal lines for the top and bottom of the hole. Scribe one line at 51 inches and the other at 75 inches from the floor. Use a hammer and a 6d finishing nail to poke holes in the wall until you find the inside edge of each stud. You can also use a drill with a small bit for this job. Use the level to draw plumb lines along the inside edges. Connect the level lines and form a box measuring 14$\frac{1}{2}$ by 24 inches. Now remove the wall material inside the box. See "Removing Wallboard," page 28. Measure to make sure the distance between the two studs is 14$\frac{1}{2}$ inches. If the stud spacing is a little off, you'll want to adjust the cabinet dimensions to fit.

Medicine Cabinet Materials List

Qty	Part	Dimensions	Qty	Part
Carcase, frame, and door			**Hardware**	
2	Solid-wood cabinet sides	3/4" x 3½" x 24"		6d Finishing nails
2	Solid-wood top/bottom panels	3/4" x 3½" x 13½"		1¼" Drywall screws
1	Plywood cabinet back	1/4" x 14½" x 23½"		7/8" Brads
4	Solid-wood rails	3/4" x 1½" x 16"		4d Finishing nails
4	Solid-wood stiles	3/4" x 1½" x 25"		#8 x 1½" Flathead wood screws
1	Plywood mirror back	1/4" x 13⅞" x 22⅞"	1 pair	3/4" x 2" Butt hinges
2	Horizontal retaining strips	1/8" x 1/2" x 14³⁄₁₆"		#4 x 1/2" Brass flathead wood screws
2	Vertical retaining strips	1/8" x 1/2" x 23³⁄₁₆"		#10 x 2" Oval head wood screws
Glass				#10 Finishing washers
3	Shelves	1/4" x 3½" x 12⅞"	1	Small cabinet-doorknob
1	Mirror	1/8" x 13⅞" x 22⅞"	1	Magnetic latch
			12	Adjustable shelf pins

Overall View

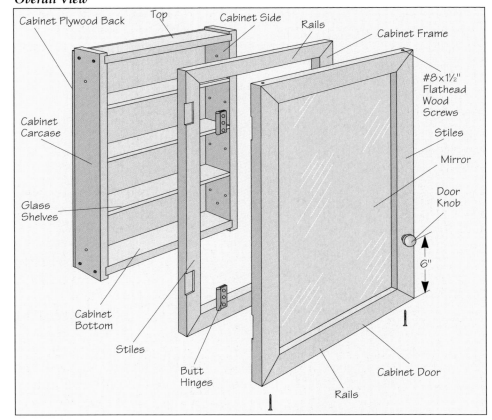

Side Panel Layout

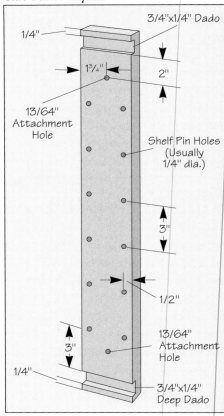

BUILDING THE CABINET CARCASE

1. **Cut the parts.** Cut the cabinet sides, top, bottom, and plywood back to the dimensions in the Materials List.

2. **Dado the sides.** Dado the side panels as shown in the *Side Panel Layout*. See "Dadoes, Grooves, and Rabbets," page 10.

3. **Drill the sides.** Drill attachment hole and shelf pin holes in the cabinet sides as shown in *Side Panel Layout*. Use a template to drill the shelf pin holes. See "Installing Shelf Pins," page 22.

4. **Assembling the carcase.** Assemble the top and bottom panels into the dadoes in the side panels with glue and two 1¼-inch drywall screws at each connection. Install the back panel with glue and 7/8-inch brads.

BUILDING AND INSTALLING THE CABINET FRAME

1. Cut the parts. The cabinet frame and the door frame have the same dimensions. Cut both sets of rails and stiles to the dimensions in the Materials List with 45-degree miters on all ends.

2. Attach the cabinet frame. Put glue along one front vertical edge of the cabinet. Put one stile in place over the glue, flush to the inside of the cabinet, and secure it with 4d finishing nails. Put glue on the top mitered end of the stile and on the top front edge of the cabinet. Nail the top rail in place. Repeat this process for the other stile, then the last lower rail. Secure each miter joint with two 7/8-inch brads as shown in *Cabinet Frame Details*.

3. Make the hinge mortises. Cut hinge mortises in the frame as shown in *Cabinet Frame Details*. See "Installing Doors and Hinges," page 19.

BUILDING THE CABINET DOOR

1. Cut the parts. Cut the mirror back from 1/4-inch plywood. Cut the retaining strips to the dimensions in the Materials List with a 45-degree miter on each end.

2. Rabbet the rails and stiles. These stepped rabbets are shown in *Door Details*. First, cut a 1/8-inch-deep, 3/4-inch-wide rabbet for the retaining strip; then mill the second rabbet to 1/2x3/8 inch for the mirror and back, which will modify the first rabbet to 1/4x1/8 inch.

3. Assemble the door frame. Use corner clamps to clamp the frame together without glue. At each miter joint, counterbore through the top of the top rail and the bottom of the bottom rail, through the rail into the stile for one #8x1½-inch flathead wood screw at

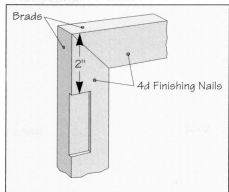

Cabinet Frame Details

each location as shown in *Overall View*. Locate the screws no more than 1/2 inch from the corners so they won't interfere with the rabbets. Put glue on the mitered ends, assemble the frame in the corner clamps, then insert the screws. Plug the screw holes.

4. Mortise the door frame. Lay the cabinet frame face up. Align the door frame immediately to the left, face down. Using the hinges as templates, mark the door frame for hinge mortises as you did the cabinet frame. Then mortise the door frame the same way.

5. Drill the hinge and knob holes. Using the hinges as templates, mark the cabinet and door frames for hinge-screw holes. Drill small pilot holes for the hinge screws, and temporarily install the hinges. Drill the doorknob hole six inches up from the bottom right corner of the frame.

6. Sand the cabinet and door frames. It's important to sand these frames together, so they'll mate perfectly when finished. With the door and frame clamped in the closed position, sand the top, bottom, and right surfaces with 120- and 220-grit sandpaper, gently easing the sharp edges and corners as you proceed. Remove clamps and hinges, reclamp the frames, and sand the left sides. Then sand the face of the door frame.

7. Complete the door. It's easiest to sand and varnish or paint the door frame before you install the mirror. When the finish is dry, lay the door frame face down; then lay the mirror

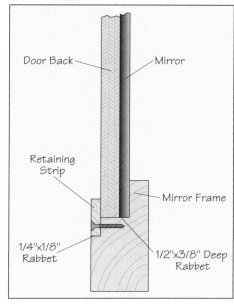

Door Details

and door back in place. Attach the retaining strips with #4x1/2-inch brass flathead wood screws driven through countersunk pilot holes.

FINISHING AND INSTALLING THE CABINET

1. Finish the cabinet. Do any necessary sanding. Apply the finish of your choice to the cabinet and the back of the door.

2. Install the cabinet. Set the cabinet into the wall cavity, making sure it is level. Then use four oval head wood screws with finish washers to attach it to the studs.

3. Hang the door and attach the knob and magnetic latch. Attach the hinges to the cabinet and door with the screws provided. Then install the knob. Attach the magnetic portion of a magnetic latch to the inside of the unhinged frame stile. Put the little metal latch plate opposing it on the inside of the door.

4. Install the shelves. Install each shelf with four metal shelf supports, and your new medicine cabinet is ready for duty.

for the Bath...

Vanity

A vanity is an attractive and useful addition to any bathroom. You can buy a vanity, but by building your own you can create a unit that perfectly fits your space and decor.

The handsome vanity shown here is designed for a large bathroom where there is 7 feet of wall space available, but you can easily adapt the design and dimensions to your own situation.

This practical vanity provides a spacious countertop and plenty of storage in its six drawers and behind its three cabinet doors. It uses a post-formed plastic-laminate countertop available at home centers in standard width with the length cut to order. See "Counter-tops," page 26.

Space beside the bank of drawers on the right is for a chair or stool. Install a well-lit mirror, and this becomes the perfect place for applying makeup.

Vanity Materials List

Qty	Part	Dimensions
Carcase and face frame		
2	Plywood side panels	3/4" x 20¼" x 31¼"
1	Plywood bottom panel	3/4" x 17" x 20"
1	Plywood bottom panel	3/4" x 40½" x 20"
2	Plywood partitions	3/4" x 20" x 31¼"
1	Plywood back panel	1/4" x 31¼" x 83¼"
1	Solid-wood nailer	3/4" x 3½" x 83¼"
1	Solid-wood kickplate	3/4" x 4¼" x 18"
1	Solid-wood kickplate	3/4" x 4¼" x 41½"
1	Solid-wood rail	3/4" x 1½" x 81"
1	Solid-wood rail	3/4" x 1½" x 38½"
1	Solid-wood rail	3/4" x 1½" x 24½"
1	Solid-wood rail	3/4" x 1½" x 22"
5	Solid-wood rails	3/4" x 1½" x 15"
2	Solid-wood stiles	3/4" x 1½" x 27¾"
2	Solid-wood stiles	3/4" x 1½" x 26¼"
1	Solid-wood short stile	3/4" x 1½" x 24¾"
4	Plywood corner blocks	3/4" x 3½" x 3½" x 5"
1	Preformed countertop	3/4" x 22½" x 85"
1	Solid-wood fixed panel	3/4" x 5" x 22¾"
Drawers (with 3/8" overlay)		
For 4¼" x 15" openings:		
8	Sides	3/4" x 3¾" x 19"
4	Fronts	3/4" x 3¾" x 14"
4	Backs	3/4" x 3⅛" x 14"
4	Bottoms	1/4" x 13½" x 18½"
4	False fronts	3/4" x 5" x 15¾"

Qty	Part	Dimensions
For 4¼" x 24½" opening:		
2	Sides	3/4" x 3¾" x 19"
1	Front	3/4" x 3¾" x 23"
1	Back	3/4" x 3⅛" x 23"
1	Bottom	1/4" x 18½" x 23"
1	False front	3/4" x 5" x 25¼"
For 7½" x 15" opening:		
2	Sides	3/4" x 7" x 19"
1	Front	3/4" x 7" x 14"
1	Back	3/4" x 6⅛" x 14"
1	Bottom	1/4" x 13½" x 18½"
1	False front	3/4" x 8¼" x 15¾"
Doors (with 3/8" overlay)		
1	Door	3/4" x 15¾" x 19¾"
2	Doors	3/4" x 11⁵⁄₁₆" x 19¾"
Hardware		
	4d Finishing nails	
	7/8" Brads	
	1/4" x 1¼" Dowels	
	#10 x 3½" Wood screws	
	#10 x 1¼" Wood screws	
	Bottom-mounted metal drawer slides	
3	Doorknobs	
6	Drawer pulls	
	Self-closing hinges	

Overall View

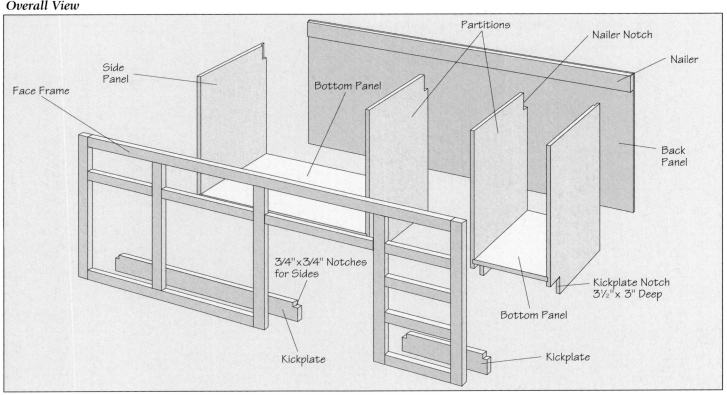

Partitions
Nailer Notch
Nailer
Side Panel
Bottom Panel
Face Frame
Back Panel
3/4" x 3/4" Notches for Sides
Kickplate Notch 3½" x 3" Deep
Bottom Panel
Kickplate
Kickplate

BUILDING THE CARCASE

1. Cut the parts. Cut side and bottom panels, partitions, back panel, nailer, and kickplates to the dimensions in the Materials List. Then cut kickplate notches in the bottom front edge of each side partition. Cut nailer notches in the top rear edge of both partitions. These details are shown in *Side Panel Layout* and *Partition Layout*.

2. Rabbet and dado the panels. Rabbet the back of the side panels as shown in *Side Panel Layout*. See "Dadoes, Grooves, and Rabbets", page 10. Then widen the top of the rabbets to 1 inch to accept the nailer. Square off the nailer rabbet with a 1-inch chisel. Dado side and partition panels as shown in *Side Panel Layout* and *Partition Layout*. Note that these drawings show only one side panel

Side Panel Layout

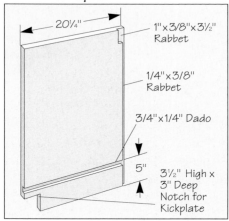

Partition Layout

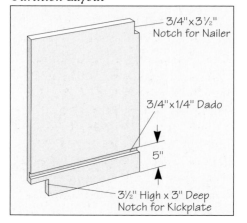

and one partition. The other side panel is a mirror of the one shown. The other partition gets dadoes on the other face. See the *Overall View*.

3. Install the bottoms. Secure the bottom panels into the dadoes in the side panels and partitions with glue and 4d finishing nails.

4. Attach the nailer and back. Attach the nailer to the side panels and partitions with glue and 4d finishing nails. Set the back panel in place, and secure with 7/8-inch brads.

5. Notch and attach kickplates. Notch the kickplates as shown in the *Overall View*. Attach the kickplates in their notches with glue and 4d finishing nails.

BUILDING AND INSTALLING THE FACE FRAME

1. Cut the parts. Cut all face-frame rails and stiles to the dimensions in the Materials List.

2. Assemble the face frame. Assemble the face frame with glue and two dowels at each joint, locating the

parts as shown in *Face Frame Construction*. See "Reinforcing Joints with Dowels," page 9.

3. Install the face frame. Fasten the face frame to the carcase with glue and 4d finishing nails, spaced about 12 inches apart.

INSTALLING AND FINISHING THE VANITY

1. Cut plumbing holes. With the vanity near the rear wall, measure the distance from the wall and floor for the plumbing pipes. Use a drill and saber saw to cut pipe holes in the vanity back, allowing about an inch of clearance around each pipe.

2. Install the vanity. Scribe a level line along the rear wall 31¼ inches from the high point in the floor as shown in *Installing the Vanity*. Slide the vanity in place, and level with shims as necessary. Then drive two #10x3½-inch wood screws through the nailer into each stud. See "Installing Cabinets and Built-ins," page 28.

Face Frame Construction

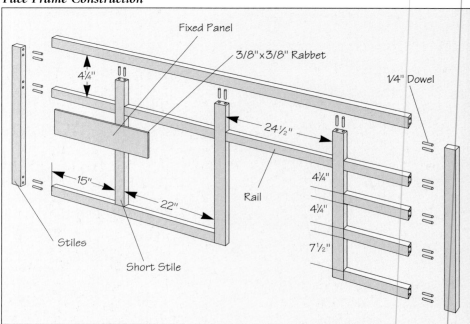

Installing the Vanity

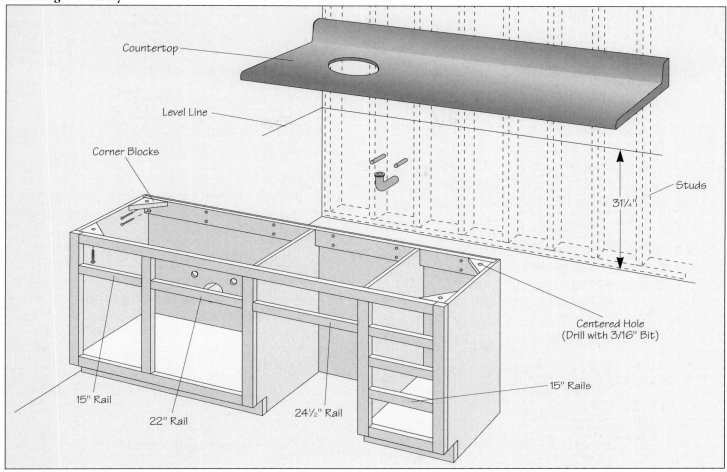

Countertop

Level Line

Corner Blocks

Studs

31¼"

15" Rail

22" Rail

24½" Rail

Centered Hole
(Drill with 3/16" Bit)

15" Rails

3. Finish the vanity. Before installing the countertop, fill nailholes with wood putty. Sand as necessary, and apply the finish of your choice.

INSTALLING THE COUNTERTOP

1. Cut and install corner blocks. Cut four triangular plywood corner blocks to the dimensions in the Materials List. On each block, apply glue to the two edges forming the 90-degree angle, press one in place in each top corner, and secure with 4d finishing nails. Drive nails from inside the vanity, being careful to avoid driving them through the vanity exterior. Let the glue dry.

2. Install the countertop. With a 13/64-inch bit, drill a centered hole through each corner block. Lay the countertop in place, and attach it from the underside with four #10x1¼- inch wood screws through the corner blocks.

BUILDING AND INSTALLING DRAWERS AND DOORS

1. Make the Drawers and Doors. The cabinet shown here has plain solid wood drawer fronts and raised panel doors for a traditional look. The dimensions in the Materials List are for inset doors that overlay the face frame by 3/8 inch on all sides. You may build drawers and doors to suit your decor. The drawers use bottom-mounted metal slides, so be sure to leave enough room between the bottom panel and the drawer bottom to accommodate the slides that you purchase. See "Building Drawers," page 23 and "Making Cabinet Doors," page 15.

2. Make and install the fixed panel. Because of plumbing, there is no room for a drawer under the sink. Instead, make a fixed panel to match the false drawer fronts. If you are making inset drawers, rabbet the panel all around as you did for the drawers. Glue and clamp the panel over the opening.

3. Finish drawer faces and doors and install hardware. Finish drawer faces and doors to match the vanity. Then install pulls and slide hardware according to manufacturers' directions. Attach self-closing hinges to doors and face frames. See "Installing Doors and Hinges," page 19 and "Installing Drawer Slide Hardware," page 25.

for the Bath...
Clothes Hamper

This hamper is so handy that your family might even be encouraged to use it instead of leaving dirty clothes around the house. It features a double-bin design to separate clothes into "lights" and "darks," and the self-closing door couldn't be easier to operate.

The laundry baskets in this project are actually a pair of plastic, kitchen-size trash receptacles. You'll find these durable containers at just about any hardware store or home center. If you'd prefer a hamper with just one container, or if your containers are a different size than those shown here, you can adjust the project's dimensions accordingly. The design and construction basics will remain the same.

Your choice of wood and plywood depends largely on how you want to finish the unit. If you plan to paint your finished project, pine or poplar are two economical choices for the solid-wood parts.

The easiest way to make the top is to cut it from commercially available edge-glued stock, but if you can't find suitable stock, it's not much harder to glue up your own from clear nominal 1-inch stock. See "Edge-Gluing Stock," page 8.

Clothes Hamper Materials List

Difficulty Level 🔨🔨

Qty	Part	Dimensions	Qty	Part	Dimensions
Carcase			***Top***		
2	Plywood sides	3/4" x 11¾" x 29⅝"	1	Solid-wood top	3/4" x 13¼" x 36½"
1	Tempered pegboard back	1/4" x 29⅝" x34¼"	***Hardware***		
2	Solid-wood front edge strips	3/4" x 3/4" x 29⅝"		4d Finishing nails	
2	Solid-wood crosspieces	3/4" x 2¾" x 33½"		#6 x 1½" Flathead wood screws	
2	Solid-wood top corner blocks	3/4" x 3½" x 3½"		7/8" Brads	
2	Solid-wood stop blocks	3/4" x 1½" x 1½"		#6 x 1¼" Flathead wood screws	
4	Solid-wood bottom corner block	1¼" x 1½" x 2¾"	20	3/8" Wood plugs	
2	Tilt-stop blocks	3/4" x 1½" x 1½"		#6 x 1⅝" Flathead wood screws	
Door/platform assembly			4	3/4" dia. Self-adhesive rubber or plastic cushions	
1	Plywood door	3/4" x 25¼" x 31⅞"	1	Doorknob	
2	Solid-wood side edge strips	3/4" x 3/4" x 25¼"	2	2½" Butt hinges	
1	Solid-wood top edge strip	3/4" x 3/4" x 33⅜"	2	Garbage bins	
1	Plywood platform	3/4" x 11" x 33⅜"			
2	Plywood braces	3/4" x 10¼" x 10¼"			

Overall View

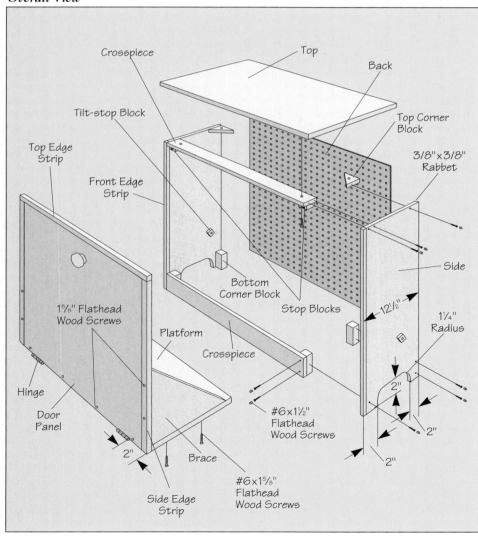

BUILDING THE CARCASE

1. Cut the parts. Cut the sides from 3/4-inch plywood, the back from tempered pegboard, and all the other carcase parts from solid wood to the dimensions in the Materials List. Rabbet the side panels for the back as shown in the *Overall View*. See "Dadoes, Grooves, and Rabbets" page 10.

Use a saber saw to cut out the curved openings at the bottom of each side panel.

2. Attach the edge strips. Apply glue to the rear edge of each edge strip. Attach the strips to the front edge of each side panel with 4d finishing nails.

3. Counterbore screw holes. Use a counterbore bit or a combination of 3/8-inch and 3/16-inch bits to drill and counterbore screw holes in the crosspieces as shown in the *Overall View*. See "Countersink and Counterbore Bits," page 35.

4. Attach the crosspieces and back panel. Glue and screw the bottom corner blocks onto both ends of the bottom crosspiece so that they are flush with the ends. Use #6x1½-inch flathead wood screws. Next, attach the top and bottom crosspieces to the side panels with glue and 1½-inch wood screws, as shown in the *Overall View*.

Apply glue to both rabbets in the back of the side panels and position the pegboard back in place. Attach the back with ⅞-inch brads nailed into the rabbets.

5. **Attach the top corner blocks.** Cut the top corner blocks into a triangular shape, then glue and screw them in place as shown in the *Overall View*. Use two 1¼-inch screws for each block.

6. **Plug the screw holes.** Fill the counterbored holes with glued wood plugs and sand flush.

7. **Make the top.** Rip three pieces of stock to 5½ inches, and cut them to a rough length of 38 inches. Apply glue to the edges of the boards to be joined and clamp them together with three bar or pipe clamps. See "Edge-Gluing Stock," page 8.

After the glue has dried, scrape away any squeeze out and cut the top to the finished size given in the Materials List. To finish the edge of the top, use a router equipped with a chamfering bit. Chamfer only the bottom edges.

8. **Install the top.** Using a 3/16-inch bit, drill two holes in the top crosspiece and one in each rear top-corner block, as shown in the *Overall View*. Since a solid wood top will expand and contract in response to changes in relative humidity, it is important to allow it some room to move. You can allow for this simply by wiggling the drill bit perpendicular to the length of the crosspiece. The oversized hole will provide adequate space for movement.

Position the top so that it overhangs both the sides and front by 3/4 inch and is flush with the back panel. Attach the top to the crosspiece and corner braces with 1¼-inch flathead wood screws.

MAKING AND INSTALLING THE DOOR/PLATFORM ASSEMBLY

1. **Cut the parts.** Cut the door, platform, and triangular braces from 3/4-inch plywood to the dimensions in the Materials List. Cut the three edge strips from solid wood.

2. **Build the door.** Attach edge strips to the door panel top and sides with glue and 4d finishing nails. Secure the door panel to the door with four countersunk 1⅝-inch screws as shown in the *Overall View*.

Secure each triangular brace to the side edge strips and platform with two countersunk 1⅝-inch screws. Fill the screw holes with glued wood plugs and sand the plugs flush.

3. **Install the doorknob.** Drill a centered hole for the knob screw 1½ inches from the door's top edge. Attach the knob with the screws provided.

4. **Install the stop blocks.** Glue and screw each stop block, with its rubber pad, against the cabinet side and top crosspiece, as shown in the *Overall View*. Make sure the pad surface is 3/4 inch inside the front edge of the side panel. Use #6x1¼-inch flathead wood screws.

5. **Hang the door.** Position the hinges 2 inches inside the bottom corners of the door. Mortise the hinges in the door front. Then center the door in the cabinet opening, and mark the mortise location for each hinge. See "Installing Doors and Hinges," page 19.

6. **Install tilt-stop block.** Cut the tilt-stop blocks to the dimensions in the Materials List. Measure the width of your bins. Open the door enough so you will be able to take the bins in and out. Reach in with a pencil and mark where you want one of the tilt-stop blocks to be located. Attach one tilt-stop block to the marked location with glue and and one 1¼-inch wood screw. Let the door tilt forward and install the second block.

Locating Tilt-Stop Blocks

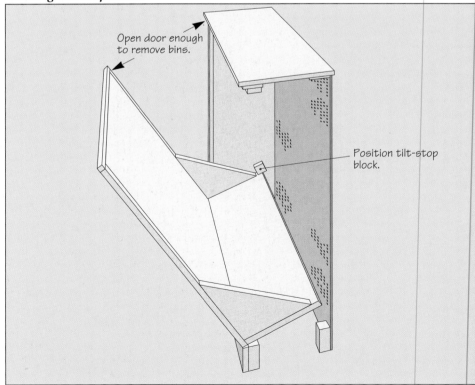

Open door enough to remove bins.

Position tilt-stop block.

for the Bedroom...
Chest of Drawers

This chest of drawers is a great example of how you can use modern methods and materials to create a traditional heirloom-quality piece that will serve your family for generations to come. Old-time cabinetmakers used hand tools, great skill, and patience to plane boards by hand and cut complex joints. You'll still need the patience, but plywood, power tools, modern fasteners, and glue simplify joinery and eliminate the need for great skill.

In this project, the plywood is used for the big flat expanses—the sides and back. Select a hardwood plywood such as cherry, walnut, or oak, then make the rest of the project from solid hardwood to match.

Chest of Drawers Materials List

Qty	Part	Dimensions
Base		
1	Solid-wood base front	3/4" x 3½" x 31"
1	Solid-wood base back	3/4" x 3½" x 29½"
2	Solid-wood base sides	3/4" x 3½" x 17½"
4	Solid-wood base cleats	1¼" x 1¼" x 3½"
1	Solid-wood apron front	3/4" x 2½" x 31½"
2	Solid-wood apron sides	3/4" x 2½" x 18½"
1	Solid-wood apron back	3/4" x 2½" x 26½"
Carcase		
2	Plywood side panels	3/4" x 17" x 40½"
1	Plywood back panel	1/4" x 29¼" x 40½"
12	Drawer supports front & back	3/4" x 3½" x 29¼"
12	Drawer supports sides	3/4" x 3½" x 9¾"
6	Runners	1/4" x 3/4" x 16¾"
1	Apron cleat front	3/4" x 3½" x 28½"
1	Apron cleat back	3/4" x 3½" x 22½"
2	Apron cleat sides	3/4" x 3⅛" x 13¼"
2	Face frame stiles	3/4" x 1½" x 40½"
7	Face frame rails	3/4" x 1½" x 27"

Qty	Part	Dimensions
4	Corner blocks	3/4" x 3½" x 3½"
1	Top panel	3/4" x 18½" x 31½"
Drawers		
6	Drawer false fronts	3/4" x 5¾" x 28"
12	Drawer sides	3/4" x 4½" x 16½"
6	Drawer fronts	3/4" x 4½" x 25¾"
6	Drawer backs	3/4" x 4" x 25¾"
6	Plywood drawer bottoms	1/4" x 16¾" x 25¾"
12	Runner tracks	1/4" x 3/4" x 16½"
Hardware		
	#6 x 1¾" Flathead wood screws	
48	1/4" x 1¼" Wood dowel pins	
	#6 x 3/4" Flathead wood screws	
	7/8" Brads	
	2½" Wood screws	
	6d Finishing nails	
	#6 x 1¼" Flathead wood screws	
12	Drawer pulls	

Overall View

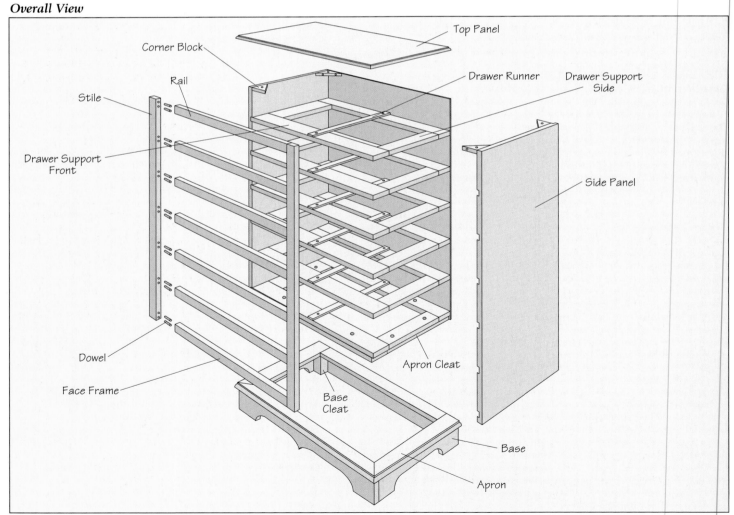

Top Panel

Corner Block

Rail

Stile

Drawer Support Front

Drawer Runner

Drawer Support Side

Side Panel

Dowel

Face Frame

Base Cleat

Apron Cleat

Base

Apron

BUILDING THE BASE

1. Cut the parts. Cut the base front, back, sides, and base cleats to the dimensions in the Materials List. Use a band saw or saber saw to make the decorative cuts shown in *Base and Apron Construction*.

2. Assemble the base. With 1¾-inch flathead wood screws, glue and screw two base cleats to the back of the base and one cleat flush with the front end of each side piece. Apply glue to the mating sides of the rear cleats, then assemble the sides to the back. Next, apply glue to the mating sides of the front cleats and assemble the front to the sides. Clamp the base together, then measure across diagonals to make sure the base is square. Secure the joints with screws through the cleats into the base.

3. Make and attach the apron. Cut the apron front to the dimensions in the Materials List with a 45-degree miter on each end. Clamp the apron front in place so that it creates a 1/4-inch overhang along the front. Next, cut the two mitered side pieces a bit longer than the given dimensions. Position them in place and mark the square back cuts in place. Clamp the side pieces in place. Cut the back piece to fit.

Glue and clamp the entire apron assembly onto the base. When the glue dries, use a router equipped with a 3/4-inch half-round bit to rout the front and side edges of the apron. See "Router, Bits, and Accessories," page 36, for details on routing options.

BUILDING THE CARCASE

1. Cut the side and back panels. Cut the sides and back panels to the dimensions in the Materials List. Rabbet and dado the side panels as shown in *Side Panel Details*. Note that the drawing shows one side panel. Don't forget to make the other panel as a mirror image. See "Dadoes, Grooves, and Rabbets," page 10.

2. Build the drawer supports. Cut the pieces for the drawer supports, drawer runners, and apron cleats to the dimensions in the Materials List. Note that only the bottom drawer support will be attached to the apron

Base and Apron Construction

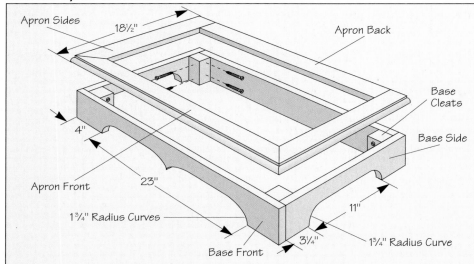

Side Panel Details

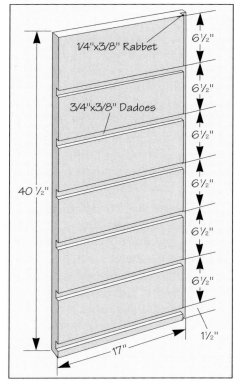

Drawer Support Construction

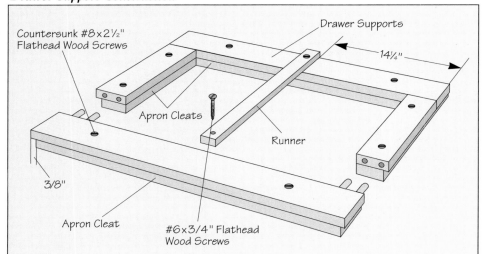

cleats. Assemble the supports with glue and dowels as shown in *Drawer Support Construction*. Clamp the supports together, measuring the diagonals to ensure that the assembly is square. Using 3/4-inch flathead wood screws, attach the runner centered across the front and rear support pieces as shown in *Drawer Support Construction*.

3. **Assemble the carcase.** Apply glue to the dadoes in the side panels, and slide the drawer supports in place so that they are flush with the front edges of the side panels. Attach the back panel to the assembly with glue and 7/8-inch brads. Glue and clamp the apron cleats in place beneath the bottom drawer support as shown in *Drawer Support Construction*.

4. **Attach the carcase to the apron.** Place the carcase on the apron, making sure they are flush at the back. Make sure the apron extends past the carcase by 3/4-inch all around the front and sides. Predrill countersunk holes for 2½-inch flathead wood screws through the bottom drawer supports and apron cleats into the apron. Remove the carcase. Apply glue to the top of the apron, then screw the carcase to the apron.

5. **Building and installing the face frame.** Cut the stiles and rails to the dimensions in the Materials List. Join the rails to the stiles with dowels. See "Reinforcing Joints With Dowels," page 9. Be sure that the top of each rail is 6½ inches from the top of the rail below so that the rail tops will be flush to the top of the drawer supports. Assemble the face frame to the carcase with glue and 6d finishing nails.

6. **Build the top.** Cut boards to be edge-glued to form the top panel. Cut the boards so the top will be slightly larger than the dimensions given in the Materials List. Glue and clamp the boards together. Cut the glued panel to its finished dimensions. Use a 3/4-inch half-round bit to rout the front and side edges of the top trim to match the apron.

7. **Install the corner blocks.** Predrill and countersink each corner block for two 1¼-inch wood screws. Position so as not to penetrate the exterior of the carcase. Glue and screw the blocks into the top corners of the carcase, flush with the top of the carcase. As you predrill the screw holes in the corner blocks for the chest top, wiggle the bit to elongate the hole from front to back. This allows room for wood movement.

8. **Attach the top.** Lay the top in place, flush with the back edge of the carcase and with an equal overhang at front and sides. Secure the top with 1¼-inch screws driven up through the center of each corner block. Do not use glue in this step; the screws will allow the top to move in response to seasonal changes in humidity.

BUILDING THE DRAWERS

1. **Cut the drawer parts.** Cut the drawer sides, fronts, and backs to the dimensions in the Materials List. Dado the sides and groove the front and sides as shown in *Drawer Construction*.

2. **Build the drawers.** Follow directions in "Building Drawers," page 23, to build the six drawers in this project using the dimensions in the Materials List.

3. **Make the false drawer fronts.** Cut the false drawer fronts according to dimensions in the Materials List. Round over the outside edges of the false fronts with your router and a 3/8-inch roundover bit set to round the edges slightly. Attach the drawer front with four 1¼-inch screws. Attach the drawer pulls with screws provided.

4. **Attach the runner tracks.** Apply glue to the runner tracks and attach them to the plywood drawer bottoms, clamping them in place. After the glue has dried, test the drawers in the carcase. If the drawers don't slide smoothly when installed, you can use a block plane or sandpaper on the runners or runner tracks until the drawers slide easily.

Drawer Construction

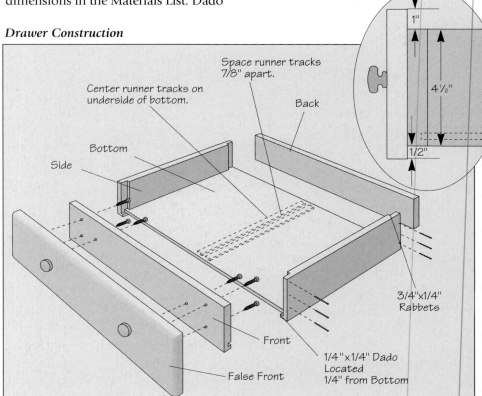

Center runner tracks on underside of bottom.

Space runner tracks 7/8" apart.

Bottom

Side

Back

Front

False Front

3/4"x1/4" Rabbets

1/4"x1/4" Dado Located 1/4" from Bottom

1"

4½"

1/2"

Bunk Bed

Kids love bunk beds, and so should you, especially if your children share a small bedroom. This project really maximizes floor space; not only do the bunk beds take up less room than a pair of conventional twin beds, they also provide two dressers' worth of built-in drawers! You can install the bottom bunk as shown here, or you can turn it so that the length of both beds are along the same wall in conventional bunk bed fashion.

These beds will be permanently installed in a corner of the room, so you must prepare the room prior to installation. First, you'll need to remove any trim

or molding (see "Removing Trim," page 30) so that the headboards and sideboards can be fastened onto the walls. Once you've located and marked the studs, scribe a level line on the walls 16 inches above the floor for the sideboard and headboard of the lower bed, and 56¼ inches above the floor for the upper bed.

These beds are designed to work with 4x39x75–inch foam mattresses. If you intend to use the beds with thicker mattresses, make the upper bunk rail supports longer so that the top of the rails is at least 5 inches above the mattress.

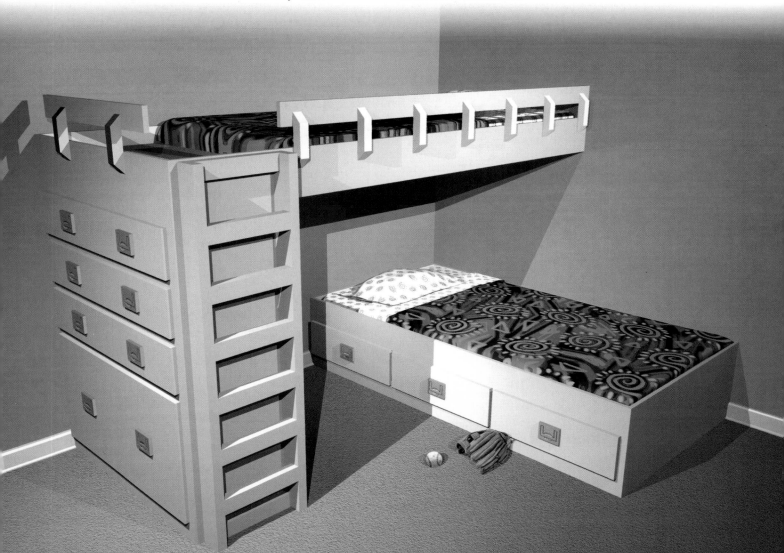

Bunk Bed Materials List

Difficulty Level ♪♪♪

Qty	Part	Dimensions	Qty	Part	Dimensions
Cabinet			6	Plywood side panels	1/2" x 6½" x 30"
			3	Plywood bottom panels	3/8" x 22" x 29¾"
2	Plywood side panels	3/4" x 17¾" x 49"			
2	Plywood top & bottom panel	3/4" x 17½" x 39¾"	**Ladder and guardrails**		
1	Plywood back panel	1/4" x 39¾" x 49"	2	Solid-wood sides	1½" x 3½" x 56"
2	Solid-wood stiles	3/4" x 2" x 49"	8	Solid-wood steps/nailers	1½" x 2½" x 16"
4	Solid-wood rails	3/4" x 2" x 36½"	1	Solid-wood foot guardrail	3/4" x 3½" x 30"
1	Solid-wood bottom rail	3/4" x 3½" x 36½"	1	Solid-wood side guardrail	3/4" x 3½" x 77¾"
8	Solid-wood guide hangers	1¼" x 1½" x 17½"	9	Solid-wood supports	1½" x 1½" x 8"
Lower bunk			**Cabinet drawers (overall dimensions:**		
2	Plywood headboard/footboard	3/4" x 15¾" x 39¾"	**1 at 18¼" x 16½" x 35½"; 3 at 5¾" x 16½" x 35½")**		
1	Plywood sideboard	3/4" x 15¾" x 75"	1	Solid-wood false front	3/4" x 19½" x 37¼"
1	Plywood long support	3/4" x 12" x 75"	1	Plywood front panel	3/4" x 18¼" x 35"
6	Plywood platform supports	3/4" x 12" x 38⅝"	1	Plywood rear panel	3/4" x 17½" x 35"
2	Screen molding	1/4" x 3/4" x 39¾"	2	Plywood side panels	3/4" x 18¼" x 16½"
1	Screen molding	1/4" x 3/4" x 75"	3	Solid-wood false fronts	3/4" x 7" x 37¼"
2	Solid-wood long stiles	3/4" x 1½" x 16"	3	Plywood front panels	1/2" x 5¾" x 35"
2	Solid-wood short stiles	3/4" x 1½" x 7"	3	Plywood rear panels	1/2" x 5" x 35"
1	Solid-wood rail	3/4" x 3½" x 73½"	6	Plywood side panels	1/2" x 5¾" x 16½"
1	Solid-wood rail	3/4" x 5½" x 73½"	4	Plywood bottom panels	3/8" x 16¼" x 35"
6	Plywood cleats	3/4" x 1½" x 23½"	**Hardware**		
1	Plywood mattress platform	1/2" x 39" x 75"		4d Finishing nails	
Upper bunk				7/8" Brads	
1	Solid-wood headboard	3/4" x 7¼" x 39¾"		1/4" x 1¼" Dowels	
1	Solid-wood inner sideboard	3/4" x 7¼" x 93½"		1¾" Drywall screws	
2	Solid-wood headers	1½" x 3½" x 93½"	4 sets	16" Side-mounted metal drawer slides	
5	Solid-wood joists	1½" x 3½" x 36"		#10 x 1¼" Flathead wood screws	
1	Plywood backerboard	1/4" x 39" x 93½"		#10 x 3½" Flathead wood screws	
1	Solid-wood outer sideboard	3/4" x 7¼" x 95"		1¼" Drywall screws	
1	Solid-wood footboard	3/4" x 7¼" x 40½"	3 sets	28" Side-mounted metal drawer slides	
1	Plywood mattress platform	1/2" x 39" x 93½"		1½" Wood screws	
Lower-bunk drawers (overall dimensions: 6½" x 22½" x 30")				3" Galvanized deck screws	
3	Solid-wood false fronts	3/4" x 7¾" x 24¼"		#6 x 2½" Flathead wood screws	
3	Plywood front panels	1/2" x 6½" x 22"	64	3/8" Wood plugs	
3	Plywood rear panels	1/2" x 5¾" x 22"		#8 x 2" Flathead wood screws	
			11	Drawer pulls	

BUILDING THE CABINET

1. Cut the parts. Cut the sides, top, bottom, and back panel to the dimensions in the Materials List. Dado and rabbet the side panels as shown in *Cabinet Construction.* Also, make a 1/4-inch-wide by 3/8-inch-deep rabbet along the inside back edge of each side panel. These rabbets will house the back panel. See "Dadoes, Rabbets, and Grooves" page 10.

2. Assemble the cabinet. Apply glue to the rabbets and dadoes and the ends of the top and bottom. Then secure the panels with 4d finishing nails. Apply glue to the side-panel rabbets and to the rear edges of the horizontal panels, and nail the back panel in place with 7/8-inch brads.

3. Build the face frame. Cut the stiles and rails to the dimensions in the Materials List. Use a doweling jig to drill 1/4-inch dowel holes. See "Reinforcing Joints with Dowels," page 9. Apply glue to dowels and insert them into the holes in the stiles and the rails. Pull the frame

Cabinet Construction

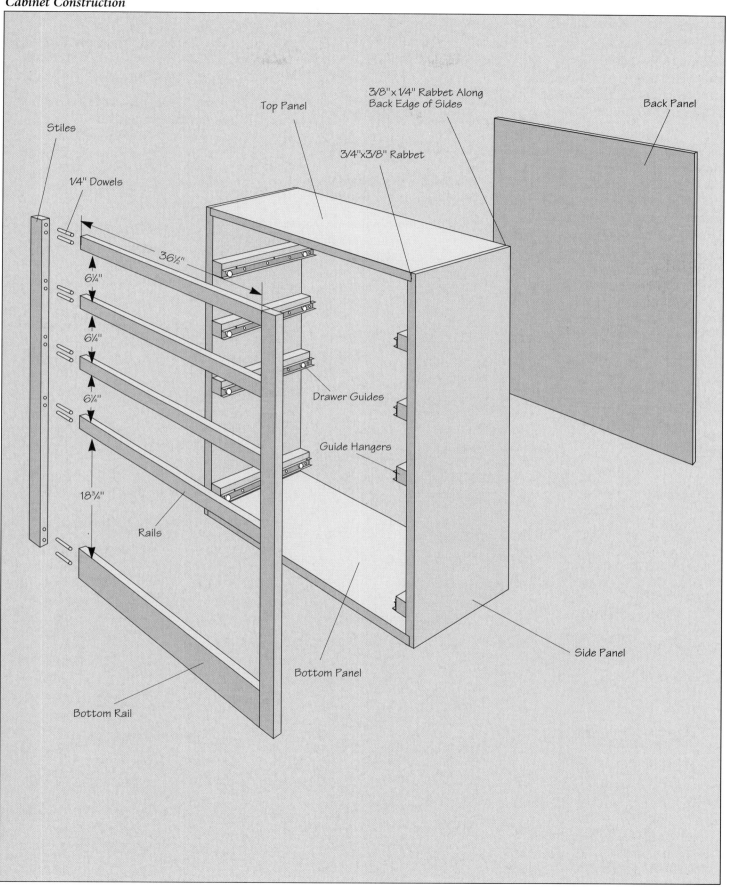

Stiles

1/4" Dowels

Top Panel

3/8" x 1/4" Rabbet Along
Back Edge of Sides

Back Panel

3/4" x 3/8" Rabbet

36½"

6¼"

6¼"

6¼"

Drawer Guides

Guide Hangers

18¾"

Rails

Bottom Panel

Side Panel

Bottom Rail

together with bar or pipe clamps. Square up the frame and let it stand until the glue sets.

4. **Attach the face frame.** Apply glue to the front edges of the cabinet. Then nail the face frame in place with 4d finishing nails every 12 inches.

5. **Attach the guide hangers and drawer guides.** Draw layout lines on the inside of the cabinet. Make the lines flush to the tops of the rails and square to the front of the cabinet. From 5/4 dimension lumber, cut the guide hangers to the dimensions in the Materials List. Align the tops of the hangers to the lines and fasten

them with glue and 1¾-inch drywall screws. Follow the manufacturer's directions and use the screws furnished to attach the guide portion of the 16-inch-long drawer slide hardware.

BUILDING THE LOWER BUNK

Building the Lower Bunk Frame

1. **Cut and assemble the parts.** Cut the lower bunk headboard, footboard, sideboard, supports, and screen molding to the dimensions in the Materials List. Rabbet and dado

the long support as shown in *Lower Bunk Construction*.

Attach screen molding to the top edges of the headboard, footboard, and sideboard with glue and 7/8-inch brads.

Apply glue to one broad side of four of the platform supports and sandwich them together to make two double-thick supports. Reinforce this joint with eight 1¼-inch flathead wood screws as shown in *Lower Bunk Construction*.

2. **Install the headboard and sideboard.** Set the headboard snugly into the corner. Level the panel with shims as necessary before attaching it

Lower Bunk Construction

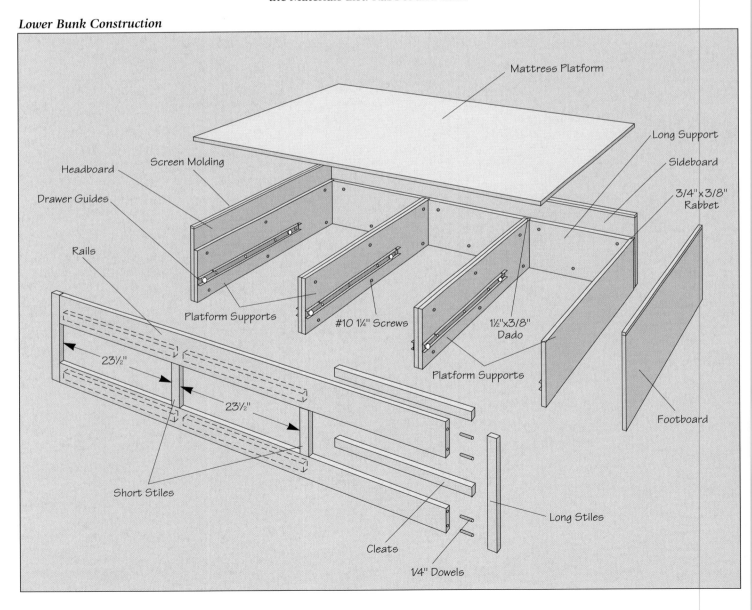

to the wall with two 3½-inch flathead wood screws into each stud. Butt the sideboard against the headboard and check for level. Make any necessary adjustments before attaching with 3½-inch screws.

3. **Install the footboard.** Apply glue to the foot end of the sideboard, and attach the footboard to it with four 4d finishing nails. Use a framing square to keep the footboard perpendicular to the wall as you nail; then let it stand until the glue sets.

4. **Install the supports.** Apply glue to the two dadoes and the two rabbets in the long support and insert the doubled platform supports in the dadoes and the single platform supports in the rabbets, securing each to the long support with 1¼-inch drywall screws.

Apply glue to the wall side of the long support, press the subassembly in place against the sideboard, and secure it with nine 1¼-inch drywall screws. Glue and screw the two single supports to the inside of the headboard and footboard. Follow the manufacturer's directions to attach the guide portion of the 28-inch-long drawer slide hardware.

Installing the Lower Bunk Face Frame and Platform

1. **Cut the parts.** Cut the stiles, rails, plywood cleats, and platform to the dimensions in the Materials List.

2. **Assemble the face frame.** Using a doweling jig, drill dowel holes in the stiles and rails. Insert dowels into the holes, apply glue and draw the pieces

together with bar or pipe clamps. Check that the face frame is square and let the frame stand until the glue sets. See "Reinforcing Joints with Dowels," page 9.

3. **Attach the face frame and platform.** Apply glue to the ends of the headboard, footboard, and the platform supports, and attach the face frame with four 4d finishing nails, tacking them in at first in case you need to make an adjustment. Position each plywood cleat between the platform supports and flush with their top or bottom edges. Then glue and screw the cleats to the inside of the rails, using four 1¼-inch screws for each connection.

Apply glue to the top edges of all platform supports and top cleats and lay

Upper Bunk Construction

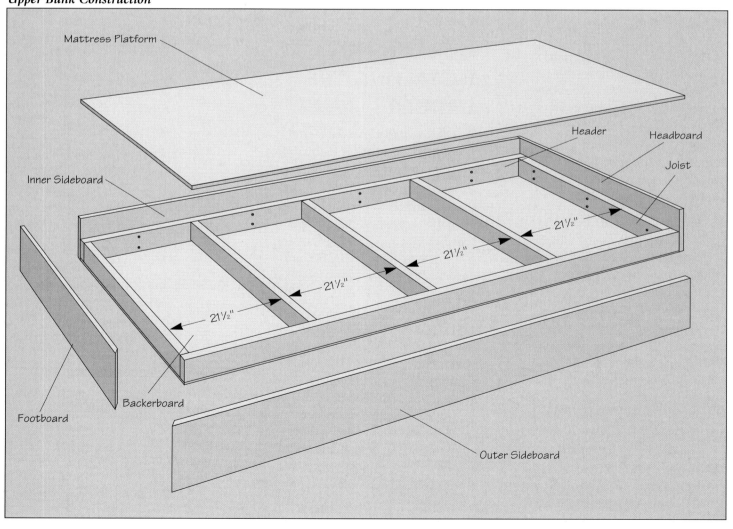

the platform atop the supports. Weigh down the platform with some books or tools until the glue dries.

BUILDING THE UPPER BUNK

1. Cut the parts. Cut the headboard and inner sideboard to the lengths in the Materials List. Cut two headers and five joists from common 2x4s to their listed lengths. Cut the backerboard from 1/4-inch plywood.

2. Attach the headboard and sideboard. Align the top edge of the headboard with the 56¼-inch level line and attach it to the wall with one 3½-inch flathead wood screw into each stud. Align the sideboard along the adjacent wall, and secure it with screws.

3. Assemble the frame. Attach the joists to the header using two 3-inch deck screws or 16d nails at each joint, spacing the joists as shown in *Upper Bunk Construction*. Attach the other header the same way. Measure diagonals to ensure the frame is square.

Attach the backerboard onto one face of the frame with glue and 4d finishing nails every 12 inches.

4. Install the frame. Place the cabinet in position. With the aid of a couple of helpers, position one end of the frame atop the cabinet. Level the frame and then attach it to the walls with two 3½-inch wood screws driven in each wall stud.

5. Attach the cabinet. Secure the cabinet to the frame with two 1½-inch wood screws driven up through the top panel of the cabinet into the bed frame. Secure the cabinet to the wall with three 3½-inch wood screws driven into a stud.

6. Install the sideboard and footboard. Cut the outer sideboard square at the wall ends and mitered at the outside corner. Apply glue to the end of the headboard and outside header and attach the sideboard with 4d finishing nails.

Miter-cut one end of the footboard, then double-check the distance from the mitered end of the outer sideboard to the wall. Cut the other end of the footboard to that finished length. Apply glue to the end of the inner sideboard, the outer face of the joist and the mitered ends of the footboard and outer sideboard; then attach the footboard with 4d finishing nails.

7. Cut and install the platform. Cut the mattress platform from 1/2-inch plywood. Apply glue to the top surfaces of the frame, lay the platform on top of the frame and secure it with 4d finishing nails every 12 inches.

BUILDING AND INSTALLING THE LADDER

1. Cut the parts. Cut the ladder sides, steps, and nailers to the dimensions in the Materials List.

2. Mark the step notches. Hold the ladder sides together, face to face, align their ends, and clamp them together with a C-clamp at each end. Starting 8 inches from the bottom ends, use a framing square to lay out seven lines 8 inches apart. Scribe a second guideline 2½ inches beneath the other guidelines.

3. Cut the step notches. Set the circular saw for a 1½-inch cutting depth. Using an angle square as a saw guide, make cuts across the 2x4s just inside each guideline. Then cut away the material between the guidelines by making several more cuts at each location and chiseling out the material.

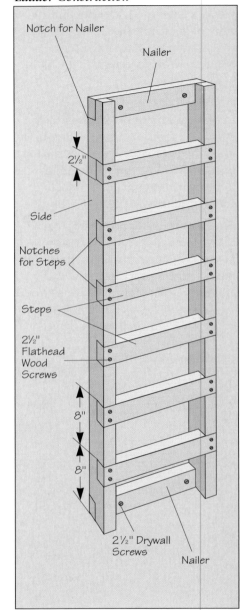

Ladder Construction

Notch for Nailer
Nailer
2½"
Side
Notches for Steps
Steps
2½" Flathead Wood Screws
8"
8"
2½" Drywall Screws
Nailer

4. Mark and cut the nailer notches. Turn the ladder sides over, and scribe lines across the rear surfaces 2½ inches from each end. Then cut away the material from the lines to the ends the way you did for the step notches.

5. Counterbore and drill the steps and nailers. Use a 3/8-inch bit to counterbore a pair of holes 3/4 inch from each end and 3/4 inch from the top and bottom of each step and nailer. Counterbore two centered holes into the front of each nailer, 3 inches from each end. Then drill through the center of each hole with an 11/64-inch bit. See "Countersink and Counterbore Bits," page 35.

6. **Attach the steps and nailers.** Apply glue to the nailer notches. Lay the nailers in place, and secure each with two 2½-inch flathead wood screws. Attach each step to the step notches with two 2½-inch screws and glue in each notch.

7. **Install the ladder.** Center the ladder against the side of the cabinet, and attach it with four 2½-inch screws. Plug all the counterbored screw holes with glued wood plugs. When the glue sets, cut the plugs off flush, and sand as required.

BUILDING AND INSTALLING THE GUARDRAILS

1. **Cut the parts.** Cut the foot guardrail, side guardrail and their nine supports to the dimensions in the Materials List. Cut a 45-degree bevel at each end of the 2x2 supports. Counterbore and drill for the two screws that will be installed at each end of each support.

2. **Attach the supports.** Attach two supports 6 inches from the ends of the foot guardrail and 1½ inches from the top edge of the rail, using two 2-inch screws in each support. Then attach a support to the center of the side rail and two more located on 12-inch centers on each side of the center support.

3. **Install the guardrails.** Using glue and two 2-inch screws in each sup-

port, attach the side guardrail to the sideboard and foot guardrail to the footboard, keeping a 3-inch space between the guardrails and the sideboard or footboard.

4. **Plug the screw holes.** Plug the screw holes with 3/8-inch wood plugs and glue. When the glue sets, cut off the plugs, and sand them smooth.

BUILDING THE DRAWERS

Make the cabinet drawers and bed drawers. Make the false drawer fronts from solid wood and the rest of the parts from plywood. See "Drawer

Guardrail

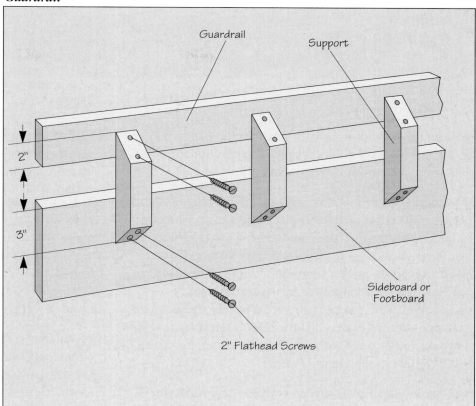

Construction," page 23, for instructions on making 3/8-inch overlay drawers, and see "Edge-Gluing Stock," page 8, for instructions on making a wide, solid-wood false drawer front from narrow boards.

Apply finish to the project before attaching the drawer pulls and the drawer sections of the side-mounted metal drawer slides. Attach hardware with the screws provided.

for the Bedroom...

Toy Box

If you have children in your household or on your gift list, here's a dandy project you can put together in a few evenings or over a weekend.

In a child's room, this box will hold all sorts of toys and games in its roomy interior. But thanks to its functional and sturdy design, this handsome chest is sure to remain in service long after its owner outgrows the need to store toys. In a teenager's room, it becomes a catchall or a gear locker for sports equipment. In a young adult's first apartment, it's a handy storage unit that doubles as an accent table or coffee table. Line it with aromatic cedar and it becomes a cedar chest worthy of a spot in any adult's home.

You can build this toy box of softwood and softwood plywood and paint it, or make it with hardwood and hardwood plywood and finish it naturally. Just make sure to use nontoxic finishing materials and special spring–loaded toy–box lid supports that prevent the lid from slamming on little fingers.

You can decorate the front and side plywood panels with wooden numbers or alphabet letters you can make yourself or buy at any home center. You could use a scroll saw to cut out geometric designs or other shapes to attach to the exterior with glue and brads. Or, simply paint or stencil decorations onto the finished surface.

To make the unit mobile, install the optional swivel casters available at any hardware store or home center. Match the casters to the flooring in the child's room and follow the manufacturer's directions for installation.

Toy Box Materials List

Qty	Part	Dimensions	Qty	Part
2	Plywood front and rear panels	3/4" x 17¼" x 38½"		**Hardware**
2	Plywood side panels	3/4" x 17¼" x 18"		4d Finishing Nails
2	Solid–wood top trim strips	3/4" x 1½" x 20"		1 ¼" Brads
2	Solid–wood top trim strips	3/4" x 1½" x 40"		1" Brads
2	Solid–wood base trim strips	3/4" x 2½" x 20"	1	36" Piano hinge
2	Solid–wood base trim strips	3/4" x 2½" x 40"	2	Toy–box lid supports
4	1" Corner guard	1/4" x 1" x 1" x 13¼"	2	Chest or trunk handles
2	Cleats	3/4" x 3/4" x 37"		
2	Cleats	3/4" x 3/4" x 15½"		
1	Plywood bottom panel	3/4" x 16⅞" x 36⅞"		
1	Solid–wood lid	3/4" x 21" x 42"		

Overall View

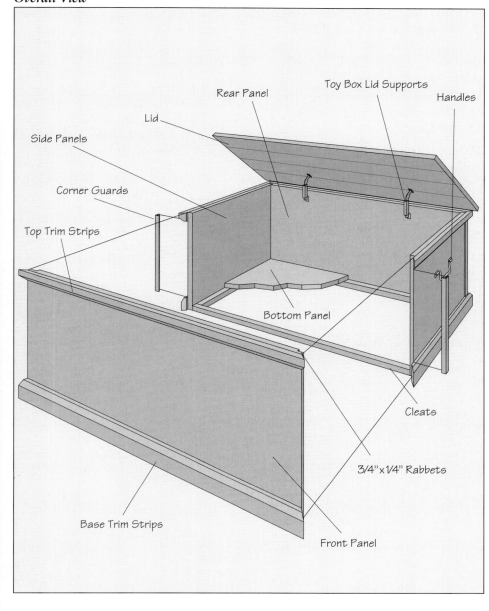

Rear Panel

Toy Box Lid Supports

Handles

Lid

Side Panels

Corner Guards

Top Trim Strips

Bottom Panel

Cleats

3/4"x1/4" Rabbets

Base Trim Strips

Front Panel

ASSEMBLING THE FRONT, REAR, AND SIDE PANELS

1. Cut the parts. Cut the front, rear, and side panels to the dimensions in the Materials List.

2. Rabbet the front and rear panels. Rabbet the ends of the front and rear panels as shown in the *Overall View*. See "Making Rabbets with a Router," page 14.

3. Assemble the parts. Assemble the side panels to the rabbets in the front and back panels with glue and 4d finishing nails. Square up the box with corner clamps at two diagonal top corners and the two opposite diagonal bottom corners, and let stand until the glue sets. See "Squaring a Carcase," page 14.

ATTACHING THE TRIM AND CORNER GUARD

1. Chamfer the trim stock. Use a router with a chamfering bit or a table saw to cut a 1/2–inch chamfer along one edge of the 1x2 and 1x3 trim stock.

2. Cut and attach the top trim. Cut the top trim strips from the chamfered

1x2 stock with 45–degree miters at the ends. Then attach the trim, chamfered edge down, with glue and 1¼-inch brads flush with the top edges of the plywood panels.

3. **Cut and attach the base trim.** Cut the base trim strips from the chamfered 1x3 stock the same as you did the top trim, and install it the same way but with the chamfered edge up.

4. **Cut and attach the corner guard.** Cut four strips of corner guard to fit the corners of the box between the top and base trim. Attach the strips with glue and 1–inch brads.

INSTALLING THE TOY–BOX BOTTOM

1. **Cut the parts.** Cut the bottom panel and the four cleats to the dimensions in the Materials List.

2. **Attach the cleats.** Turn the box upside down and attach the front and rear cleats with glue and 1¼–inch brads flush with the bottom edges of the front and rear panels. Then attach the side cleats flush with the bottom edges of the side panels.

3. **Install the bottom panel.** Turn the box upright and run a bead of glue along the top edges of the cleats. Lay the bottom panel atop the cleats and let stand until the glue sets. If necessary, put several heavy objects atop the bottom panel so it maintains full contact with the cleats while the glue dries.

BUILDING THE LID; FINISHING AND INSTALLING HARDWARE

1. **Glue up the lid.** For the lid, you'll need a slab made from nominal one–inch stock to fit the dimensions in the Materials List. See "Edge–Gluing Stock," page 8, for instructions on building up large pieces from narrow boards.

2. **Apply finish.** Fill any remaining nailholes or flaws with wood filler, let dry, and sand the lid and box as required. Then apply the finish of your choice and let dry.

3. **Attach the hinge to the box.** Center the piano hinge along the top edge of the back of the box as shown in *Installing the Piano Hinge*, and use it as a template to mark for pilot holes. Drill pilot holes and mount the hinge to the box with the screws provided.

4. **Attach the lid.** Position the lid atop the box so it overhangs the front and sides by one inch and is flush with the rear edge. Use the hinge to mark for pilot holes in the rear edge of the lid, make the holes, and attach the hinge to the lid.

5. **Attach the lid supports.** With the lid propped open, attach the supports to the inside of the rear panel and underside of the lid according to the manufacturer's directions and with the screws provided.

6. **Attach the handles.** Center a chest or trunk handle on each end of the box about six inches from the top edge and mount it with the screws provided.

Installing the Piano Hinge

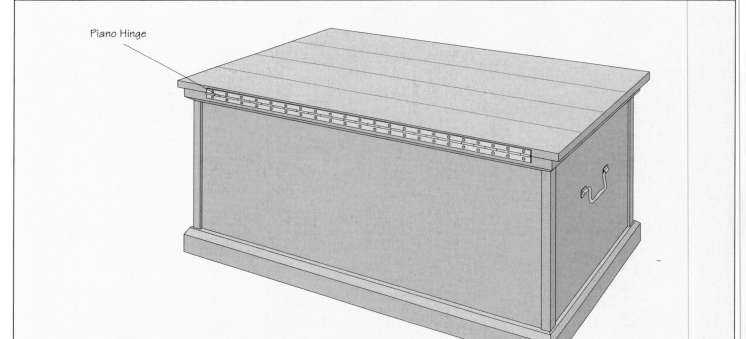

Piano Hinge

for the Bedroom...
Platform Bed

A platform bed makes sense in several ways. First, the platform provides excellent support of the mattress for comfortable sleeping and is particularly advantageous for those who suffer from back problems. Bedding expenses are cut in half because there's no need for box springs. Moreover, platform beds appeal especially to do–it–yourselfers because they can be built in the home workshop. This bed offers the added advantage of a handsome pedestal that also furnishes spacious and convenient storage.

The bed shown here is sized to accommodate a queen-sized mattress. The platform itself folds in half with a piano hinge to make it easier to maneuver in and out of the bedroom.

While the platform bed is a great project in its own right, it's designed to be combined with the bedroom wall unit, making it one of the most functional and attractive bed ensembles you can build.

Platform Bed Materials List

Qty	Part	Dimensions	Qty	Part	Dimensions
Pedestal			**Drawers (with 3/8" overlay)**		
4	Solid–wood side–frame rails	3/4" x 1½" x 74½"	8	Plywood sides	1/2" x 9" x 24"
4	Solid–wood side–frame stiles	3/4" x 3½" x 9½"	4	Plywood fronts	1/2" x 9" x 22¼"
2	Plywood side–frame panels	3/4" x 9½" x 20"	4	Plywood backs	1/2" x 8½" x 22¼"
4	Solid–wood cleats	3/4" x 1½" x 1½"	4	Plywood bottoms	3/8" x 22¼" x 23¾"
4	Solid–wood cleats	3/4" x 1½" x 3½"	4	Solid–wood false fronts	3/4" x 10¼" x 24½"
2	Solid–wood supports	1½" x 3½" x 48½"	**Hardware**		
2	Solid–wood supports	1½" x 1½" x 48½"	28	5/16" x 1½" Wood dowels	
2	Plywood headboards/footboards	3/4" x 12½" x 50"		1¼" x #6 Flathead wood screws	
4	1" corner guard	1/4" x 1" x 1" x 12½"		4d Finishing nails	
Platform			8	3" Metal corner braces with screws	
2	Plywood bed slabs	3/4" x 40¼" x 61"		6d Finishing nails	
2	Solid–wood headboards/footboards	3/4" x 2½" x 62½"	4	Side–mounted drawer slides	
4	Solid–wood sideboards	3/4" x 2½" x 40¼"		1" Brads	
4	Solid–wood platform stops	3/4" x 3/4" x 8	1	48" Piano hinge with screws	
			8	Drawer pulls	

Overall View

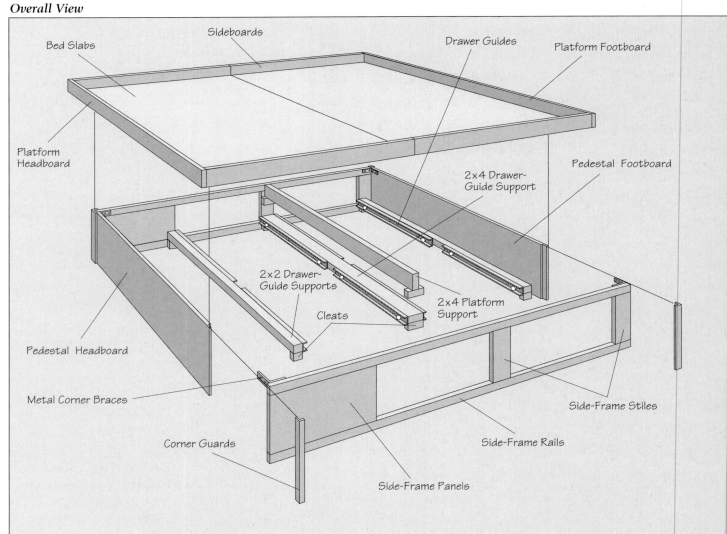

Bed Slabs

Sideboards

Drawer Guides

Platform Footboard

Platform Headboard

2x4 Drawer-Guide Support

Pedestal Footboard

2x2 Drawer-Guide Supports

Cleats

2x4 Platform Support

Pedestal Headboard

Metal Corner Braces

Side-Frame Stiles

Corner Guards

Side-Frame Rails

Side-Frame Panels

Side-Frame Construction

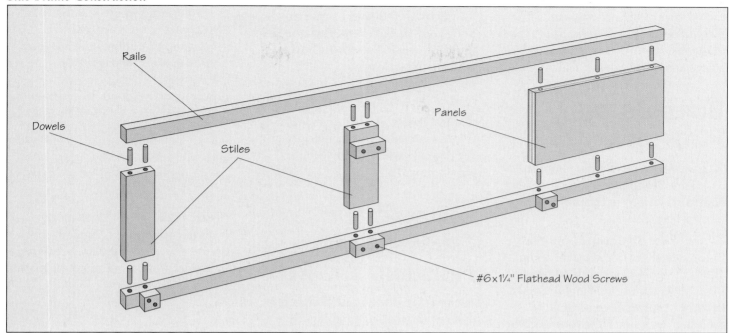

BUILDING THE PEDESTAL

1. Cut the side-frame parts and drill the cleats. Cut the side–frame rails, stiles, panels, and cleats to the dimensions in the Materials List. Use a #6 countersink bit to drill and countersink two pilot holes in each cleat as shown in *Side-Frame Construction.*

2. Assemble the side frames. Assemble the rails to the stiles and side-frame panels with glue and two dowels at each joint, locating the parts as shown in *Side-Frame Construction.* See "Reinforcing Joints with Dowels," page 9.

3. Attach the cleats. Apply glue to the back of each cleat, and install each with two #6 x 1¼-inch screws on the inside surface of each side frame, locating them as shown in *Side-Frame Construction.*

4. Cut the remaining pedestal parts. Cut the drawer–guide supports, platform supports, and pedestal headboard and footboard to the dimensions in the Materials List. (Wait until the pedestal is assembled to cut and install the corner guard.)

Pedestal Corner Detail

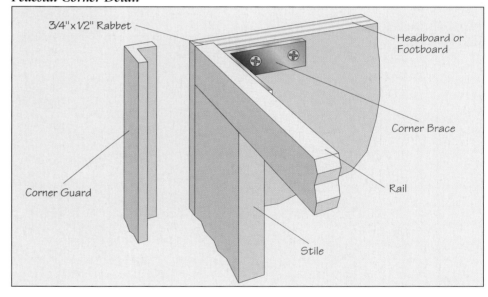

5. Rabbet the headboard and footboard. Rabbet each end of the inside surface of the headboard and footboard as shown in *Pedestal Corner Detail.* See "Making Rabbets with a Router," page 14.

6. Assemble the pedestal. Attach the headboard and footboard to the side frames with glue and 4d finishing nails as shown in *Overall View.* Then install two corner braces at each corner with screws provided as shown in *Pedestal Corner Detail.*

7. Install the supports. Apply glue to the ends of the 2x2 and 2x4 supports and to the tops of the cleats. Lay the supports atop the cleats and attach them with 6d finishing nails as shown in *Overall View.*

8. Install the drawer slides. Attach the cabinet portions of the drawer slides to the drawer–guide supports according to the manufacturer's directions. See "Installing Drawer Slide Hardware," page 25.

9. Attach the corner guard. Measure each corner of the pedestal, and cut a piece of corner guard to fit. Apply glue to the inside surfaces of the corner guard, and attach it with 1-inch brads.

BUILDING THE PLATFORM

1. Cut the parts. Cut the platform bed slabs, headboard, footboard, sideboards, and stops to the dimensions in the Materials List.

2. Build the platform. Apply glue to the side edges of each slab, and attach the sideboards with 4d finishing nails as shown in *Platform Construction.* Apply glue to one end of each slab, and attach the footboard to one and headboard to the other with 4d finishing nails.

3. Attach the stops. Use a #6 countersink bit to drill and countersink pilot holes in each stop. Turn the slabs upside down and attach each stop with glue and two #6 x 1¼-inch screws, positioning them as shown in *Platform Construction.*

4. Attach the piano hinge. With the slabs positioned together, attach the piano hinge to them with the screws provided.

BUILDING THE DRAWERS AND FINISHING THE BED

The pedestal drawers are designed to overlay the pedestal openings by 3/8 inch on all sides. Make the false fronts from solid wood and the rest of the parts from plywood according to the dimensions in the Materials List. See "Drawer Construction," page 23, for instructions on making 3/8-inch overlay drawers, and see "Edge-Gluing Stock," page 8, for instructions on making solid-wood false drawer fronts from narrow boards.

Fill any remaining nailholes or flaws with wood filler, let dry, and sand all components. Then apply the finish of your choice and let dry.

Attach a drawer pull to the false front of each drawer. Then attach the drawer portions of the drawer slides to the drawers according to the manufacturer's directions.

Platform Construction

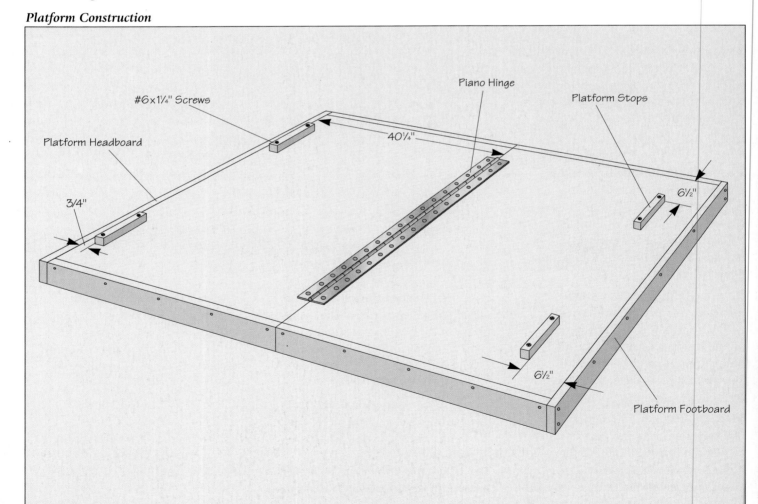

for the Bedroom...
Bedroom Wall Unit

Here's an ideal project for the master bedroom— a modular unit that stands 6 feet tall and spans nearly 11 feet of wall space. Combine this project with the platform bed on page 113, and you'll have the perfect bedroom ensemble. In each bedside cabinet are three roomy drawers and three spacious shelves.

Two large bridge shelves span the head of the bed and join the two cabinets. The lower shelf also features built–in fluorescent lighting.

You can build the project from softwood or hardwood, and then paint it or finish it naturally. Plans call for trimming the cabinets with 1–inch corner guard. This finishing touch conceals plywood edges and provides a pleasing contemporary visual appeal. The softwood version of the corner guard has 1–inch outside and 3/4–inch inside dimensions. Hardwood corner guard might be as much as 1/8 inch wider, but will work just as well. Although dimensions are provided in the Materials List, be sure to carefully measure and miter-cut each strip individually.

Holes drilled in cabinet panels and fitted with brass hardware help keep electrical cords out of sight. Because of the narrow diameters of the holes and hardware, it's necessary to remove plugs from lights and other electrical appliances before threading the cords through. You can then replace the plugs with new snap–on or other standard two–prong plugs.

Bedroom Wall Unit Materials List

Difficulty Level 𝍐𝍐𝍐

Qty	Part	Dimensions	Qty	Part	Dimensions
Face frames			**Top Drawers (with 3/8" overlay)**		
12	Solid–wood rails	3/4" x 1½" x 25½"	4	Solid–wood false fronts	3/4" x 7¼" x 12¾"
2	Solid–wood bottom rails	3/4" x 3½" x 25½"	4	Plywood fronts	1/2" x 5½" x 11"
2	Solid–wood stiles	3/4" x 1½" x 6½"	4	Plywood backs	1/2" x 4⅝" x 11"
4	Solid–wood stiles	3/4" x 1½" x 22½"	8	Plywood sides	1/2" x 5½" x 16"
4	Solid–wood stiles	3/4" x 1½" x 48"	4	Plywood bottom panels	3/8" x 11" x 15¾"
Carcases			**Bottom Drawers (with 3/8" overlay)**		
2	Plywood cabinet tops	3/4" x 11½" x 29½"	2	Solid–wood false fronts	3/4" x 10¼" x 26¼"
2	Plywood night stand tops	3/4" x 17¼" x 28½"	2	Plywood fronts	1/2" x 8½" x 24½"
6	Plywood cabinet shelves	3/4" x 10⅛" x 28⅜"	2	Plywood backs	1/2" x 7⅞" x 24½"
2	Solid–wood night stand edging	1/2" x 3/4" x 28½"	4	Plywood sides	1/2" x 8½" x 16"
2	Solid–wood top panel edging	1/2" x 3/4" x 29½"	2	Plywood bottom panels	3/8" x 24½" x 15¾"
4	Plywood side panels	3/4" x 18" x 72"	**Hardware and electrical items**		
2	Plywood back panels	1/4" x 29½" x 71¾"		2½" Drywall screws	
12	Solid–wood shelf cleats	1/2" x 3/4" x 10¼"		1" Brads	
4	Solid–wood face frame stops	1/2" x 3/4" x 22½"		1" x #6 Flathead wood screws	
4	Solid–wood back cleats	3/4" x 1½" x 28½"		7/8" Brads	
2	Solid–wood bottom back cleats	3/4" x 3½" x 28½""		4d Finishing nails	
4	Rear corner guard	1/4" x 1" x 1" x 72½"		1" Brads	
4	Top horizontal corner guard	1/4" x 1" x 1" x 12½"	6	Drawer pulls	
4	Top vertical corner guard	1/4" x 1" x 1" x 49¾"	6	17" Bottom–mount drawer slides	
4	Night stand corner guard	1/4" x 1" x 1" x 7"		18", 15–watt Under–cabinet fluorescent lamps	
4	Bottom vertical corner guard	1/4" x 1" x 1" x 23¾"		1/4" x 1½" Brass roundhead machine screws	
4	Bottom horizontal corner guard	1/4" x 1" x 1" x 18½"		1/4" Brass flat washers	
Bridge Shelves				1/4" Brass hex nuts	
2	Plywood bridge shelves	3/4" x 9¾" x 65"		2" 3/8 IP Brass nipples	
2	Solid–wood bridge shelf faces	3/4" x 2½" x 66½"		3/8 IP Brass knurled locknuts	
4	Solid–wood bridge shelf ends	3/4" x 2½" x 9¾"		3/8 IP Brass hex nuts	
				Snap–on, two–prong electrical plugs	

MAKING THE FACE FRAMES

1. Cut the parts. Cut all the face–frame rails and stiles to the dimensions in the Materials List.

2. Build the upper face frames. Clamp the four upper face frame stiles together face up, making sure they are flush at top and bottom. Draw lines across all the stiles laying out the positions of the bottom of each rail as shown in *Upper Face Frame*

Construction. Use an 11/64-inch bit to drill pilot holes through the sides of the stiles. Drill one hole 3/4 inch above each layout line. Then assemble the two upper face frames with glue and 2 1/2-inch drywall screws.

3. Build the lower face frame. Clamp the four lower face frame stiles together as you did for the upper face frames and lay out the position of one side of the center rails as shown in *Lower Face Frame Construction.* Then do the same with the 1x2 upper rails to lay out the

positions of the center stiles. Predrill, glue, and screw the lower face frames together as you did the upper face frames, using two screws for each bottom rail connection as shown.

MAKING THE CABINET TOPS AND SHELVES

1. Cut the parts. Cut the cabinet and night stand tops, cabinet shelves, and

Overall View

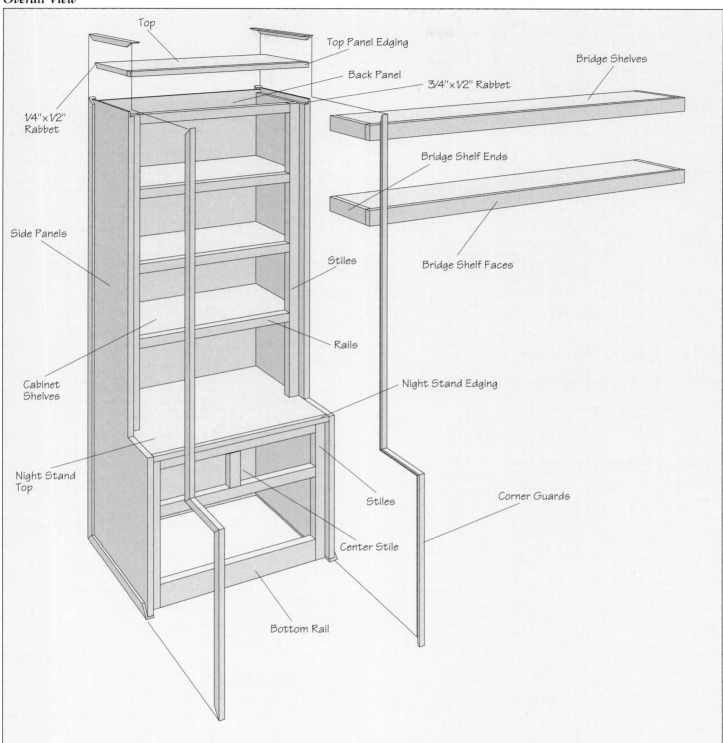

Top

Top Panel Edging

Back Panel

3/4"x1/2" Rabbet

Bridge Shelves

1/4"x1/2" Rabbet

Side Panels

Cabinet Shelves

Bridge Shelf Ends

Stiles

Bridge Shelf Faces

Rails

Night Stand Edging

Night Stand Top

Stiles

Corner Guards

Center Stile

Bottom Rail

the night stand and top panel edging to the dimensions in the Materials List.

2. Rabbet the cabinet tops. Rabbet the back edge of each cabinet top as shown in *The Overall View*. See "Dadoes, Grooves, and Rabbets," page 10.

3. Attach the shelf edging. Use glue and 1-inch brads to attach the edging to the front of the top panels and night stands.

4. Predrill the shelves. To make the wall units lighter and easier to

maneuver, don't install the shelves until you assemble the unit in the bedroom. For now, just drill pilot holes for the 1-inch brads that will secure the shelves to the cleats. Use a 1/16-inch-diameter bit to drill two holes through the top of each shelf

Upper Face Frame Construction

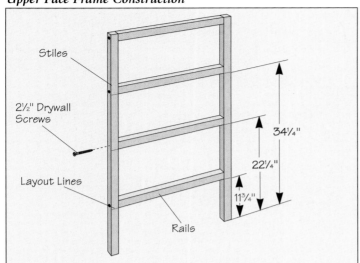

Lower Face Frame Construction

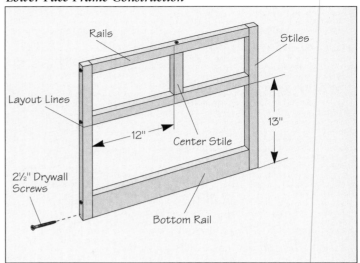

about 1 inch from the front and rear edges and 1/4 inch from the ends.

MAKING THE SIDE AND BACK PANELS

1. Cut the parts. Cut the cabinet sides, back panels, shelf cleats, face-

frame stops, and back cleats to the dimensions in the Materials List. If you don't want to rip your own stock for the cleats and stops, you can buy 1/2 x 3/4-inch stock called parting bead.

2. Make the night stand cutaways. As shown in *Side and Back Panel*

Side and Back Panel Construction

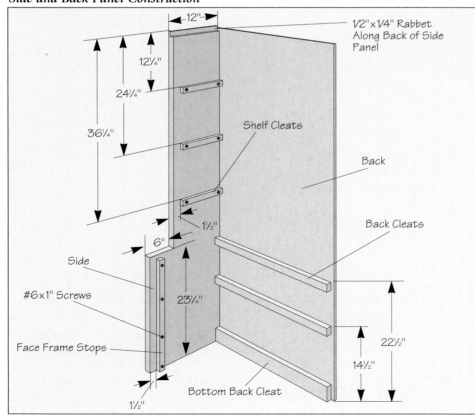

Construction, lay out the cuts that will reduce the cabinet sides to 12 inches wide above the night stand. Make the cuts with a saber saw and saw guide.

3. Rabbet the cabinet sides. Rabbet the top and back edges of the cabinet sides as shown in *Side and Back Panel Construction*. See "Making Rabbets with the Router," page 13. Remember to rout the right sides on faces that will oppose the left sides.

4. Attach the side cleats. Use a pencil to lay out the positions of the shelf cleats and face frame stops as shown in *Side and Back Panel Construction*. Drill and countersink two holes for #6 x 1-inch screws in a wide edge of each cleat and four holes in each face-frame stop as shown. The cleats and stops are attached with glue and screws. Align the top of each cleat and the front of the stops to the layout lines and attach them with #6 x 1-inch wood screws.

5. Attach the back cleats. Lay out the position of the back cleats on the back panels as shown in *Side and Back Panel Construction*. Then, flip the panels over and lay out nailing lines on the outside face of the back panel. Apply glue to the back of each bottom back cleat and clamp each cleat in place flush with the bottom of each back panel. Glue and clamp the remaining cleats the same way. Turn the panels over and drive 7/8-inch brads, about 6 inches apart, through the back panels and along the nailing lines.

ASSEMBLING THE CARCASES

1. Install the lower face frames. In these cabinets, the face frames fit between the side panels, against the face frame stops and recessed 3/4 inch from the front edges of the side panels. Apply glue to the front edges of the face frame stops and the side edges of the lower face frames, and attach the side panels to the face frames with 4d finishing nails spaced about 6 inches apart.

2. Attach the back panels. Apply glue to the rabbets in the rear edges of the side panels and to the side edges

Corner Guard Details

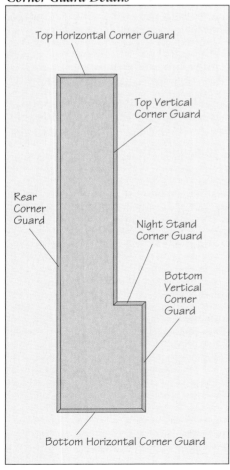

Top Horizontal Corner Guard

Top Vertical Corner Guard

Rear Corner Guard

Night Stand Corner Guard

Bottom Vertical Corner Guard

Bottom Horizontal Corner Guard

of the back panels. Lay each back panel in place, check it for square (see "Squaring a Carcase," page 14), and secure it with 4d finishing nails spaced about 8 inches apart.

3. Install the night stand tops. Apply glue to the side and rear edges of each night stand top, the top of each face frame stop, and the top edge of the upper cleat on each back panel. Lay the tops in place and secure them with 4d finishing nails driven through the side and rear panels.

4. Install the upper face frames. Apply glue to the front edges of the shelf cleats and side edges of each upper face frame. Set each face frame in place, snug against the night stand top, and secure with 4d finishing nails driven through the cabinet sides about 8 inches apart.

5. Install the cabinet tops. Apply glue to the upper rabbets in the side panels, the rabbets in the rear of the top panels, the top edges of the back panels, and the top edges of the upper face frames. Then secure the tops with 4d finishing nails.

ATTACHING THE CORNER GUARD

Note: When attaching the corner guard put glue on both inside surfaces of the guard and on all the miter joints.

1. Attach the rear corner guard. Measure and miter-cut corner guard to fit the rear of the cabinet side panels as shown in *Corner Guard Detail.* Attach the guard with glue and bar clamps placed across the side panels. If you don't have bar clamps, you can attach the guard with glue and 1-inch brads.

2. Attach the top corner guard. Miter-cut strips of corner guard to fit the top horizontal edges of the side panels. Attach the guard with glue and 1-inch brads.

3. Attach the remaining corner guard. Cut corner guard pieces to fit the top vertical edges at the front of the side panels and attach them with glue and bar clamps or glue and brads. Cut guard pieces to fit the night stand cutaway and attach them with glue and brads. Cut guard pieces to fit the bottom vertical front edge and attach them with glue and bar clamps or glue and brads. Finally, cut guard pieces to fit the bottom horizontal edges and attach them with glue and brads.

BUILDING THE BRIDGE SHELVES AND DRAWERS

1. Cut and assemble the shelves. Cut the bridge shelves, shelf faces, and shelf ends to the dimensions in the Materials List. Attach each shelf end and then both shelf faces with glue and 4d finishing nails as shown in *Bridge Shelves Details.*

2. Drill the shelf ends. Lay each shelf upside down and counterbore two 1/2-inch diameter attachment holes 3/8 inch deep into the inside surface of each shelf end, 1 inch inside the front and rear edges of each shelf end. Then drill through each hole with a 1/4-inch bit. In the bottom shelf only, drill a centered 13/32-inch wiring hole through each shelf end.

3. Build the Drawers. The drawers are designed to overlay the face frames by 3/8 inch on all sides. Make the false drawer fronts from solid wood and the rest of the parts from plywood according to the dimensions in the Materials List. See "Drawer Construction," page 23, for instructions on making 3/8–inch overlay drawers, and see "Edge–Gluing Stock," page 8, for instructions on making solid–wood false drawer fronts from narrow boards.

Bridge Shelf Details

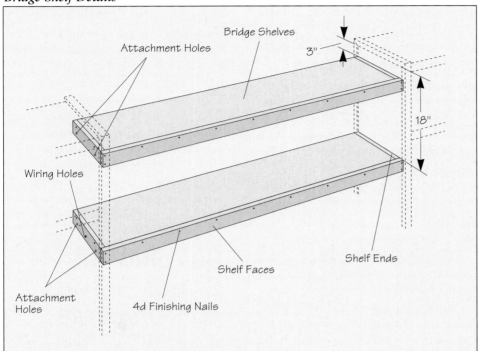

BORING HOLES AND APPLYING FINISH

1. **Drill the cabinet sides.** Lay the left cabinet on its left side and the right cabinet on its right side. Lay out the positions of the bridge shelves as shown in *Bridge Shelf Details*. Stand the top bridge shelf on end on the left side panel, aligned with the guide marks, and drill 1/4-inch holes through the holes in the shelf ends. Align the bottom shelf with the lower marks and drill through with 1/4-inch and 13/32-inch bits. Do likewise on the right side panel.

2. **Drill the cabinet backs.** Drill a 13/32-inch hole through the back of each cabinet, near the same-size hole in the side panel. If you will need access to an electrical outlet from the night stand top (for clock, radio, etc.), drill a 13/32-inch hole in the cabinet back near a bottom corner of the open area.

3. **Fill, sand, and finish the unit.** Fill any remaining nailholes or flaws

with wood filler, let dry, and sand all components. Then apply the finish of your choice and let dry.

ASSEMBLING THE UNIT

1. **Attach the pulls.** Attach one drawer pull to each small drawer and two pulls to each large drawer with the screws provided by the manufacturer.

2. **Attach the drawer slides.** Follow the manufacturer's directions and use the screws provided to attach a drawer section of a slide to the bottom center of each drawer. Attach the cabinet sections to the lower face frames and rear supports as shown in the *Overall View.*

3. **Install the lamps.** Lay the lower bridge shelf upside down and mount a light fixture $3\frac{1}{2}$ inches inside each end, snug against the back of the shelf face, according to the manufacturer's directions. Cut the plug off the cord end with wire cutting pliers.

4. **Assemble the unit.** In the bedroom, lay the cabinets on their backs and attach the bridge shelves with brass machine screws, washers, and nuts. Insert a brass nipple into each 13/32-inch hole and secure with a knurled locknut on the outside and hex nut on the inside. With a helper, stand the assembly upright and move it back against the wall. Thread the lamp cords through the brass nipples and attach the snap–on plugs. See to other wiring chores, and plug the lamps into extension cords if necessary, then into wall outlets. Lay the cabinet shelves atop the cleats, snug against the upper face frame rails, and secure them with 1-inch brads driven through the pilot holes.

Installing the Fluorescent Lamps

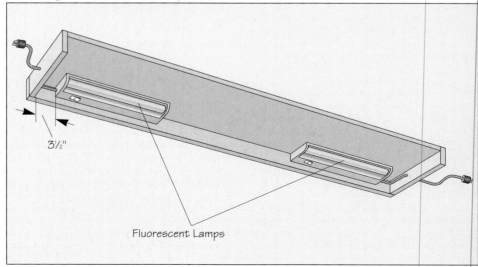

for the Bedroom...
Under-Bed Drawer

In the search for storage around the house, most of us overlook an area with excellent potential: the space under the bed. This project provides under-bed storage that's out of sight but readily accessible. This pull-out drawer is designed to fit under your bed, and it's just the place for storing off-season clothing or children's toys. It has an easy-open top that keeps stored items free from dust. And you'll never have to struggle to pull the unit in and out because installed near the drawer's bottom corners are four wooden

wheels (available at most hobby and craft shops or through mail-order suppliers).

Before you begin cutting parts to size, measure the clearance under your bed. The dimensions in the Materials List will yield a drawer that measures 6¼ inches high—a size that will fit under most beds—but you can adjust the width of the drawer's sides and ends if your under-bed clearance demands a shallower drawer, or a deeper one, if space allows.

Under-Bed Drawer Materials List

Difficulty Level

Qty	Part	Dimensions	Qty	Part
2	Plywood sides	3/4" x 5¼" x 24"		**Hardware**
2	Plywood front & back	3/4" x 5¼" x 23¼"		6d Finishing nails
1	Plywood bottom	3/8" x 23¼" x 23¼"		1" Brads
1	Plywood top	1/4" x 22¾" x 22¾"		4d Finishing nails
1	Solid-wood edging blank	3/4" x 2⅛" x 50"	1	Wood knob
			4	2" to 4" Wooden wheels with axles

Overall View

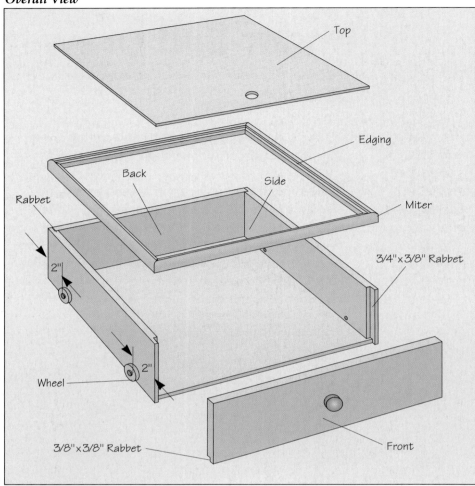

MAKING THE PARTS

1. Cut the parts. Cut the parts to the dimensions in the Materials List using clear pine for the solid-wood edging.

2. Cut the rabbets. Rabbet the ends of the side panels and the bottoms of the front and back as shown in the *Overall View*. Rabbet the bottoms of the side panels as shown in *Section Through Side*. See "Dadoes, Grooves, and Rabbets," page 10.

Making the Edging

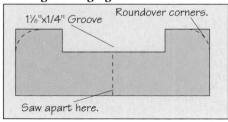

3. Make the top edging. Groove the edging as shown in *Making the Edging*. With a router and 3/8-inch or 1/2-inch roundover bit, round-over two corners of the blank as shown. Then rip the blank in half to form two strips of top edging.

ASSEMBLING THE DRAWER

1. Assemble the box. Fasten the front and back to the end rabbets in the sides with glue and 6d finishing nails. Fasten the bottom to the bottom rabbets in the box with glue and 1 inch brads.

2. Install the top edging. Use a miter box and backsaw or suitable power saw to miter-cut four strips of edging to fit the top edges of the

drawer with the rabbet in each strip facing the inside of the drawer. Attach the strips with glue and 4d finishing nails so that the outside surfaces of the edging and drawer panels are flush, as in *Section Through Side*.

3. Drill the top. Use a 1-inch spade or Forstner bit to drill a finger hole centered about 2 inches from one edge of the plywood top.

FINISHING THE DRAWER

1. Apply the finish. After sanding, stain and varnish or paint the drawer and top. Paint or stain the wheels before installation.

2. Install the knob. Center the screw hole for the knob in the front panel, and screw the knob in place.

3. Install the wheels. Drill two axle holes in each side panel 2 inches inside each front and rear corner and at a distance from the bottom edge to provide 1/4-inch clearance when wheels are attached. Then insert an axle through each wheel hub, and glue each axle in a hole, being careful to keep glue off the axle where it contacts the wheel.

Section Through Side

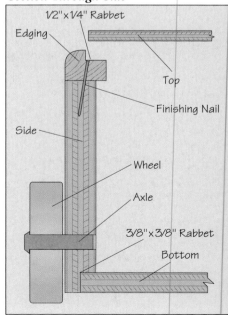

Decorative Shelf

Part of the appeal of a fireplace is its mantelpiece— the decorative over-the-hearth shelf meant for displaying special items. With this project, you can have such a mantelpiece, even if you don't have a fireplace to go with it. The shelf shown here is designed with the same built-up thickness and mitered molding that distinguishes many traditional mantelpieces.

As shown in the *Overall View*, the shelf top has a small box, or subassembly, attached to its underside. The subassembly consists of a front, bottom, and two ends. It provides structural support for attaching the project to the ledger strip that is fastened to the wall. It also serves as backing for the crown molding.

The shelf shown here is 48 inches long. You can adjust shelf length to fit available wall space. The installation instructions at the end of this project apply to a wood-frame wall. If you need to install your shelf against a masonry wall, refer to the instructions in "Solid-Wall Fasteners," page 47.

If you plan to paint the shelf, make it from a softwood. For a clear finish, you can choose an attractive hardwood. Unfortunately, you'll find that most lumberyards stock crown molding only in pine or oak. One attractive option is to paint the crown and apply clear finish to the shelf. Even if you build your shelf from hardwood, use softwood for the ledger.

Decorative Shelf Materials List

Difficulty Level

Qty	Part	Dimensions	Part
1	Solid-wood top	3/4" x 8½" x 48"	**Hardware**
1	Solid-wood bottom	3/4" x 4⅜" x 39¾"	6d Finishing nails
1	Solid-wood front	3/4" x 2½" x 41¼"	4d Finishing nails
2	Solid-wood sides	3/4" x 2½" x 5⅛"	#8 x 2½" Drywall screws
1	Front crown molding	11/16" x 3½" x 50"	8d Finishing nails
2	Side crown molding	11/16" x 3½" x 10"	
1	Solid-wood ledger	3/4" x 1¾" x 39⅝"	

Overall View

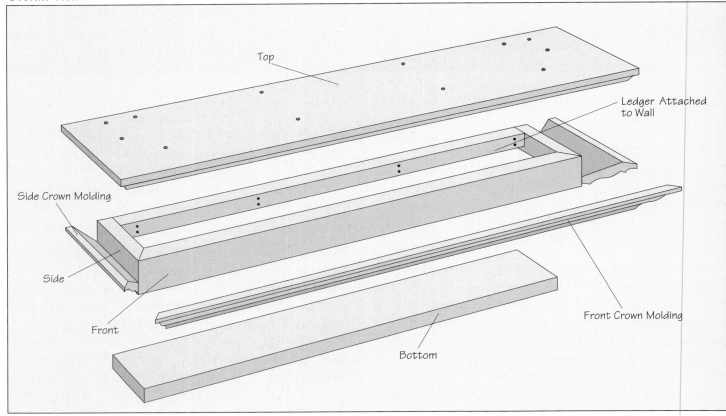

Top

Ledger Attached to Wall

Side Crown Molding

Side

Front

Front Crown Molding

Bottom

BUILDING THE SHELF

1. **Cut the shelf parts.** Cut the top and bottom to the dimensions in the Materials List. Cut the front and side pieces to the dimensions in the Materials List with 45-degree miters on both ends of the front piece and one end of each side piece.

2. **Rout the top.** Use a router and 3/8-inch cove bit to mill a cove along the front and side edges of the shelf top, as shown in the *Overall View*. Sand the shelf top with 120- and 220-grit sandpaper.

3. **Assemble the bottom, front, and sides.** Apply glue to the front and side edges of the bottom and to the mitered ends of the front and side pieces. Attach the front and sides to the bottom with 6d finishing nails to form the subassembly. Use four nails into the front and two nails into each side.

4. **Attach the top.** Glue and nail the subassembly to the top with 6d finishing nails. Use two nails for each side piece and four nails for the front. Predrill for the nails if the top is made of hardwood.

CUTTING AND INSTALLING THE CROWN

1. **Cut and attach the front crown.** Miter-cut one end of the molding. Position the molding against the front of the shelf assembly, as shown in the *Overall View*, and mark the second cut in place. Glue and nail the front crown to the top and to the subassembly front piece, using 4d finishing nails. See"Cutting and Installing Crown Molding," page 31.

2. **Cut and install the side molding.** Miter-cut each crown molding side piece a little longer than the dimen-

sions in the Materials List. Position each against the mitered end of the front crown molding piece and mark where it meets the rear edge of the shelf assembly. Square-cut that end for a flush fit. Apply glue to the mitered ends and contact surfaces of the side molding pieces. Install the pieces with 4d finishing nails into the top and into the subassembly side pieces.

INSTALLING THE SHELF

1. **Install the ledger.** Use a stud finder to locate the wall framing. See "Finding Studs," page 28. Scribe a level line that crosses at least two studs at the height of your choice. Attach the ledger with 2½-inch screws driven in at each stud.

2. **Attach the shelf to the ledger.** Fit the shelf over the ledger, and secure the shelf with four 8d finishing nails driven into the ledger.

for the Living Room...
Window Seat with Drawers

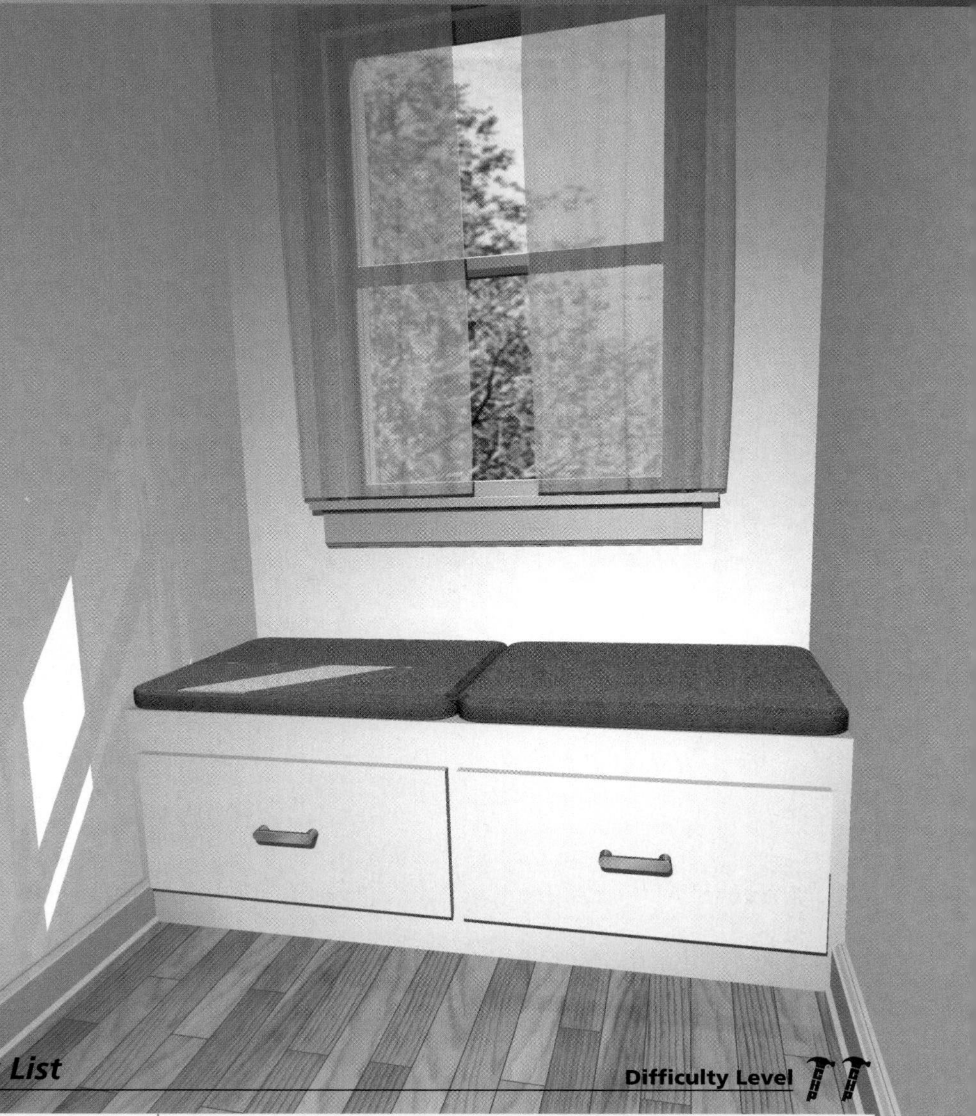

A window seat is a warm and cozy addition to any room. It's equally suitable in a den as an inviting break in a wall full of floor-to-ceiling bookcases as it is in a bedroom flanked by his-and-her closets. This handsome window seat was designed for double duty with its comfortable cushions and spacious drawers. It is designed to fit a space 48 inches wide, but you can alter its dimensions to fit any available space.

If you have experience upholstering, or if you simply enjoy the challenge, by all means, make your own cushions. Otherwise, you can have them custom made to your specifications at a local upholstery shop.

If you need to remove carpeting and woodwork in the area where you plan to build your window seat, see "Removing Wallboard," page 28 and "Removing Carpet," page 29.

Window Seat with Drawers Materials List

Difficulty Level

Qty	Part	Dimensions
Carcase and face frame		
2	Solid-wood face frame rails	3/4" x 3½" x 48"
3	Solid-wood face frame stiles	3/4" x 1½" x 9¾"
2	Plywood side panels	3/4" x 16" x 18½"
1	Plywood back panel	3/4" x 16" x 48"
1	Plywood top panel	3/4" x 19½" x 48"
Drawers		
4	Sides	3/4" x 8¾" x 18"
2	Backs	3/4" x 8⅛" x 20¾"
2	Fronts	3/4" x 8¾" x 20¾"
2	Bottoms	1/4" x 17½" x 20¾"
2	Solid-wood false fronts	3/4" x 10½" x 22½"

Qty	Part
Hardware	
12	1/4" x 1¼" Wooden dowels
	3" Screws (if attaching side panel to wall)
	1½" Screws (if attaching side panels to cabinet)
	4d Finishing nails
2	Bottom-mount roller-bearing drawer slides
2	Drawer pulls
Miscellaneous	
2	Upholstered foam cushions 4" x 20" x 24"

Overall View

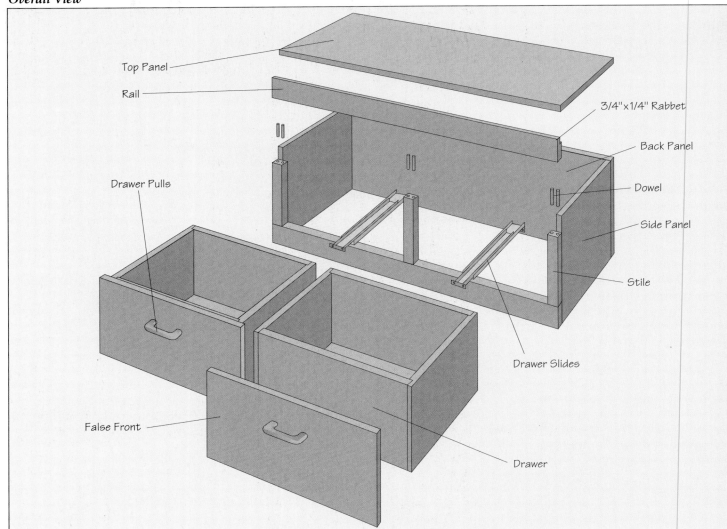

Top Panel

Rail

3/4"x1/4" Rabbet

Back Panel

Drawer Pulls

Dowel

Side Panel

Stile

Drawer Slides

False Front

Drawer

1. **Cut and rabbet the face frame.**
Cut the rails from clear 1x4 stock and
the stiles from clear 1x2 stock to the
dimensions in the Materials List.
Rabbet the top rear edge of the top
rail as shown in the *Overall View*.

2. **Assemble the face frame.** Use
a doweling jig to make two holes in
each end of each stile. Drill corresponding holes in the center and at
both ends of each rail, as shown in
the *Overall View*. See "Reinforcing
Joints with Dowels", page 9.

Attach the rails to the stiles with
12 glued dowels. Draw the rails to the
stiles with three bar clamps or pipe
clamps. Check the frame for square
and make any necessary adjustments
before the glue sets.

3. **Cut the carcase panels.** Cut the
sides, back, and top to the dimensions in the Materials List.

4. **Attach the back and side panels.**
Place the back panel against the wall
beneath the window, and secure it
to the studs with 3-inch screws. Attach the side panels the same way if
you are securing them to another
wall. If you are securing the side panels to another cabinet, use 1½-inch
screws instead.

5. **Install the face frame.** Apply glue
to the front edges of the side panels,
press the face frame against the glued
sides, and secure it with four 4d finishing nails.

6. **Install the drawer slides.** Attach
the cabinet portions of the drawer

slides to the bottom rail and back
panel according to the manufacturer's directions.

7. **Attach the top panel.** Apply glue
to the top edges of the carcase and the
rabbet in the top of the face frame.
Lay the top panel in place, and secure
it with 4d finishing nails.

8. **Cut and build the drawers.** Cut
the drawer parts to the dimensions in
the Materials List. The solid-wood
false fronts are larger than the drawer
to allow a 3/8-inch overhang on all
sides. Build the drawers according to
the directions in "Building Drawers,"
page 23.

Attach the drawer portion of the slides
to the drawer bottoms. Attach the
drawer pulls with the screws provided.

Entertainment Center

This traditional-looking entertainment center is a sophisticated solution for housing your entire entertainment system. At 3 feet wide by 7 feet high, it has plenty of room for a TV, VCR, stereo system, and all of the discs or tapes in your collection.

Depending on your needs and space, you can build the entertainment center alone, or you can create a wall unit by adding the tall bookcase featured on page 133.

Inside the center's traditional exterior is a space designed specifically for storing today's electronic equipment. The shelves are open at the back to vent heat and allow plenty of space for wiring. The doors are mounted with inset hinges, which open a full 180 degrees.

Before the age of plywood, large cases like this were backed with narrow boards. This entertainment center recreates that look simply and inexpensively by using wood-grain paneling for the back. Wood paneling is available in dozens of colors and grain patterns.

The wall unit here is painted with a semi-gloss enamel latex paint, except for the crown molding and shelf edge strips which are made of pine. The pine parts are stained cherry then varnished.

Entertainment Center Materials List

Qty	Part	Dimensions	Qty	Part	Dimensions
Carcase			**Trim (crown & baseboard dimensions for stand-alone entertainment center)**		
1	Plywood top panel	3/4" x 22¾" x 36¼"	1	Front crown molding	3/4" x 2" x 41"
2	Plywood fixed shelf & bottom panel	3/4" x 22¾" x 36¼"	2	Side crown molding	3/4" x 2" x 25¾"
2	Plywood side panels	3/4" x 23" x 86"	1	Front base molding	3/4" x 4" x 38½"
1	Wood-grain paneling back panel	1/4" x 36¼" x 85⅜"	2	Side base molding	3/4" x 4" x 24½"
3	Plywood adjustable shelves	3/4" x 20" x 35¼"	**(Dimensions for three-piece wall unit)**		
2	Shelf edges	3/4" x 3/4" x 35¼"	2	Bookcase front crown molding	3/4" x 1½" x 32"
2	Stiles	3/4" x 2½" x 86"	2	Bookcase side crown molding	3/4" x 1½" x 17"
1	Middle rail	3/4" x 2½" x 32"	1	Cabinet front crown molding	3/4" x 2" x 41"
1	Top rail	3/4" x 3" x 32"	2	Cabinet side crown molding	3/4" x 2" x 10"
1	Bottom rail	3/4" x 5½" x 32"	2	Bookcase front base molding	3/4" x 4" x 30¾"
Doors			2	Bookcase side base molding	3/4" x 4" x 17"
10	Rails	3/4" x 2½" x 11¹⁵⁄₁₆"	1	Cabinet front base molding	3/4" x 4" x 38½"
4	Top-door stiles	3/4" x 2½" x 50¾"	2	Cabinet side base molding	3/4" x 4" x 8¾"
4	Bottom-door stiles	3/4" x 2½" x 24¾"	**Hardware**		
4	Top-door plywood panels	1/4" x 11⅞" x 22⁵⁄₁₆"		4d Finishing nails	
2	Bottom-door plywood panels	1/4" x 11⅞" x 20⁷⁄₁₆"		1¼" Screws	
2	Bottom-door plywood panels	1/4" x 11⅞" x 20⁷⁄₁₆"		7/8" Brads	
			12	Adjustable shelf pins	
			8	Inset hinges	
			4	Knobs	

BUILDING THE CASE

1. Cut the parts. Cut the top and bottom panels, the fixed shelf, the side panels, and the back panel to the dimensions in the Materials List. Rabbet and dado the side panels as shown in *Side Panel Layout.* Note that the drawing shows only one side panel. Don't forget to make the other panel in a mirror image. Drill 1/4-inch holes into the side panels for the shelf pins. See "Installing Shelf Pins," page 22. If you plan to house electronic equipment in your entertainment center, bore a row of 1¹/₂-inch holes in the back of the top panel to provide ventilation.

Cut the three adjustable shelves and their solid-wood edges to the dimensions in the Materials List. Attach the edges to the front of the shelves with glue and 4d finishing nails. (If you want to paint the shelves but not the edges, don't add the edges

until after the bookcase is assembled and painted.)

2. Assemble the carcase. Attach the fixed shelf and bottom panel to the dadoes in the side with glue and 4d finishing nails. Next, attach the top panel to the case with glue and 1¹/₄-inch screws (the crown molding will conceal the screw heads). Install the back panel flush to the top of the cabinet and secure it with glue and 7/8-inch brads. (The space at the bottom is to accommodate uneven floors.) If you plan to house electronic equipment in your entertainment center, drill a 1¹/₂-inch hole for power-strip cord access.

3. Building and installing the face frame. Cut the two stiles and attach them flush with the outside of the carcase, using glue and 4d finishing nails. Cut the three rails to fit and install them so that their top edges are flush with the fixed shelf and the top and bottom panels.

Side Panel Layout

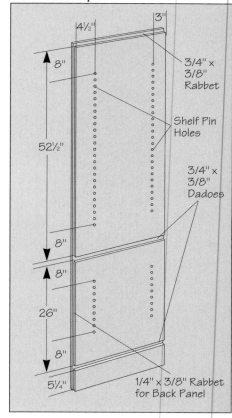

3"
4½"
8"
3/4" x 3/8" Rabbet
Shelf Pin Holes
52½"
3/4" x 3/8" Dadoes
8"
8"
26"
8"
5¼"
1/4" x 3/8" Rabbet for Back Panel

Overall View

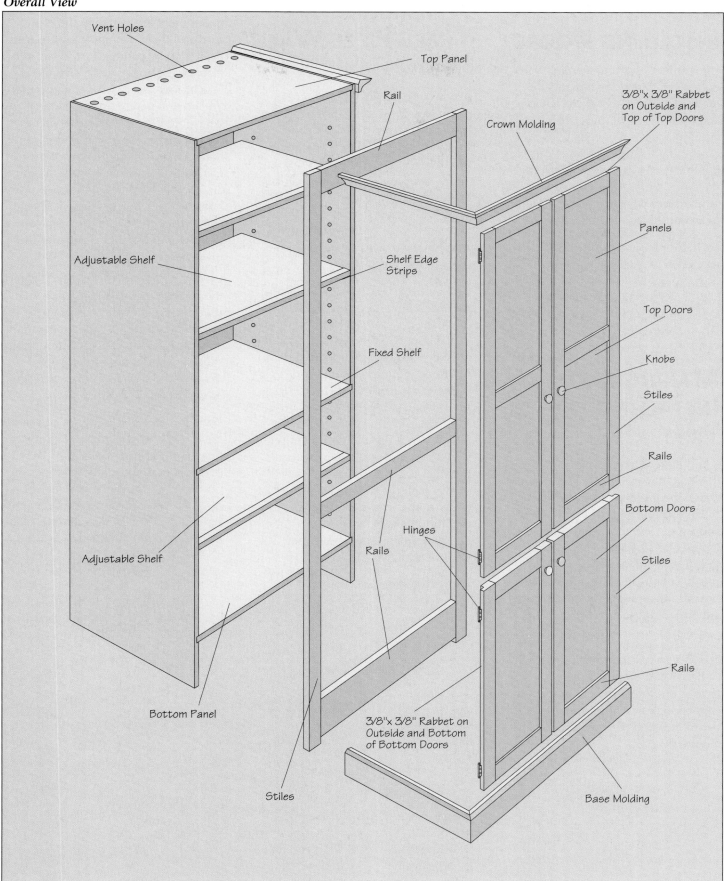

Vent Holes

Top Panel

Rail

3/8"x 3/8" Rabbet on Outside and Top of Top Doors

Crown Molding

Panels

Adjustable Shelf

Shelf Edge Strips

Top Doors

Knobs

Fixed Shelf

Stiles

Rails

Adjustable Shelf

Bottom Doors

Rails

Hinges

Stiles

Bottom Panel

Stiles

Rails

3/8"x 3/8" Rabbet on Outside and Bottom of Bottom Doors

Base Molding

MAKING AND INSTALLING DOORS

This cabinet uses frame-and-panel doors. The panels are flat and are made of 1/4-inch plywood. The top and bottom sets of these doors are virtually identical in construction, except that the top pair has a center rail that serves as a visual break for the larger panel. Don't forget to groove both edges of the center rails to accept the door panels.

Each door has a 3/8-inch x 3/8-inch rabbet on two sides which allows the doors to be inset in the door opening. See "Building a Frame-and-Panel Door," page 16 and "Installing Inset Doors," page 20.

MAKING AND INSTALLING THE TRIM

If you plan to use this cabinet without the matching side bookcases, simply attach the molding with glue and 4d finishing nails when it is still in the shop, and then proceed to finishing. If you'll be adding the bookcases, install the trim after the entertainment center is in place. For information about coping joints and cutting crown moldings, see "Cutting and Installing Crown Molding," page 31.

Feel free to select any style of crown or baseboard molding that you wish to trim out the cabinet. However, it is easy enough to make your own baseboard molding with your router and a decorative bit.

ASSEMBLING THE THREE-PIECE WALL UNIT

Assembling the wall unit entertainment center is slightly different from installing the pieces individually. Installing the crown and baseboard moldings on the entire assembly allows the units to fit against each other and creates a more finished look. The trick is to trim the multi-piece unit in an order so that any gaps will be concealed by the next piece of molding.

1. Position the cabinets. Position the entertainment center in place and check the case for level and plumb just as you would do with a base cabinet. See "Installing Cabinets and Built-ins," page 28. If your floor is uneven, it is possible at this time to insert small shims (no greater than 3/16 inch). Put the bookcases on either side of the entertainment center so that the back edges are flush and the sides touch. Use four 1¼-inch screws to fasten the carcases together. Position the screws directly beneath the middle shelf or top panel of the entertainment center where they will not be readily visible.

Crown Molding Installation

2. Install the trim. The sequence and joinery for installing the base trim and the crown molding are identical. Start by cutting the trim for the front of the bookcases. These pieces butt against the entertainment center and are mitered on their outside edges. Next, cut the two side pieces for the bookcases. Position the front and side pieces of trim so that they fit tightly at the outside corner and attach with glue and 4d finishing nails. (Don't worry if there is a small gap in the butt end of the front trim; that will be covered up with another piece of molding.)

Cut the trim for the front of the entertainment center. To ensure that the molding is cut exactly to size, you may want to cut it a little longer than you need, tack it in place with double stick tape and try to fit matching miters to both ends. Don't install this piece just yet.

The short side pieces for the entertainment center are the trickiest because they have a coped end and a mitered end. Cut each piece a little long, cope one end, put the piece in place and mark the miter cut. Test the front and side pieces to make sure that they fit before attaching both with glue and 4d finishing nails.

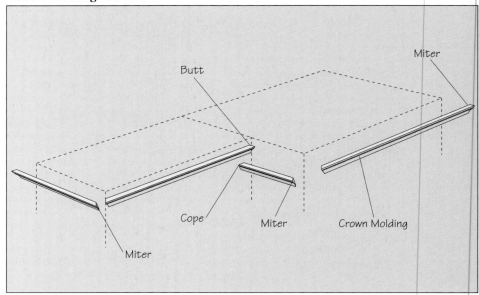

While it can be quite handsome standing alone, this bookcase is designed specifically to flank both sides of the entertainment center on page 129. The dimensions of this case are proportional with those of the entertainment center, and because the construction steps are virtually identical, both units can be built at the same time. Like the entertainment center, the bookcase is made of plywood except for the shelf edge strips, rails and molding. The back panel is made of a sheet of decorative paneling. It is especially important to purchase or mill all of your crown and baseboard molding at one time for all the units, because the entire assembly will be trimmed as one piece to create a finished look.

Tall Bookcase Materials List

Difficulty Level

Qty	Part	Dimensions
1	Plywood top panel	3/4" x 14¾" x 29¼"
1	Plywood bottom	3/4" x 14¾" x 29¼"
2	Plywood side panels	3/4" x 15" x 86"
1	Wood-grain paneling back panel	1/4" x 29¼" x 85⅝"
4	Plywood adjustable shelves	3/4" x 13¾" x 28¼"
3	Edge strips	3/4" x 3/4" x 28¼"
2	Stiles	3/4" x 1½" x 86"
1	Top rail	3/4" x 2" x 27"
1	Bottom rail	3/4" x 5½" x 27"

Qty	Part	Dimensions
Trim (crown & baseboard dimensions for stand-alone bookcase)		
1	Front crown molding	3/4" x 1½" x 34"
2	Side crown molding	3/4" x 1½" x 17¾"
1	Front base molding	3/4" x 4" x 31½"
2	Side base molding	3/4" x 4" x 16½"
Hardware		
	4d Finishing nails	
	1¼" Screws	
	7/8" Brads	
16	Adjustable pins	

Overall View

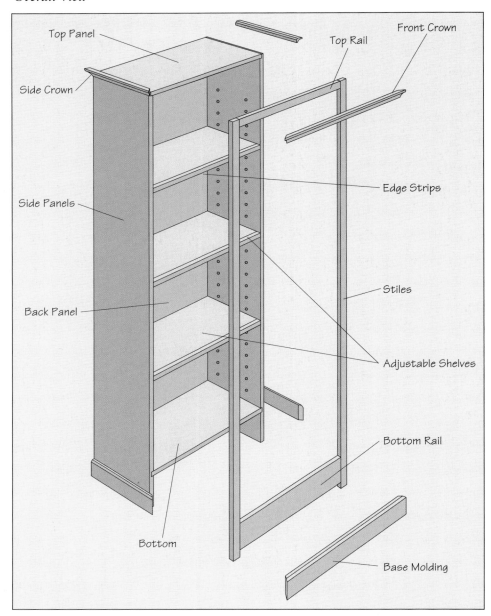

Top Panel

Side Crown

Side Panels

Back Panel

Bottom

Top Rail

Front Crown

Edge Strips

Stiles

Adjustable Shelves

Bottom Rail

Base Molding

1. **Cut the parts.** Cut the top, bottom, side, and back panels to the dimensions in the Materials List. Rabbet and dado the side panels as shown in *Side Panel Layout.* Note that the drawing shows only one side panel. Don't forget to make the other panel in a mirror image. See "Dadoes, Grooves, and Rabbets," page 10. Drill 1/4-inch holes into the side panels for the shelf pins. See "Installing Shelf Pins," page 22.

Cut the four adjustable shelves and their solid wood edges to the dimensions in the Materials List. Attach the

edging to the shelves with glue and 4d finishing nails. (If you want to paint the shelves but not the edging, don't add the edging until after the bookcase is assembled and painted.)

2. **Assemble the carcase.** Glue the top and bottom to the side pieces. Attach the top with 1¼-inch screws. (The crown molding conceals the screw heads). Attach the bottom with 4d nails. Install the back panel flush to the top of the cabinet and secure it with glue and 7/8-inch brads. (The space at the bottom is to accommodate uneven floors.)

3. **Building and installing the face frame.** Cut the two stiles and attach them to the carcase with 4d finishing nails. Cut the top and bottom rails to fit and install them so that their top edges are flush with the top panel and bottom shelf, respectively.

4. **Installing the trim.** If you are planning to build the bookcase to stand alone, cut the crown and baseboard moldings to the dimensions in the Materials List and attach with glue and 4d finishing nails. Installing the trim on the wall-unit entertainment center is a little different. See "Assembling the Three-Piece Wall Unit," page 132.

Side Panel Layout

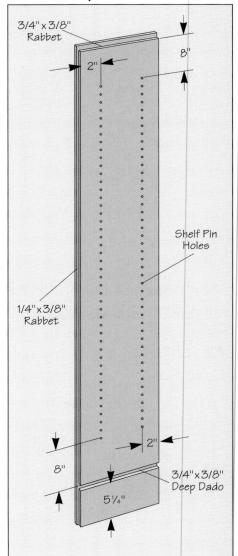

3/4" x 3/8" Rabbet

8"

2"

1/4" x 3/8" Rabbet

Shelf Pin Holes

2"

8"

3/4" x 3/8" Deep Dado

5¼"

for the Living Room...
Short Bookcase

Here's a lovely classical bookcase that you can assemble in less than a day. Although its construction is simple, this bookcase will impress you with its pleasant proportions and its versatility. Its compact size and adjustable shelves serve well in a bedroom, family room, den or study, to display books or showcase your favorite momentos.

The cove and baseboard moldings give the piece a formal appearance, reminiscent of larger, built-in cabinets. The appearance is further enhanced by the solid-wood top with a quarter-round edge detail. If you choose, you can make the side panels of hardwood plywood to match the solid-wood top. Or you can emphasize the solid-wood top by painting the case.

Short Bookcase Materials List

Difficulty Level 🔨🔨

Qty	Part	Dimensions	Qty	Part	Dimensions
Carcase			1	Front cove molding	3/4" x 7/8" x 37½"
2	Plywood side panels	3/4" x 11¼" x 48"	2	Side cove molding	3/4" x 7/8" x 12¾"
2	Plywood top/bottom panels	3/4" x 11" x 35¼"	**Shelves**		
1	Plywood back	1/4" x 35¼" x 48"	2	Plywood shelves	3/4" x 10½" x 34¼"
Face frame			2	Half-round shelf edge	3/8" x 3/4" x 34¼"
2	Solid-wood stiles	3/4" x 1½" x 48"	**Hardware**		
2	Solid-wood rails	3/4" x 3½" x 33"		4d Finishing nails	
Top & Molding				#6 x 1¼" Flathead wood screws	
1	Solid-wood top	3/4" x 13½" x 39"		1" Brads	
1	Front base molding	3/4" x 2½" x 37½"	4	48" Metal shelf standards	
2	Side base molding	3/4" x 2½" x 12¾"	8	Metal shelf supports	

Overall View

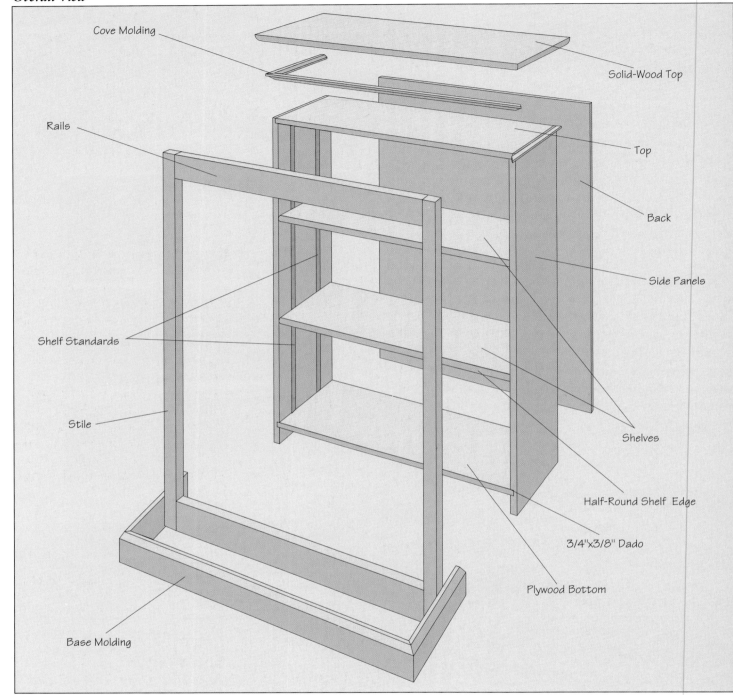

Cove Molding

Solid-Wood Top

Rails

Top

Back

Side Panels

Shelf Standards

Shelves

Stile

Half-Round Shelf Edge

3/4"x3/8" Dado

Plywood Bottom

Base Molding

BUILDING THE CASE

1. **Cut the parts.** Cut the side panels, top and bottom from 3/4-inch plywood and the back from 1/4-inch plywood to the dimensions in the Materials List.

2. **Cut rabbets and dadoes.** Rabbet and dado the side panels as shown in *Side Panel Layout*. Note that the drawing shows only one panel. Don't forget to make the other panel as a mirror image. See "Dadoes, Grooves, and Rabbets," page 10.

3. **Assemble the carcase.** Assemble the top and bottom to the side panels

with glue and 4d finishing nails. Install the back panel with glue and 4d finishing nails.

4. **Make and attach the face frame.** Cut the two stiles and the rails to the dimensions in the Materials List. Attach the rails and stiles to the carcase with glue and 4d finishing nails.

Side Panel Layout

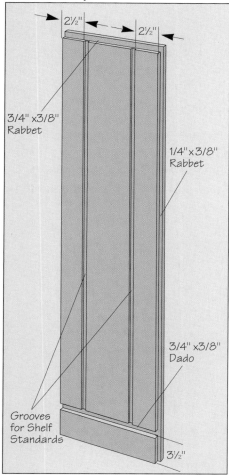

- 2½"
- 2½"
- 3/4" x3/8" Rabbet
- 1/4" x 3/8" Rabbet
- 3/4" x3/8" Dado
- Grooves for Shelf Standards
- 3½"

MAKING THE SOLID-WOOD TOP

1. **Edge-glue the boards.** Make the top by edge-gluing several boards and then cutting the solid-wood panel to the final dimensions. See "Edge-Gluing Stock," page 8.

2. **Lay out the top.** After sanding the solid-wood top to 220-grit, decide which surface will be the bottom. Then mark layout lines on the bottom to indicate how the solid-wood top will be positioned on the case. The top should overhang the case by 1½ inches at the front and sides. The top and case should be flush at back.

3. **Roundover the edge.** Fit a router with a 1/2-inch roundover bit. Shape the bottom edges of the front and two sides of the solid-wood top, making

several progressively deeper passes until the three bottom edges are rounded over 1/2 inch. Turn over the workpiece, then round the front and side edges with sandpaper.

INSTALLING THE TOP AND MOLDING

1. **Cut and install the baseboard molding.** Cut the front piece of base molding to its finished length, mitered at each end. Glue and nail it along the front edge. Use 4d finishing nails. Miter cut one end of each side piece of base molding to rough length. Set each side piece in place, mark the rear of each, cut it to finished length, and install it with glue and 4d finishing nails.

2. **Install the top.** Turn the top upside down and position the case upside down on the top. At each corner, predrill for 1¼-inch flathead wood screws into the top piece. Remove the top. Make the holes in the case oblong by inserting the drill in the holes and rocking from the front of the case to the back. (This will allow the solid wood top to expand and contract with humidity changes.)

Then counterbore the holes. Replace the top and screw it in place.

3. **Cut and install the cove molding.** Cut the front piece of cove molding to rough length, mitered at one end. Test its fit beneath the overhanging top, mark the squared end, miter cut it to finished length, and install it with 4d finishing nails. Test fit and install the side pieces as you did the base molding.

MAKING THE SHELVES

1. **Cut the shelves.** Cut the shelves to the dimensions in the Materials List. Cut two pieces of half-round molding to the length of the shelves. Attach the molding to the shelves with glue and 1-inch brads.

2. **Install the shelves.** Use a hacksaw to cut the shelf standards to fit between the top and bottom panels, and install the standards inside the grooves in the bookcase sides, using the screws or nails provided or recommended. Install each shelf with four metal shelf supports. See "Installing Metal Standards," page 21.

Installing Molding

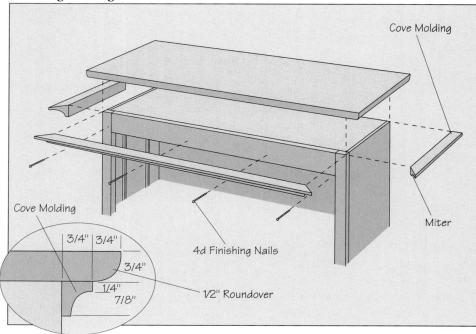

- Cove Molding
- Cove Molding
- 3/4" 3/4"
- 3/4"
- 1/4"
- 7/8"
- 4d Finishing Nails
- 1/2" Roundover
- Miter

Fold-Down Desk

I f you need a desk for occasional paperwork, or workbench for building models, tying flies, matting and framing pictures, making candles, wrapping gifts, or any of several dozen handicrafts, consider this practical project. This desk is easy to build, is attached to a wall, and folds up when not in use. For security, you can substitute a hasp and padlock for the hook and eye.

The plans call for six drawers, but they're optional. Make as many as you want to suit your purposes, or you can omit them altogether. Because the drawers require no mounting hardware, you can also build the unit and add drawers later, as needs dictate.

Fold-Down Desk Materials List

Difficulty Level

Qty	Part	Dimensions
Cabinet		
2	Plywood side panels	3/4" x 11¼" x 20¼"
2	Plywood top/bottom panels	3/4" x 11¼" x 46"
3	Plywood main partitions	3/4" x 11" x 19½"
1	Plywood back panel	1/4" x 19½" x 46"
4	Nailing cleats	3/4" x 3" x 10³⁄₁₆"
12	Plywood shelves	1/4" x 11¼" x 11"
6	Plywood envelope partitions	1/4" x 7¾" x 11"
5	Solid-wood edging	1/4" x 3/4" x 18¾"
2	Solid-wood edging	1/4" x 3/4" x 46¾"
Desktop and legs		
1	Plywood desktop	3/4" x 19¾" x 46¼"
2	Solid-wood legs	1½" x 1½" x 29¼"
1	Solid-wood leg rail	3/4" x 3½" x 40¾"
2	Solid-wood edging	1/4" x 3/4" x 46¾"
2	Solid-wood edging	1/4" x 3/4" x 20¼"

Qty	Part	Dimensions
Drawers		
6	Solid-wood front panels	3/4" x 3⁷⁄₁₆" x 10⅝"
6	Solid-wood rear panels	3/4" x 2¹⁵⁄₁₆" x 9⅞"
8	Solid-wood side panels	3/4" x 3⁷⁄₁₆" x 10⅞"
4	Solid-wood side panels	3/4" x 3⁷⁄₁₆" x 10⅛"
4	Plywood bottom panels	1/4" x 9⅞" x 10⅞"
2	Plywood bottom panels	1/4" x 9⅞" x 10⅛"
Hardware		
	7/8" Brads	
	#6 x 3/4" Flathead wood screws	
	#10 x 3½" Wood screws	
	1/2" Brads	
	1" Brads	
4	1/4" x 1¼" Wood dowels	
1	Hook-and-screw-eye set	
2	48" Piano (continuous) hinges	
	#6 x 5/8" Flathead wood screws	
2	Locking leg braces	

Cabinet Overall View

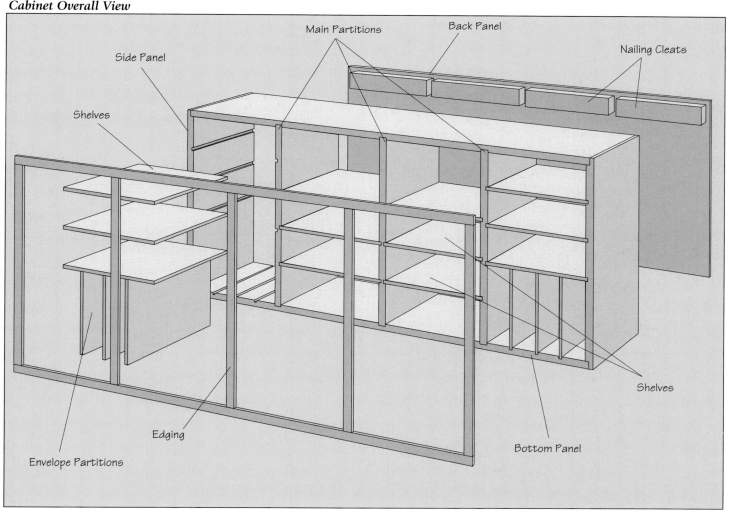

Side Panel

Main Partitions

Back Panel

Nailing Cleats

Shelves

Envelope Partitions

Edging

Bottom Panel

Shelves

BUILDING THE CABINET

1. Cut the cabinet parts. Cut the side panels, top, bottom, three main partitions, and the back panel to the dimensions in the Materials List.

2. Rabbet and dado the parts. Rabbet and dado the top and bottom panels as shown in *Top and Bottom Panel Joinery*. Rabbet and dado the side panels as shown in *Side Panel Joinery*. Note that the drawing shows one side panel; be sure to make the other side panel in a mirror image. Dado the main partitions as shown in *Main Partition Joinery*. Note that both faces of the center partition have the same dado layout, but the other partitions have different dado layouts on each face. See "Dadoes, Grooves, and Rabbets," page 10.

3. Assemble the cabinet. Glue and clamp the main partitions to the top and bottom panels. Install the back with glue and 7/8-inch brads. Cut the nailing cleats to fit and attach them to the back with glue and 3/4-inch wood screws in counter-bored holes in the back.

4. Install the cabinet. Use a stud finder to locate the studs in the wall where the unit will hang. Scribe a

Top and Bottom Panel Joinery

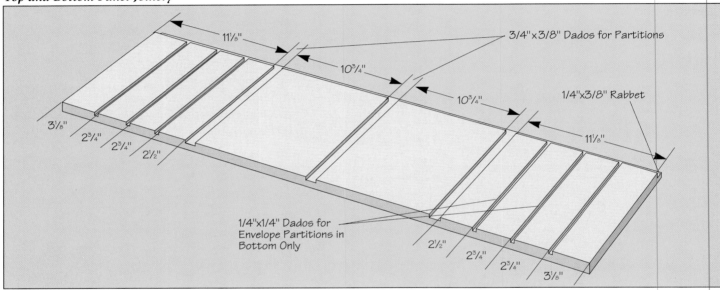

Side Panel Joinery

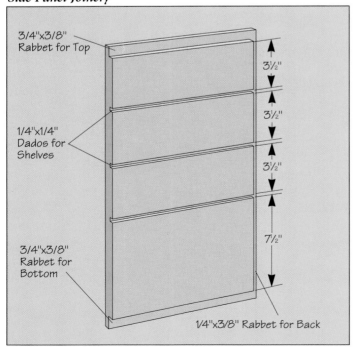

Main Partition Joinery

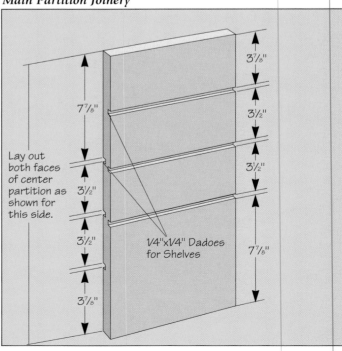

level line 30 inches from the floor. You'll need a helper or two and perhaps one or two temporary 2x4 braces cut to 30 inches to align the bottom edge of the unit to the line. Attach the unit to the wall by driving #10x3½-inch wood screws through counterbored holes in the nailing cleats and into each stud. (See "Installing Wall Cabinets," page 30.)

INSTALLING SHELVES, PARTITIONS, AND MOLDING

1. **Cut the shelves and partitions.** Cut the shelves and envelope partitions to the dimensions in the Materials List.

2. **Install the shelves and partitions.** Glue the six envelope partitions into the dadoes in the bottom panel, as shown in *Cabinet Overall View*. Glue the two shelves that go over the envelope partitions into their dadoes in the main partitions and side panels. Make sure the envelope partitions are aligned, then

Desktop and Leg Construction

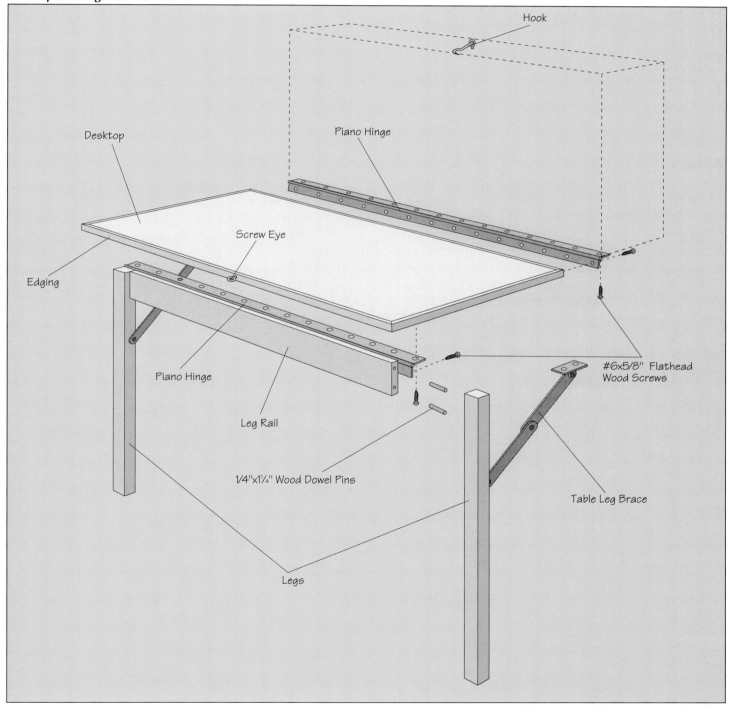

secure them with 1/2-inch brads driven through the two shelves. Glue the remaining shelves in place.

3. Cut and attach the edging. Cut edging to fit the front edges of the top and bottom panels, and attach it with glue and 1-inch brads. Cut five pieces to fit the vertical edges, and attach them the same way.

BUILDING AND INSTALLING THE DESKTOP AND LEGS

1. Cut the parts. Cut the desktop, legs, and leg rail to the dimensions in the Materials List. Use clear stock for the legs and rail.

2. Cut and attach the edging. Cut pieces of solid-wood edging with 45-degree miters at each end to fit the edges of the desktop. Then attach the edging with glue and 1-inch brads.

3. Join the legs to the rail. Join the legs to the rail with glue and dowels, making the rail flush to the back of the legs. Make sure the legs remain parallel when you clamp them to the rail. If necessary, add a temporary spacer at the bottoms of the legs and affix another clamp. Let stand until the glue sets. See "Reinforcing Joints with Dowels" page 9.

4. Attach the hook and eye. Install the screw eye in the center of the front edge of the desktop. Attach the hook in a corresponding spot on the top surface of the cabinet.

5. Cut and attach the piano hinges. Use a hacksaw to cut one piano hinge at 46³/₄ inches and the other at 43³/₄ inches. Attach the longer hinge to the rear edge of the desktop with seven #6x5/8-inch flathead wood screws and to the underside of the cabinet with seven more screws. Attach the shorter hinge to the underside of the desktop 3 inches from the front edge and centered from side to

side. Then attach the hinge to the leg assembly.

6. Attach the leg braces. Following the manufacturer's directions and using the screws provided, attach a locking leg brace to the left side of the left leg and right side of the right leg. Then attach the braces to the underside of the desktop.

BUILDING THE DRAWERS

1. Cut the parts. Cut the front, rear, and side pieces and the bottom panels to the dimensions in the Materials List. Use clear stock for the front pieces. Note that four of the side pieces and two of the bottom pieces are shorter to allow room for the nailing cleats.

2. Cut and sand the finger notches. Set a compass for a 3/4-inch radius, and scribe a circle on a piece of cardboard. Cut out the circle, and cut it in half. Use this template to scribe a semicircle at the top center of each

drawer front. Then cut out the notches with a saber saw and smooth them with a drum sander or by hand.

3. Rabbet and groove the parts. Cut rabbets and grooves in the front and side pieces as shown in *Drawer Construction*.

4. Assemble the drawers. Apply glue to the rabbets in the front and side panels. Then attach the front and rear panels to the side panels with 4d finishing nails, keeping the top edges flush. Slide the bottom panels in place, and secure with three 1-inch brads driven up into each rear panel.

5. Sand and fit the drawers. Slip the two short drawers in the top-corner openings and the long drawers in the openings beneath the top corners. The drawers have been designed to have 1/16 inch gaps all around; however, if a drawer fits too tightly, adjust the sides and top edges with either sandpaper or a plane until the drawer fits and slides smoothly. Rub the bottom edges with a little paraffin (a candle works well) to help the drawer slide more smoothly.

Drawer Construction

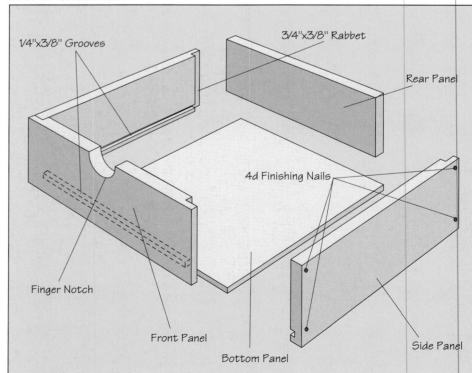

1/4"x3/8" Grooves

3/4"x3/8" Rabbet

Rear Panel

4d Finishing Nails

Finger Notch

Front Panel

Bottom Panel

Side Panel

Computer Center

Today, with more than 34 million Americans working at home, personal computers have become a necessity. Equally essential is a convenient workstation to house the computer, printer, monitor, and other peripherals, as well as software, manuals, computer paper, diskettes, and supplies.

This large, roomy unit is a comfortable computer center that keeps everything within easy reach. What's more, this project is designed to be customized to accommodate your own personal setup. Included are two different shelving units that can be used to elevate your monitor to eye level, or to store manuals, or the shelves can be omitted entirely if you are more interested in desk space. The instructions for building these shelves follow the instructions for constructing the desk.

The plans call for a paper slot to be cut in the desktop, which is designed to accommodate printers that use continuous-feed paper. If you have a laser or other type of printer that requires single sheets, you needn't cut the slot.

Make the desk from a hardwood plywood such as cherry, oak, or walnut. Use a matching or contrasting solid wood for the edging.

Computer Center Materials List

Qty	Part	Dimensions	Qty	Part	Dimensions
Desk			2	Solid-wood edging	1/4" x 3/4" x 14"
1	Plywood desktop	3/4" x 29¾" x 75"	1	Solid-wood edging	1/4" x 3/4" x 22½"
2	Solid-wood cleats	3/4" x 3/4" x 23¾"	2	Solid-wood edging	1/4" x 3/4" x 7¼"
2	Solid-wood cleats	3/4" x 3/4" x 23"	**Shelf Unit**		
1	Plywood batting strip	3/4" x 6" x 75"	1	Plywood top panel	3/4" x 13¼" x 23¼"
4	Plywood cabinet panels	3/4" x 23¾" x 25¾"	2	Plywood side panels	3/4" x 14" x 27¾"
2	Plywood fixed shelves	3/4" x 23¾" x 21¼"	1	Plywood middle shelf	3/4" x 14" x 23¼"
2	Plywood adj. shelves	3/4" x 23" x 20¼"	2	Plywood back support	3/4" x 3" x 23¼"
1	Plywood back support	3/4" x 11¼" x 72¾"	2	Solid-wood edging	1/4" x 3/4" x 14"
1	Solid-wood desk edging	3/4" x 1½" x 76½"	3	Solid-wood edging	1/4" x 3/4" x 22½"
2	Solid-wood desk edging	3/4" x 1½" x 30½"	2	Solid-wood edging	1/4" x 3/4" x 28"
4	Solid-wood cabinet edging	1/4" x 3/4" x 25"	**Hardware**		
2	Solid-wood shelf edging	1/4" x 3/4" x 20½"	1	Paper slot grommet, to fit	
2	Solid-wood shelf edging	1/4" x 3/4" x 20¼"		#6 x 1¼" Wood screws	
				4d Finishing nails	
Monitor Stand				6d Finishing nails	
1	Plywood top panel	3/4" x 14" x 23¼"		1" Brads	
2	Plywood side panels	3/4" x 14" x 7"	8	Adjustable shelf pins	
2	Plywood diagonal supports	3/4" x 3" x 4¼"		1" Flathead wood screws	

BUILDING THE DESK

1. Make the desktop. Cut the top, the cleats, and the batting strip to the dimensions in the Materials List. Use a 1-inch drill and saber saw or a router and 1-inch straight bit to cut a paper slot in the right side of the top as shown in the *Overall View*. See "Dadoes, Grooves, and Rabbets," page 10. Depending on the width of the paper you use, make the slot either 12½ or 16¾ inches long. Plastic grommets are available to conceal the plywood edges and prevent paper snags.

Predrill holes for 1¼-inch wood screws, then glue and screw the outer cleats and the batting strip flush to the front and side edges of the bottom of the desktop as shown in *Desktop Construction*. Glue and screw the middle cleats in place making sure they are square to the batting strip.

2. Cut, dado, rabbet, and notch the cabinet panels. Cut the cabinet panels to the dimensions in the

Materials List. Dado each panel for the fixed shelves as shown in *Desktop Construction*. Starting at the top back corners of the two end panels, cut an 11¼-inch-long stopped rabbet as shown. Square the stopped end of the rabbet with a 3/4-inch chisel. At the top back corners of the other two panels, draw an 11¼-inch-long line 3/4 inch from the back edge as shown. Cut along the line with a saber saw and then across, to make a notch that will house the back support.

3. Drill shelf pin holes. Drill shelf pin holes on 1½-inch centers in the cabinet panels, positioning the holes as shown in *Desktop Construction*. See "Installing Shelf Pins," page 22.

4. Cut the shelves and back support. Cut the fixed and adjustable shelves and the back support piece to the dimensions in the Materials List.

5. Assemble the carcase. Glue and screw the the rabbetted panels to the outer cleats and the notched panels to the center cleats as shown in *Desk-*

top Construction. Use countersunk #6x1¼-inch wood screws to make these connections. Then glue and screw the back support to the notches. Secure the back support in the rabbets with glue and 4d finishing nails.

Attach the fixed shelves in their dadoes with glue and 4d finishing nails.

6. Roundover, cut, and install the desk edging. Cut stock for the desk edging to the thickness and width in the Materials List. Round the front edges of the stock with a 3/8-inch-radius roundover bit in a router. Cut three pieces to fit around the desktop with miters at the corners. If the edging is hardwood, predrill it for 6d finishing nails. Glue and nail the edging to the desktop.

7. Cut and attach the cabinet edging. Cut cabinet edging stock to the thickness and width in the Materials List. If you will be making the monitor stand and shelf unit, mill enough stock for those projects at the same time. Cut the edging to length to fit the front edges of the cabinet panels and attach it with

Overall View

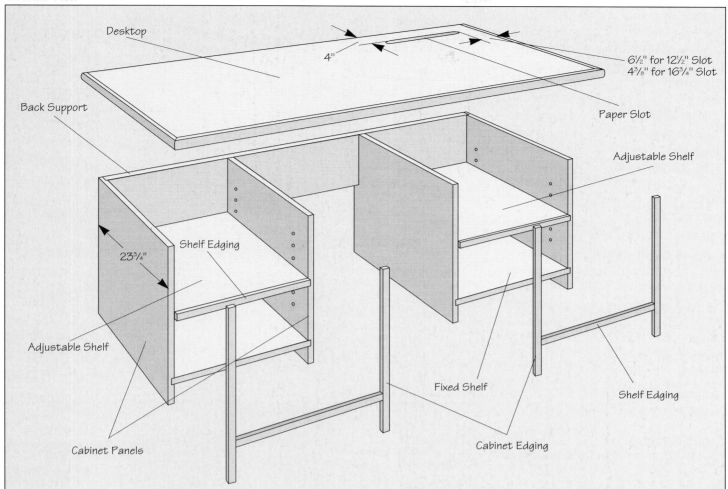

Desktop

4"

6½" for 12½" Slot
4⅜" for 16¾" Slot

Paper Slot

Back Support

Adjustable Shelf

23¾"

Shelf Edging

Adjustable Shelf

Cabinet Panels

Fixed Shelf

Shelf Edging

Cabinet Edging

glue and 1-inch brads. Likewise, cut and install the fixed-shelf edging. Again, in hardwood, you'll have to predrill for the brads. Cut strips to fit the front edges of the adjustable shelves. Attach the edging with glue and 1-inch brads. Sand edging to smooth it and round over the edges slightly.

8. **Install the shelves.** Install the shelf pins and adjustable shelves after applying finish to the desk.

BUILDING THE MONITOR STAND

1. **Cut and assemble the unit.** Cut the top and side panels to the dimensions in the Materials List. Dado the side panels as shown in *Monitor Stand Construction*. Assemble the panels with glue and 4d finishing nails.

Desktop Construction

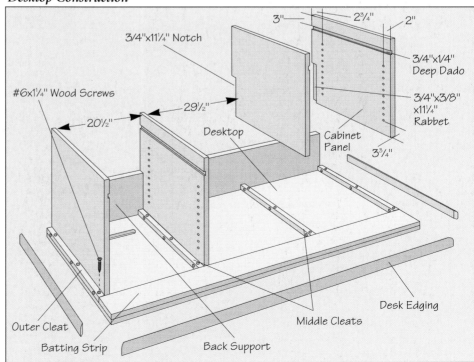

3"   2¾"   2"

3/4"x11¼" Notch

3/4"x1/4" Deep Dado

3/4"x3/8" x11¼" Rabbet

#6x1¼" Wood Screws

20½"

29½"

Desktop

Cabinet Panel

3¾"

Desk Edging

Outer Cleat

Batting Strip

Middle Cleats

Back Support

2. Cut and install the diagonal supports. Cut a scrap of plywood into a 3x3-inch square. Then use a miter box to cut the square diagonally into two right triangles. Position these diagonal supports in the back corners under the top panel. Drill two pilot holes in each block, one into the top panel and one into the side panel, then counterbore the holes. Apply glue to the sides of the supports and screw them in place with 1-inch flathead wood screws.

3. Cut and install the edging. Cut 1/4-inch-thick edging into lengths to cover the front and top plywood edges. Attach the top pieces first with glue and 1-inch brads, and then apply edging to the front of the side panels. Finish by edging the front of the top panel. Predrill in hardwood. Sand the edging to smooth it and to round the edges slightly.

BUILDING THE SHELF UNIT

1. Cut the parts. Cut the top, sides, shelf, and back supports to the dimensions in the Materials List. Rabbet and dado the side pieces as shown in *Shelf Unit Construction*. Square the ends of the stopped rabbets with a 3/4-inch chisel.

2. Assemble the shelf. Attach the back supports in the rabbets in the side panels with glue and 4d finishing nails. Attach the shelves in their dadoes with glue and 4d finishing nails.

3. Cut and install the edging. Cut 1/4-inch-thick edging to fit the front edges of the side panels and attach it with glue and 1-inch brads. Cut edging to fit the tops of the side panels and attach with glue and 1-inch brads. Cut edging to fit the top of the back support and the fronts of the shelves. Attach with glue and 1-inch brads. Predrill in hardwood. Sand the edging to smooth it and to round the edges slightly.

Monitor Stand Construction

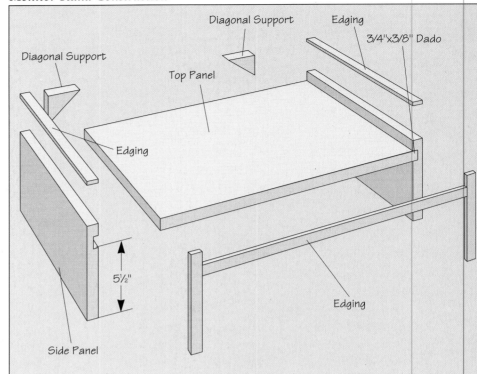

Shelf Unit Construction

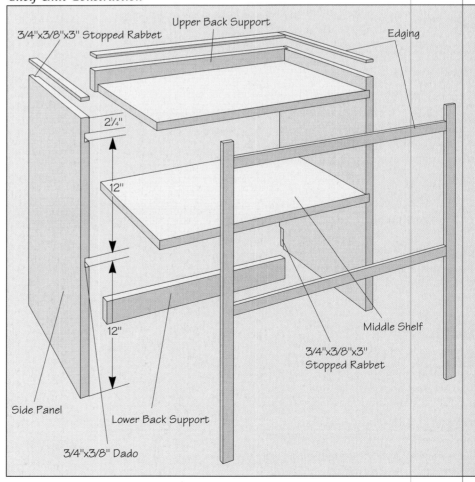

for the Utility Room...
Utility Shelving

Utility shelving is a quick and simple solution to storage problems. It requires only inexpensive materials and basic tools and techniques. You can fill a wall with shelves in one easy evening.

The utility room is an obvious place to install utility shelving, but don't overlook other parts of the house where clutter tends to accumulate and where wall space is available. These shelves will also serve well in a basement, pantry, garage, or utility shed.

The accompanying plans, though specific, can also serve as general guidelines for other shelving jobs. They call for 3/4-inch particleboard shelves, because this is the least expensive shelving material, usually available in lengths from 6 to 12 feet and widths from 10 to 15 inches. Nominal 1x10 and 1x12 boards are also good, as is 3/4-inch plywood. Whichever material you choose, be sure to support the shelves at least every 36 inches to prevent them from sagging.

In most rooms, you'll attach the cleats with #10x3½-inch wood screws, driven into the studs. For masonry walls, use #10x2-inch screws and plastic wall anchors.

Utility Shelving Materials List

Difficulty Level

Qty	Part	Dimensions	Part
10	Solid-wood shelf cleats & ribs	3/4" x 1½" x 72"	**Hardware**
3	Solid-wood shelf supports	3/4" x 1½" x 80"	#10 x 3½" Wood screws
5	Particleboard shelves	3/4" x 12" x 72"	#10 x 2" Screws (if attaching to a masonry wall)
1	Solid-wood temporary brace	1½" x 3½" x 15¼"	Plastic wall anchors (if attaching to a masonry wall)
			4d Finishing nails
			1¼" Drywall screws

Overall View

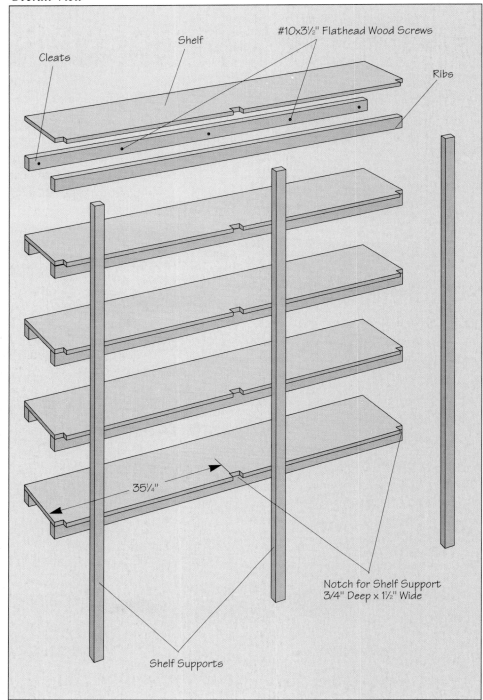

Cleats

Shelf

#10x3½" Flathead Wood Screws

Ribs

35¼"

Notch for Shelf Support
3/4" Deep x 1½" Wide

Shelf Supports

INSTALLING THE CLEATS

1. **Scribe level lines.** Measure 15¼ inches up the wall from the floor, and scribe the first 72-inch-long level line. Then scribe four more, each 16 inches above the previous one.

2. **Mark the studs.** Using a stud finder, locate the studs that will be located behind the shelf. Drop plumb lines to indicate where the studs intersect each of the shelf lines.

3. **Cut the cleats.** Cut five cleats and five ribs to the dimensions in the Materials List.

4. **Mark, drill, and install the cleats.** Align each cleat immediately beneath a level line and attach it with one 3½-inch wood screw driven into the middle stud. Next mark where the other four studs cross the cleat and predrill and attach with screws at each location. Secure the other four cleats in the same manner.

INSTALLING THE SHELVES

1. **Cut the parts.** Cut three vertical shelf supports to the dimensions in the Materials List. Cut the shelves to length. Cut a 15¾-inch temporary brace from a scrap of 2x4.

2. **Notch the shelves and install the ribs.** Use a saber saw to cut a notch in the center of the front edge of each shelf as shown in the *Overall View*. Cut another notch at each front corner. Fasten the ribs flush to the back of the notches with glue and 4d finishing nails driven through the top of the shelves.

3. **Install the shelves.** Lay a shelf on the bottom cleat in place atop a cleat, and prop it by placing the temporary brace behind the rib at the center notch. Check that the shelf is level from back to front. Put the center vertical support in place and screw it to the rib with a 1¼-inch drywall screw. Move the prop to behind one side notch. Check the shelf for level along its length and from front to back. Attach a side vertical support. Repeat for the other side. Then, repeat the process for all the shelves, supporting the brace on the shelf below.

for the Utility Room...
Sewing Center

S ewing is an enjoyable, creative, and money- saving pastime in many households; it's essential maintenance in most others.

This cabinet will store and organize all of your sewing tools and supplies. Best of all, setting up the sewing machine requires no more effort than opening a cabinet door and folding down a handy platform where your machine can be permanently installed.

In addition to spacious storage areas behind top and bottom cabinet doors, to the right of the handy sewing machine compartment is a convenient space divided by shelves. You can build flush-fitting drawers for this section. See "Building Drawers," page 23. Or buy plastic utility boxes that will stack on the shelves.

The fold-down platform provides a work surface where you can set up the machine whenever you need it, or you can permanently install the machine in the platform by following directions in your owner's manual. When the platform is in its folded-up position, the 15 inches of depth remaining behind it should accommodate most sewing machines. Nevertheless, measure the height of your machine, and make the cabinet deeper if you need to.

You can make this cabinet out of good quality softwood plywood and then paint it.

For classier appearance, make the cabinet of hardwood plywood and apply a clear finish. If you use hardwood, and you like the slab doors shown here, cut all six doors from the same panel, then install them in the same position that they were in the panel. This will give you a continuous-grain pattern on the front of the cabinet.

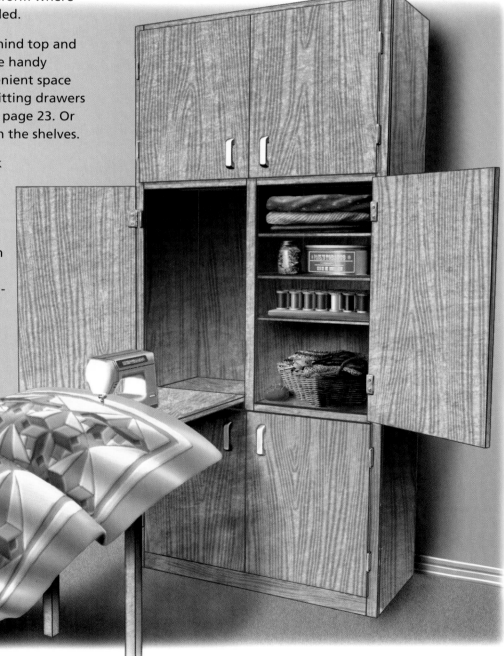

Sewing Center Materials List

Difficulty Level

Qty	Part	Dimensions
Cabinet		
1	Plywood top panel	3/4" x 17¼" x 37¼"
2	Plywood side panels	3/4" x 17¼" x 84"
3	Plywood horizontal panels	3/4" x 17" x 37¼"
1	Plywood upper partition	3/4" x 17" x 32"
1	Plywood lower partition	3/4" x 17" x 23⅞"
3	Plywood shelves	1/2" x 17" x 18⅝"
1	Plywood back panel	1/4" x 37¼" x 83⅝"
Face frame		
2	Solid-wood stiles	3/4" x 1½" x 84"
1	Solid-wood center stile	3/4" x 1½" x 79"
1	Solid-wood top rail	3/4" x 1½" x 35"
1	Solid-wood bottom rail	3/4" x 3½" x 35"
4	Solid-wood short rails	3/4" x 1½" x 16¾"
Leg assembly & fold-down platform		
2	Solid-wood legs	1½" x 1½" x 28"
1	Solid-wood leg rail	3/4" x 3½" x 11"
1	Plywood platform	3/4" x 16" x 30"

Qty	Part	Dimensions
1	Platform edging	1/4" x 3/4" x 16½"
2	Platform edging	1/4" x 3/4" x 30¼"
2	Stop block pieces	3/4" x 2" x 8"
Overlay-style doors		
4	Top and bottom doors	3/4" x 17½" x 23⅜"
2	Center doors	3/4" x 17½" x 31½"
Hardware		
	4d Finishing nails	
	7/8" Brads	
32	1/4" x 1¼" Wooden dowels	
	1" Finishing nails	
1	11" Piano (continuous) hinge	
	#6 x 5/8" Flathead wood screws	
2	Locking, folding leg braces	
	#8 x 1¼" Flathead wood screws	
6	Door pulls	
6 pairs	Overlay hinges	
1	14" Piano (continuous) hinge	
2	Bullet catches	

BUILDING THE CABINET

1. Cut the parts. Cut the top, sides, horizontal panels, partitions, shelves, and back to the dimensions in the Materials List.

2. Cut the dadoes and rabbets. Rabbet and dado the side panels and upper partition as shown in *Cabinet Joinery.* Note that the dadoes for the shelves are 1/2 inch wide. See "Dadoes, Grooves, and Rabbets," page 10.

3. Assemble the cabinet. Assemble the top and bottom panels and the shelves to the dadoes in the side panels with glue and 4d finishing nails.

4. Install the back. Attach the back in the rabbets in the sides with glue and 7/8-inch brads.

5. Install the face frame. Cut the stiles and the top and bottom rails to the dimensions in the Materials List. Join the center stile to the top and bottom rails with two 1/4-inch wood

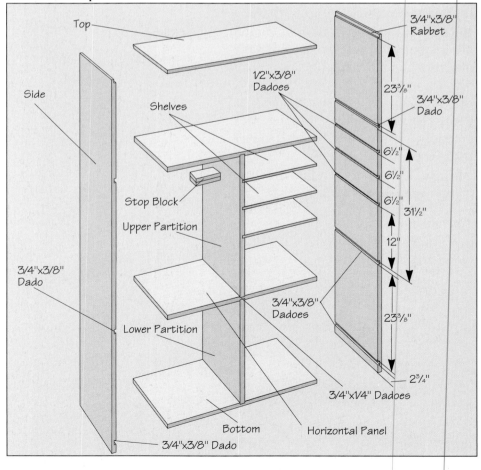

Cabinet Joinery

Top

Side

Shelves

1/2"x3/8" Dadoes

Stop Block

Upper Partition

Lower Partition

3/4"x3/8" Dado

Bottom

3/4"x3/8" Dado

Horizontal Panel

3/4"x1/4" Dadoes

3/4"x3/8" Dadoes

3/4"x3/8" Rabbet

23⅜"

3/4"x3/8" Dado

6½"

6½"

6½"

31½"

12"

23⅜"

2¾"

Overall View

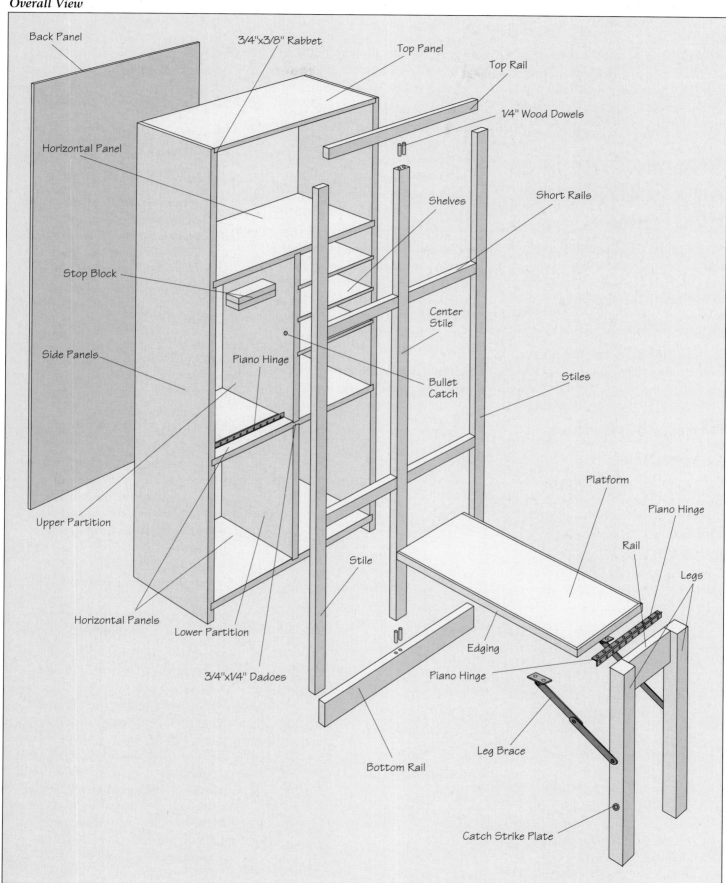

Back Panel

3/4"x3/8" Rabbet

Top Panel

Top Rail

1/4" Wood Dowels

Horizontal Panel

Stop Block

Shelves

Short Rails

Center Stile

Side Panels

Piano Hinge

Bullet Catch

Stiles

Platform

Piano Hinge

Rail

Legs

Upper Partition

Horizontal Panels

Lower Partition

Stile

Edging

Piano Hinge

3/4"x1/4" Dadoes

Leg Brace

Bottom Rail

Catch Strike Plate

dowels in each joint as shown in *Overall View.* See "Reinforcing Joints with Dowels," page 9. Attach this assembly to the cabinet with glue and 4d finishing nails. Then install the outer stiles with glue and nails. Cut the short rails to fit before installing them with glue and nails.

BUILDING THE LEGS AND FOLD-DOWN PLATFORM

1. **Build the leg assembly.** Cut the legs and leg rail to the dimensions in the Materials List. Join the rail flush to the back of the legs with glue and two dowels at each joint as shown in *Platform and Leg Construction.*

2. **Make the platform.** Cut the platform to the dimensions in the Materials List. Cut platform edging to the dimensions in the Materials List. If

you are making slab plywood doors, you may want to cut door edging at the same time. Miter-cut the edging to fit around the front and sides of the platform. Attach the edging with glue and 1-inch finishing nails.

3. **Attach the leg assembly.** Use a hacksaw to trim a piano hinge to 11 inches, and attach the hinge to the top inside of the leg rail with three #6x5/8-inch flathead wood screws. Then attach the hinge to the underside of the platform, centered 2¼ inches from the front edge.

4. **Install the leg braces.** With the platform upside down and legs fully extended, follow the manufacturer's directions to attach a locking leg brace to the outside of each leg and the underside of the platform with the screws provided.

5. **Build and attach the stop block.** Cut the stop block pieces to the dimensions in the Materials List. With glue

and countersunk 1¼-inch wood screws, attach one block under the top of the platform compartment, positioning it two inches from the cabinet face and centered side to side. Then glue and screw the other block on top of the first to create a 1½-inch thick stop.

INSTALLING DOORS AND PLATFORM

1. **Build the doors.** The cabinet uses doors that overlay the face frame. The doors shown are flat plywood panels edged in solid wood. See "Building a Slab Door," page 15. If you choose to make frame and panel doors, see "Building a Frame-and-Panel Door," page 16.

2. **Install the doors and door hardware.** After applying finish to the project, attach the pulls and hinges to the doors with the screws provided. Use the screws provided to attach the doors to the cabinet face frame. See "Installing Doors and Hinges", page 19.

3. **Install the platform.** Trim a piano hinge to 14 inches with a hacksaw, and attach the hinge to the rear edge of the platform with four #6x5/8-inch flathead wood screws, as shown in the *Overall View.* Drill pilot holes for each screw. Then attach the hinge to the horizontal panel behind the left center door so that the hinge barrel is 2 inches inside the front edge of the face frame.

4. **Attach the bullet catches.** The bullet catches ensure that the platform won't flop open when you open the door. Drill holes in both sides of the compartment for the spring-loaded bullet, locating them about halfway up the compartment and 3/4 inch from the front of the cabinet. Install the bullets and fold the platform into the compartment. Mark the location of the catch strike plates on the outside of the legs. Install the strike plates.

Platform and Leg Construction

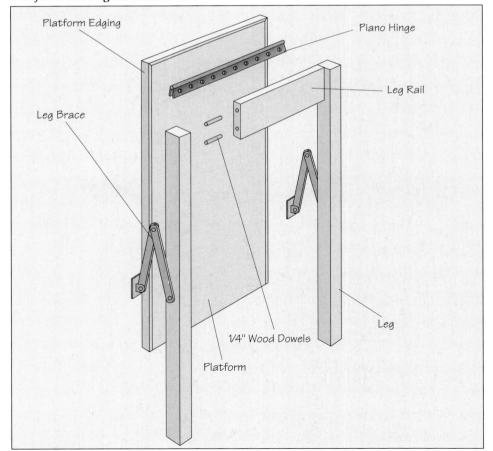

Ironing Board

Who hasn't wrestled with the unwieldy collection of springs, hinges, and spindly legs known as an ironing board, and thought wistfully about the convenience of a built-in model? Well, yearn no more, and build one yourself. It's easier than you may think, and will certainly take up less space in the tight quarters of a utility room than a standard board.

When not in use, this ironing board tucks into a small cabinet installed in the wall between studs. See "Removing Wallboard," page 28.

If you cannot find a pad and cover (usually sold as a unit) to fit this board, then you'll have to cut a standard-size pad to fit. This won't be a problem if you know your way around a sewing machine; however, for those who don't, fabric adhesives and adhesive tapes are available at fabric shops that can be used instead.

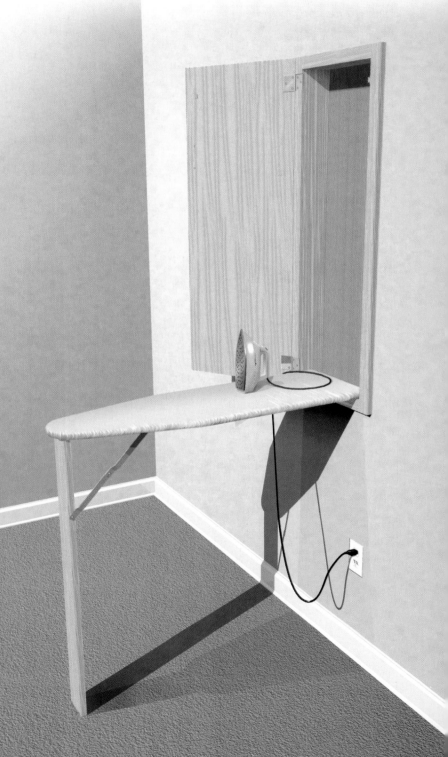

Ironing Board Materials List

Qty	Part	Dimensions	Qty	Part
Carcase & Ironing Board			**Hardware**	
2	Plywood top/bottom panels	3/4" x 3½" x 13¾"		4d Finishing nails
2	Plywood cabinet sides	3/4" x 3½" x 42"		7/8" Brads
1	Plywood cabinet back	1/4" x 14½" x 42"		6d Finishing nails
1	Solid-wood leg	3/4" x 3½" x 36"	3	3" Butt hinges
1	Plywood ironing board	3/4" x 12" x 39"	1	Locking leg brace (or card-table leg brace)
Face frame and door			2	3/4" Screw eyes
2	Solid-wood stiles	3/4" x 1½" x 43½"	1	Small bungee cord
2	Solid-wood rails	3/4" x 1½" x 13"	2	2" Butt hinges
1	Plywood cabinet door	3/4" x 16" x 43½"	1	Magnetic door catch
			1	Door pull
			1	Ironing-board pad and cover
			1	Self-adhesive felt pad

Overall View

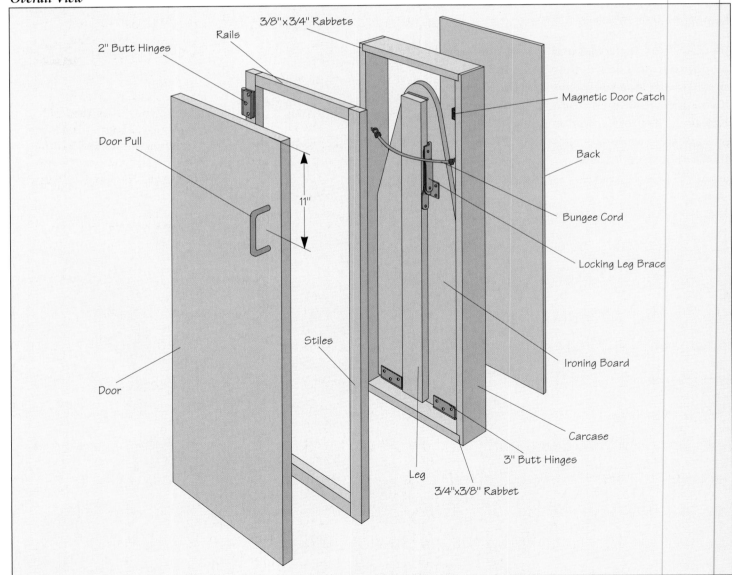

MAKING AND INSTALLING THE CARCASE

1. Preparing the wall. Locate the studs with a stud finder. Then use a level to scribe level lines from stud to stud at 35¼ inches and 77¼ inches from the floor.

Find the stud edges with a hammer and small nail or electric drill and small bit, and scribe plumb lines along the studs' inside edges, connecting the level lines and forming a box measuring 14½ x 42 inches. Cut out the wall material with a utility knife or drywall saw.

2. Cut the parts. Cut the cabinet top, bottom, sides, leg, and back panel to the dimensions in the Materials List.

3. Cut rabbets. Rabbet the sides as shown in the *Overall View*. See "Dadoes, Grooves, and Rabbets," page 10.

4. Assemble the carcase. Attach the sides to the top and bottom with glue and 4d finishing nails. Attach the back with glue and 7/8-inch brads about every 12 inches.

5. Install the carcase. Set the cabinet into the wall cavity with its front edge flush with the wall's exterior surface. Then attach the cabinet to the studs with four 6d finishing nails in each side. Use shims to fill any gaps between the carcase and the studs.

BUILDING AND INSTALLING THE IRONING BOARD

1. Cut the board. Cut the ironing board from 3/4-inch plywood. First cut out a rectangle measuring 12 x 39 inches. Mark the long sides 16 inches back from the front edge, and make a third mark 3 inches back from the center of the front edge as shown in *Cutting the Ironing Board*. Set a compass for a 3-inch radius, put the point on the 3-inch mark, and scribe an arc from the front edge, as shown in *Cutting the Ironing Board*. Connect the sides of the arc with lines scribed to the 16-inch marks made earlier. Then use a saber saw to cut along the lines. Sand the edges smooth.

2. Attach the hardware and leg. Measure 2 inches from the front edge, and scribe a line across the underside of the board. Center a 3-inch butt hinge on the line with the hinge barrel toward the front as shown in *Ironing Board Construction*, and attach the hinge with the screws provided. Attach the leg to the hinge. With the leg extended, attach the leg brace to the leg and board with the screws provided.

3. Install the board. Screw two 3-inch butt hinges to the bottom of the carcase so that they can open out as shown in *Ironing Board Construction*. Set the ironing board inside the carcase, make sure it is centered, then screw the butt hinges into the bottom of the ironing board.

4. Attach the safety-cord eyes. Measure 10 inches down the inside of each cabinet side panel, and install a centered screw eye at each location. Stretch the bungee cord from eye to eye to hold the ironing board in place.

Cutting the Ironing Board

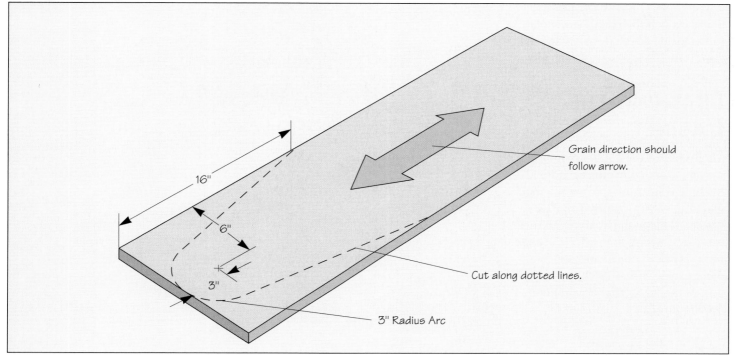

16"

6"

3"

Grain direction should follow arrow.

Cut along dotted lines.

3" Radius Arc

ASSEMBLING AND INSTALLING THE FRAME AND DOOR

1. **Cut and install the face frame parts.** Cut the stiles and rails to the dimensions in the Materials List. Attach the stiles first with glue and 6d finishing nails, making sure the stiles are flush with the inside of the carcase, then cut the rails to fit between the stiles and attach the same way.

2. **Build the door.** The cabinet shown here is a slab style door, but you can build a raised panel door or whichever type of door matches your decor. See "Making Cabinet Doors," page 15.

3. **Install the hardware.** Cut hinge mortises for 2-inch butt hinges in the left stile and in the door. Locate the hinges 2 inches from the top and bottom of the door. If you are using plywood doors, they can't be mortised. In this case, make a double-depth mortise in the stiles. Screw the door to the hinges and the hinges to the stile. Then attach the cabinet catch, placing the magnetic part inside the carcase where it won't interfere with the ironing board. Attach the latch's strike plate to the inside of the door. Attach the door pull.

FINISHING THE CABINET

After making any necessary modifications, slip the ironing board pad over the ironing board, per the manufacturer's instructions. You may have to remove the board from the cabinet to install the pad. Unless the room is carpeted, cut and attach a piece of self-adhesive felt to the bottom of the leg so that it won't damage the floor.

Ironing Board Construction

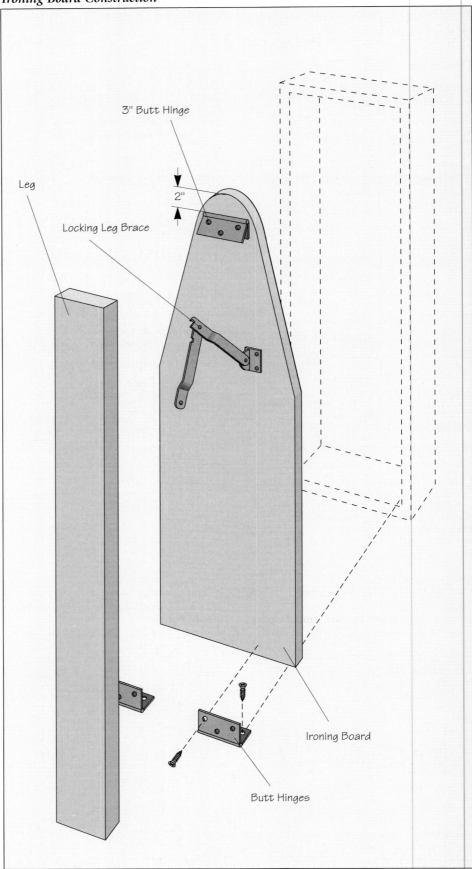

3" Butt Hinge

2"

Leg

Locking Leg Brace

Ironing Board

Butt Hinges

Actual Dimensions The exact measurements of a piece of lumber after it has been cut, surfaced, and left to dry. Example: A 2x4's actual dimensions are 1½ x 3½.

Air-Dried Wood Lumber that is stacked with spacers to allow air to circulate and is usually marked indicating its maximum moisture content at the time it leaves the mill.

Aluminum-Oxide Sandpaper A tan-colored sandpaper that is commonly used on sanding belts and disks.

Angle Square Often called by the brand name Speed Square. A durable triangular square used as a protractor and for scribing lines at 45 and 90 degrees.

Bevel An edge that is angled or slanted, but not 90 degrees.

Biscuit Pressed wood that is shaped like flat footballs. Biscuits fit into slots cut by a biscuit joiner to make wood joints.

Black Silicone-Carbide Sandpaper A sandpaper which is made with water-resistant glue to attach the abrasives to the paper. This sandpaper is often referred to as "wet-or-dry" sandpaper because it can be used with a water or oil lubricant, or no lubricant at all.

Blotching A staining problem where the stain is unevenly absorbed causing dark and light areas. This is caused by a swirly grain or uneven density of a piece of wood.

Brad A finishing nail smaller than 4d.

Butt Joint A joint in which one piece of wood is simply butted against the other.

Carcase The basic case of a cabinet.

Carpenter's Wood Glue Aliphatic resin glue that is the adhesive of choice for bonding wood to wood.

Combination Square A graduated steel blade with a sliding handle that can be tightened at any position. Most combination squares come with a spirit level and scratch awl built into the handle.

Contact Cement A rubber-based liquid glue that bonds on contact.

Corner Clamps Clamps designed to hold two pieces of material together at a right angle for gluing, nailing, and screwing.

Crosscut A cut that is made across the grain on a piece of wood.

Dado A type of groove that runs across the grain.

Dado Blade A special blade used on a table saw to make dadoes.

Depth Stop On a drill, a collar that stops the bit when it reaches a desired depth.

Drywall Screws Also known as all-purpose or bugle-head screws. Drywall screws have aggressive threads that are designed to drive fast and hold tight. These screws are self-countersinking in most softwoods.

Edge-Gluing A technique in which several boards are bonded together edge-to-edge to form a panel.

Face Frame A frame of stiles and rails that is applied to the face of a cabinet for style and strength. The face frame is often used to hide plywood edges.

Featherboard A single piece of wood with slots cut into one end. Featherboards are safety devices clamped to the work surface of certain power tools to prevent kickback and eliminate the need to place hands near the blades or cutters.

Garnet Sandpaper An orange-colored sandpaper that is popular for sanding wood by hand.

Grain The direction and arrangement of wood fibers in a piece of wood.

Gray Silicone-Carbide Sandpaper A sandpaper that contains zinc stearate, a soap-like lubricant, making it easier to sand finishes without using an additional lubricant.

Groove A channel cut into a piece of wood that runs with the grain.

Hardboard Wood fibers bonded with pressure and heat to form a thin, durable panel.

Hardwood Wood that comes from deciduous trees (those that lose their leaves in fall).

Hinges Hardware used for hanging doors and lids. For cabinet doors, hinges are available in three basic types: overlay, inset, and flush-fit.

Hollow-Wall Fastener This type of fastener is designed for use in walls made of plaster or drywall. It consists of an anchor bolt with a sleeve that expands against the inside of a wall.

Jig A device for holding a workpiece, or attached to a workpiece, that allows a tool to cut the workpiece in a way that could not otherwise be done safely and accurately.

Joint Surfaces that meet to glue or otherwise fasten two pieces of wood to each other.

Kickback The dangerous action that happens when a saw suddenly jumps backward out of a cut, or when a stationary power saw throws a piece of wood back at the operator.

Kiln-Dried Wood Lumber that is dried in a kiln. Usually it is more expensive than air-dried wood, but it is less likely to shrink after it's been installed.

Knot The high-density root of limbs that is very dense but is not connected to the surrounding wood.

Lumber Grade A label that reflects the lumber's natural growth characteristics (such as knots), defects that result from milling errors, and manufacturing techniques.

Miter Joint A joint in which the ends of two boards are cut at equal angles (typically 45 degrees) to form a corner.

Mortise and Tenon Joint A joint consisting of a mortise (a slot) and a tenon (piece that fits into the slot).

Nail Set A pointed tool with one round or square end, used to drive nails flush with or below the surface of wood.

Nippers A tool used for cutting nails and wires.

Nominal Dimensions The identifying dimensions of a piece of lumber (e.g., 2x4), which are larger than the actual dimensions (1½x3½).

Particleboard A term used to describe several different types of sheet materials made from glue and ground-up bits of wood.

Penny (abbr. d) Unit of measurement for nail length; e.g., a 10d nail is 3 inches long.

Pickling A method used to give wood a whitish cast.

Plate Joiner Also called a biscuit joiner. A tool that cuts a precise semicircular slot in which a plate or biscuit is inserted.

Plywood Veneers of wood glued together in a sandwich. Each veneer is oriented perpendicularly to the next.

Oil Finish A clear finish produced by applying an oil, such as linseed, to bare or stained wood.

Rabbet A ledge cut along one edge of a workpiece.

Rail A horizontal member that is placed between stiles.

Raised Panel A board with bevels on all four sides on one face so that stock is thicker in the center than at its perimeter.

Rip Cut A cut made with the grain on a piece of wood.

Rip Fence An attachment to a table saw used to guide wood through a cut along the length of a board.

Router A power tool that is shaped like a cannister and has a bit protruding from the bottom. A router is used to do such things as making grooves, dadoes, and rabbets, and mortising door hinges.

Shellac A natural resin secreted from the lac bug that inhabits certain trees native to India and Thailand. Shellac is the only natural resin still widely used as a finish.

Shim A tapered piece of wood used to level and secure a structure.

Softwood Wood that comes from coniferous trees, such as evergreens.

Stain A substance containing pigment used to color wood.

Stain Controllers Also called wood conditioner, prestain, and grain tamer. Slow-evaporating, petroleum-distillate solvents that work by filling up the pores and less-dense parts of the wood so the stain can't penetrate.

Stile Vertical member placed perpendicular to rails.

Stud Vertical member of a frame wall, placed at both ends and usually every 16 inches on center. Provides structural framing and facilitates covering with drywall or paneling.

T-bevel Also known as the sliding T-bevel or bevel square. A simple tool that consists of a handle or stock attached to a 6- or 8-inch slotted blade.

Table Saw A stationary power saw that can be used for crosscutting, ripping (cutting a board along the grain from end to end), grooving, and joinery.

Toggle Bolt A bolt that has spring-loaded wings and opens against the inside of the wall as the bolt is tightened.

Toluene Sometimes called toluol. A solvent, like xylene, that softens glue enough so it can be scrubbed off with a coarse cloth or soft-bristle brush.

Try Square A square with a broad blade attached to a stock at a right angle.

Varnish A type of finish that is made by cooking an oil, such as linseed oil, tung oil, or modified soybean oil, with a resin.

Wood Screws Screws that are tapered so the threads bite into the wood, which makes a stronger bond than nails.

Xylene Sometimes called xylol. A solvent, like toluene, that softens glue enough so it can be scrubbed off with a coarse cloth or soft-bristle brush.

Index

Metric Conversion Tables

NAIL SIZE AND LENGTH

Penny Size	Nail Length
2d	1"
3d	1 1/4"
4d	1 1/2"
5d	1 3/4"
6d	2 "
7d	2 1/4"
8d	2 1/2"
9d	2 3/4"
10d	3"
12d	3 1/4"
16d	3 1/2"
20d	4"
30d	4 1/2"
40d	5"
50d	5 1/2"
60d	6"

METRIC LENGTHS

Meters	Equivalent Feet and Inches
1.8m	5' 10 7/8"
2.1m	6' 10 5/8"
2.4m	7' 10 1/2"
2.7m	8' 10 1/4"
3.0m	9' 10 1/8"
3.3m	10' 9 7/8"
3.6m	11' 9 3/4"
3.9m	12' 9 1/2"
4.2m	13' 9 3/8"
4.5m	14' 9 1/8"
4.8m	15' 9"
5.1m	16' 8 3/4"
5.4m	17' 8 5/8"
5.7m	18' 8 3/8"
6.0m	19' 8 1/4"
6.3m	20' 8"
6.6m	21' 7 7/8"
6.9m	22' 7 5/8"
7.2m	23' 7 1/2"
7.5m	24' 7 1/4"
7.8m	25' 7 1/8"

Dimensions are based on 1m = 3.28 feet, or 1 foot = 0.3048m.

LUMBER

Sizes: Metric cross sections are so close to their nearest Imperial sizes, as noted below, that for most purposes they may be considered equivalents.

Lengths: Metric lengths are based on a 300mm module, which is slightly shorter in length than a U.S. foot. It will, therefore, be important to check your requirements accurately to the nearest inch and to consult the table below (left) to find the metric length required.

Areas: The metric area is a square meter. Use the following conversion factors when converting from U.S. data: 100 square feet = 9.29 square meters.

Metric Sizes (Shown before Nearest U.S. Equivalent)

millimeters	inches	millimeters	inches
16 x 75	5/8 x 3	44 x 150	1 3/4 x 6
16 x 100	5/8 x 4	44 x 175	1 3/4 x 7
16 x 125	5/8 x 5	44 x 200	1 3/4 x 8
16 x 150	5/8 x 6	44 x 225	1 3/4 x 9
19 x 75	3/4 x 3	44 x 250	1 3/4 x 10
19 x 100	3/4 x 4	44 x 300	1 3/4 x 12
19 x 125	3/4 x 5	50 x 75	2 x 3
19 x 150	3/4 x 6	50 x 100	2 x 4
22 x 75	7/8 x 3	50 x 125	2 x 5
22 x 100	7/8 x 4	50 x 150	2 x 6
22 x 125	7/8 x 5	50 x 175	2 x 7
22 x 150	7/8 x 6	50 x 200	2 x 8
25 x 75	1 x 3	50 x 225	2 x 9
25 x 100	1 x 4	50 x 250	2 x 10
25 x 125	1 x 5	50 x 300	2 x 12
25 x 150	1 x 6	63 x 100	2 1/2 x 4
25 x 175	1 x 7	63 x 125	2 1/2 x 5
25 x 200	1 x 8	63 x 150	2 1/2 x 6
25 x 225	1 x 9	63 x 175	2 1/2 x 7
25 x 250	1 x 10	63 x 200	2 1/2 x 8
25 x 300	1 x 12	63 x 225	2 1/2 x 9
32 x 75	1 1/4 x 3	75 x 100	3 x 4
32 x 100	1 1/4 x 4	75 x 125	3 x 5
32 x 125	1 1/4 x 5	75 x 150	3 x 6
32 x 150	1 1/4 x 6	75 x 175	3 x 7
32 x 175	1 1/4 x 7	75 x 200	3 x 8
32 x 200	1 1/4 x 8	75 x 225	3 x 9
32 x 225	1 1/4 x 9	75 x 250	3 x 10
32 x 250	1 1/4 x 10	75 x 300	3 x 12
32 x 300	1 1/4 x 12	100 x 100	4 x 4
38 x 75	1 1/2 x 3	100 x 150	4 x 6
38 x 100	1 1/2 x 4	100 x 200	4 x 8
38 x 125	1 1/2 x 5	100 x 250	4 x 10
38 x 150	1 1/2 x 6	100 x 300	4 x 12
38 x 175	1 1/2 x 7	150 x 150	6 x 6
38 x 200	1 1/2 x 8	150 x 200	6 x 8
38 x 225	1 1/2 x 9	150 x 300	6 x 12
44 x 75	1 3/4 x 3	200 x 200	8 x 8
44 x 100	1 3/4 x 4	250 x 250	10 x 10
44 x 125	1 3/4 x 5	300 x 300	12 x 12

Dimensions are based on 1 inch = 25mm

Have a home improvement, decorating, or gardening project? Look for these and other fine Creative Homeowner books wherever books are sold.

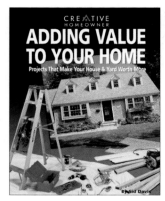

Advice for improving the value of your home. Over 400 illustrations. 176 pp.; 8¹/₂"×10⁷/₈"
BOOK #: 277006

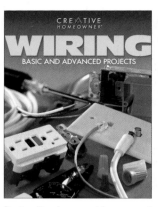

Best-selling house-wiring manual. Over 700 color photos and illustrations. 256 pp.; 8¹/₂"×10⁷/₈"
BOOK #: 277049

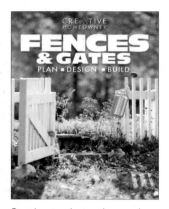

Step-by-step instructions and projects. Over 320 color photos and illustrations. 144 pp.; 8¹/₂"×10⁷/₈"
BOOK #: 277985

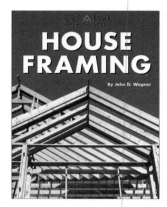

Designed to walk you through the framing basics. Over 400 illustrations. 208 pp.; 8¹/₂"×10⁷/₈"
BOOK #: 277655

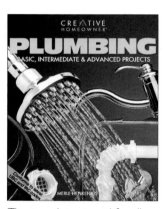

The complete manual for all plumbing projects. Over 750 color photos. 272 pp.; 8¹/₂"×10⁷/₈"
BOOK #: 278210

Proven tips for hanging and removing wallpaper. Over 250 illustrations. 144 pp.; 8¹/₂"×10⁷/₈"
BOOK #: 278910

Complete DIY tile instruction. Over 350 color photos and illustrations. 160 pp.; 8¹/₂"×10⁷/₈"
BOOK #: 277524

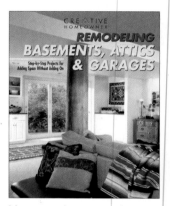

How to convert unused space into useful living area. 570 illustrations. 192 pp.; 8¹/₂"×10⁷/₈"
BOOK #: 277680

How to create kitchen style like a pro. Over 150 color photographs. 176 pp.; 9"×10"
BOOK #: 279935

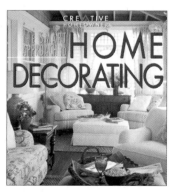

How to work with space, color, pattern, texture. Over 300 photos. 256 pp.; 9"×10"
BOOK #: 279667

An impressive guide to garden design and plant selection. More than 600 photos. 320 pp.; 9"×10"
BOOK #: 274615

For the beginning and experienced gardener. Over 500 color photos. 208 pp.; 9"×10"
BOOK #: 274032

For more information, and to order direct, call 800-631-7795; in New Jersey 201-934-7100.
Please visit our Web site at www.creativehomeowner.com